HYPNOTIC GASTRIC BAND FOR RAPID WEIGHT LOSS

EXTREME WEIGHT LOSS HYPNOSIS FOR MEN AND WOMEN TO STOP FOOD ADDICTION AND EAT HEALTHY WITH GUIDED MEDITATION AND MOTIVATIONAL AFFIRMATIONS

D1026970

Jessica Williams

Table of Contents

BOOK 1 :

GASTRIC BAND HYPNOSIS FOR WEIGHT LOSS

RAPID WEIGHT LOSS HYPNOSIS FOR MEN AND WOMEN TO BURN FAT AND LOSE WEIGHT THROUGH DEEP SLEEP MEDITATION AND MOTIVATIONAL AFFIRMATIONS

Introduction

The hypnosis band for weight loss has recently blown up in the market and to make things worse, there is a lot of hype about it out there. You might have heard about it and wondered if it's really worth the money in your pocket or if you should just ignore it. It turns out, this isn't one of those products that are too good to be true. In fact, this is a sure-fire way to shed pounds quickly and easily. It's quite simple and has helped many people lose weight around their stomachs without any unhealthy restrictions on food intake or exercise routine needed.

So what is it and is it right for your goal?

The first thing that people want to know before they even think about buying one of these is what the hell difference does it make? Basically, this band can change your body's natural response to fullness by inhibiting the production of appetite-stimulating hormones. It turns out, when your stomach becomes full, it signals that you should stop eating. The problem here is that you will not end up eating less and because there are no restrictions on how much food you eat, you will overeat and gain weight fast. The band is designed to trick your body into believing that you have eaten enough by slowly releasing the stomach contents back into the intestines. The net result of this is that it will make you feel full even after meals and you will be less likely to eat when you are not hungry.

This is not something inflicted on unsuspecting citizens, this is a device that has been tested and approved by many doctors and scientists all over the world. It should be safe for anyone who uses it correctly according to the manufacturer's guidelines. All users must sign an agreement stating that they understand the risks involved in using this product as well as prior authorization from their doctor before they can use it.

Now, this is not some miracle pill that will instantly and miraculously slim you down without effort. This is a very good way to improve your health, but it's more of a lifestyle change than a short-term fix. You can expect to use this for at least six months before you see progress and then slowly phase it out after that. Most users can expect to start seeing results after about six months.

On the other hand, those who experience weight loss in the first few weeks would be thrilled with these results. It doesn't matter what your age or weight is; you can lose up to 2 pounds per day with this malfunctioning device if you do it properly (according to the manufacturer's guidelines). You can lose up to 10 pounds per week if you eat proper food, get plenty of exercises and follow the instructions of the product. You should also be careful not to rush it or overdo things; otherwise, you will get hurt and possibly end up in a medical condition. If you are going for a fast weight loss, this is the best way of doing it without listening to your body's needs or attempting dangerous and dangerous methods that might give you more harm than good. The hypnosis band may be expensive but it is worth its price if you consider all the benefits that come with it: health improvement and less food consumed. The cherry on top is the fact that it can help you lose weight fast and with the least amount of effort possible.

Chapter 1 - Getting Into the Zone Motivation for Exercise

Welcome to your weight loss hypnosis session. This one is called "Getting into the Zone—Motivation for Exercise". During this exercise, I will guide you through a meditative journey and help you wire your body to burn fat quickly and effortlessly. As with most hypnosis, you may find yourself transported into a different level of peace, a state of total relaxation. Your mind, body, and attention will be completely absorbed. Before commencing, please make sure you are in a safe, quiet environment and not performing any tasks that require your attention, such as driving or working near safety hazards. Ideally, you should be giving this hypnotic session your full, undivided attention for the most optimum results. Pause.

When you are ready, settle into a good headspace and relax as I guide you through a satisfying, phenomenal, and highly transformative experience. You will find yourself in a state of deep relaxation, stress relief, comfort, tranquility, and inner power. Be prepared to have your entire mindset about weight loss altered and your willpower exponentially increased. Soon you will find yourself losing weight naturally and effortlessly. This is the power of hypnosis. Don't be surprised if you begin to enjoy losing weight and developing healthier habits. Pause.

Start by asking yourself what is your motivating factor to exercise? Why do you want to increase the level of activity that you put out every day? Is it for health, overall longevity in life, to keep up with your kids? Are you wanting to exercise more to gain more confidence, more muscle strength, to play sports, or compete in competitions? Are you wanting to exercise more for the physical appeal, to look better in summer clothing? To be able to go to pool parties and outdoor events feeling more secure about yourself. Pause.

Find out what your true reason is for wanting to exercise more, and for wanting to lose weight is and use this as your motivation to get through each day when you need a lift. Your weight loss journey will help you become stronger from the inside out.

You will find the strength that you never knew existed. You will see a brand new you emerge right before your eyes. Pause.

To start this session, please make sure that you are in a comfortable location and that you have about an hour or so of peace and quiet, with no interruptions. Make sure that cell phones are silenced as well. Pause.

The next step is to make sure that you are dressed in loose clothing that is free of restrictions. Breathable fabrics always work best for any type of hypnosis or meditative work. Pause.

Now that you are ready to sit comfortably. Begin by focusing on your breathing. Take a deep breath in through your nose and out through your mouth. Choose a pace that does not leave you winded afterward. Nice and slow peaceful breaths. Do this for a few minutes to let your system slow down a notch. Pause.

Now close your eyes, if you have not already, and take another breath in through your nose, completely filling your lungs and exhaling through your mouth, letting all the air out. Pause.

You may choose to do this once more or you may now continue to breathe at a normal, comfortable pace. Pause.

As you take your next breath, I want you to imagine that the air that you inhale is like a thick fog. This thick fog that you are inhaling is a positive energy that is sweeping into your body to cleanse you and rid you of any negative energy and tension that you may be carrying.

As you inhale, take a moment to visualize the white, thick fog as it enters your lungs. Pause.

Visualize this positive energy sweeping down into your arms, down to the tips of your fingers, and then back to your lungs, and out of your mouth as you exhale that breath. Pause.

This is sweeping out all the tensions and worry and is leaving you feeling very light and airy. Inhale through your nose and imagine that positive white fog traveling throughout your abdomen, cleansing as it goes. Ridding you of all stress, tension, and worry. Pause.

Imagine the positive energy going down each leg and touching each toe, then traveling back up the way it came, passing by all your areas of stress and back out of your mouth as you exhale. Pause.

You should be feeling very relaxed and calm. Every muscle and joint in your body has been massaged and feels light and relaxed. Pause.

Your body feels lighter and unrestricted now. You can easily feel yourself drifting with each breath that you inhale. Pause.

As you glide around in this state of complete relaxation; you are still aware that the inner workings of your body. In fact, you may become more aware of the inner workings of your body. You may hear your stomach growl. You may feel a muscle or a tremor. All of this is okay, as it is very natural for you to feel and sense your internal body functions as you explore this trance-like state. Pause.

You will eventually let the sounds and sensations of this room fade into the background of your mind. The only thing that you will have to focus on is the sound of my voice and the calm, steady pace of your breathing. Pause.

I want you now to imagine that you are at the top of a beautiful staircase, inside of a gorgeous home with many windows bringing in the bright sunlight. As I count to 10, you will take a step down the staircase. Pause.

With each step-down, you go deeper and deeper into this peaceful trance. I am going to count from 1 to 10 and with each step you take and each number that I say, you will feel more relaxed. Deeply relaxed and at peace.

One. You are very relaxed. Two Getting more relaxed. Three, you are deepening your relaxation. Four, getting deeper and deeper into this trance-like state. Five. You are so relaxed. Pause.

16

Six. Deeper. Seven. Very relaxed. Eight, so super calm. Pause.

Nine, you are in a complete state of bliss. Ten, you have reached the bottom of the stairs and now you can step onto the landing. Feel the warmth of the sun coming through the windows. The warmth is just right. Feel the breeze roll across your body as the windows are open and the curtains are swaying with the wind. You can now walk towards an open door. Pause.

Imagine yourself now walking down the main street of a small town. The town is like one that you might have seen on your travels in the past. You know the one; it is perfect and dream-like and you can feel a good old-fashioned, small-town vibe. It is a place that has a cute main street with old cobblestone walkways. The street has businesses that have been there for a hundred years and are still thriving. There is laughter and a feeling of pure happiness.

This is a good place that feels safe and delightful. Children ride their bikes on the sidewalks. Business owners stand just outside their doorstep with a fresh cup of coffee or tea. People greet each other by their first name. The buildings are well-kept, despite their age and they will continue to support new generations to come. Pause.

Imagine that there are no other people on this street today. You are the only one on this street and you feel comfortable and safe, and you decide to go for a walk through the town. Take a minute to stop and go into the first clothing store that you see. When you first look at the clothes, you do some browsing, but then you spot the mirrors on the wall and all you can see is your own reflection. Pause.

You smile at the sight of your slim figure. You feel healthy, athletic, confident, and determined. Your muscles are defined, and you have a very flattering athletic outfit on. You look down at the reflection and see your fitness tracker on your wrist. It is clean and bright, and you admire it because it has helped you to obtain this slimmer look by tracking all of your steps and showing you all the calories you have burned with every movement you have done through the day.

While you continue to breathe at a pace that is comfortable to you, you feel healthy, athletic, confident, and determined. Pause. You can almost feel that fitness tracker on your wrist right now. Think about it. What does it look like? How many miles can this fitness tracker take you? How many miles are you willing to go? Pause.

You are excited to find out because you know how healthy it is to exercise. After all, movement and exercise have helped you to become healthy, athletic, confident, and determined. Pause.

There are many times throughout our day that we mindlessly sit on our phones or sit on the couch and waste time away. This mindless lack of movement is going to stop because you want to keep working on your slimmer figure.

Your body is healthy, athletic, confident, and determined. Instead of sitting at free times during your day, you are going to put on your fitness tracker and walk for ten to twenty minutes. You are going to want to move every time that you see your fitness tracker. Your sneakers are a tool that will help you to stay healthy, athletic, confident, and determined. Pause.

You will place your fitness tracker and the charger near your front door, back door, or even a doorway of any room. The fitness tracker will be a new trigger for you. You are going to want to move every time that you see your fitness tracker. Pause.

Your fitness tracker will help you to feel healthy, athletic, confident, and determined. Every single time that you want to sit on your phone or spend time lounging, think of your fitness tracker. Pause.

You may have more than 1 fitness tracker or fitness watch, but all of them will have the same effect on you. All of them make you want to walk for 10 to 20 minutes. You will want to walk when you see your fitness tracker because it makes you feel healthy, athletic, confident, and determined. Pause.

Continue to focus on your peaceful feeling. Your breathing is steady, and you feel healthy, athletic, confident, and determined. You are going to use an alarm set up on your phone that is only used for fitness or exercise time, and every time you hear this alarm, you will associate it with working out and doing something movement and fitness-oriented. You have a new-found sense of being an active person who looks to exercise at all times. Pause.

You are once again in that lovely home with the beautiful windows letting in all the light and then you see that beautiful staircase. Walk towards the staircase. Pause.

I am going to count back from 10 to 1. As you take each step towards the top of the stairs, you will come back to being fully aware, fully awake. Energized and refreshed. Ten. You feel great. Nine. Coming back to the full consciousness soon. Eight. You are coming back feeling refreshed as if you've had a long rest. Seven. You can now hear the sounds in this room. Six. You are more aware. Five. You are becoming more awake. Four. Energized and refreshed. Three. More awake. Two. More awake. One.

Chapter 2 - Understanding Hypnosis

Hypnosis is a trance state, almost like sleep. In this state, you're incredibly vulnerable to hints or guidance from the hypnotist. During hypnosis, you'll enter a more focused and attentive state. A hypnotist can help you relax and become calm, making it easier for you to accept advice. Hypnosis is like daydreaming. Once you daydream, you tend to obscure other existing ideas or stimuli and focus only on your daydreams. Furthermore, you tend to consider what's happening in anesthesia without being distracted by other thoughts or sounds.

Hypnosis is often to treat various diseases, conditions, and discomforts. For instance, suggestiveness caused by anesthesia can relieve anxiety or depression. Hypnosis also can be applied to treat certain medical disorders, like gastrointestinal diseases, skin diseases, or chronic pain. However, hypnosis treatment isn't entirely feasible in all cases. The researchers also used hypnosis to get information about their effects on learning, memory, feeling, and perception. To better understand how hypnosis works, let's check out an example.

Imagine you biting your nails and need to obviate this bad habit. To the present end, please arrange a gathering with the hypnotist. Once you enter the space, the hypnotist will ask you to settle on an area to take a seat or lie.

While sitting down in a chair, the hypnotist will ask you what you would like to do. You will then tell him/her that you want to prevent biting your nails; the hypnotist then asks you to shut your eyes and imagine yourself in a place you wish, for instance, at a beach or park.

The hypnotist will guide you through some visual operations to make you feel calm and relaxed. After relaxing, the hypnotist recommends that you should not bite your nails. He/she requires you to consider healthy and well-manicured nails. In a very calm state, this suggestion may significantly impact your brain than in other situations. Your mood will be intense, calm, and relaxed, which makes it very suggestive.

After generating the suggested image, the hypnotist will use phrases like "It's time to travel back to the present" to induce you to open your eyes; at now, the session ends. There are several popular myths about hypnosis. First, many of us believe that the hypnotist has "power" over the person hypnotized. It's not valid. Even in a state of calm hypnosis, you'll fully control what you are doing and picture in the meeting; you'll never be bound by anything the hypnotist suggests. Second, some people think that hypnosis can make people unconscious. It's another myth.

Throughout the anesthesia, you'll control your thoughts and listen to what's happening around you. Finally, many of us believe what we learned about hypnosis from movies and television shows is real. Anesthesia usually describes the hypnotized person as entirely unaware of the encompassing environment around them, almost unconscious, or exhibiting weird behaviors involving animal noise and new songs. Hypnosis helps you relax and calm, which successively allows you to face and deal with your pain or bad habits.

What Do We Know About Hypnosis?

A review recently published in the Journal of Neuroscience and Biological Behavior Review defined hypnosis as a top-down regulation of consciousness, in which "psychological representation overrides physiology, perception, and behavior" because the author explains that hypnosis involves two main elements: induction and suggestion. Hypnosis induction is the first suggestion made during the hypnosis process, although its content remains controversial.

Recommendations are usually expressed as hints that cause participants to look and reply involuntarily. They believe that participants don't have much or any control (or agency) over things. Some people are more "suggested" than others, and researchers have found that folks who are highly likely to be implied are more likely to scale back agency consciousness during hypnosis.

The suggestiveness of hypnosis defines as "the ability to experience suggested changes in physiology, sensation, emotions, thoughts, or behavior."

Certain areas of the brain activated during hypnosis include the prefrontal cortex, the anterior gyrus cinguli, and the parietal network. Neuroimaging techniques show that profoundly hypnotized people show high levels of activity in the frontal area, cingulate back anterior cortex and parietal network of the brain at different hypnosis stages. These are areas of the brain that involve a series of complex functions, including memory and perception, processing emotions, and task learning. However, although scientists have begun to piece together this process's neurocognitive characteristics, it is unclear the precise brain mechanisms involved in hypnosis.

Benefits of Hypnosis

Stop Smoking

If you would like to seek out the best way to leave smoking, you'll browse an extended list of over-the-counter drugs and nicotine replacement drugs, and non-nicotine prescriptions to seek out the proper method. Of course, smoking cessation is essential: consistent with the Centers for Disease Control and Prevention; cigarettes cause quite 480,000 deaths annually. The CDC also acknowledged that seven out of ten (68%) of all current US adult smokers said they wanted to quit smoking. Herbs, behavioral therapy, and acupuncture are other ways people quit smoking.

However, for bar owner Jon Brian in Melbourne, Florida (the bar still allows smoking), hypnosis is the daily habit of kicking two packs of cigarettes.

Richard Barker, a knowledgeable hypnotist, said: "When you attend the doctor, they're going to offer you medicine, but they cannot offer you anti-habit medicine." Barker and Bryner cooperated and altered his thought process to eliminate emotional connections to rework their habits into positive ones. "At first, I thought, how would I drive, drink beer without smoking?"

Brian said: "But now I just believe in the bad smell of smoke."

No Longer Overeating

Making healthier diet choices and exercising are critical factors for weight loss. In some cases, successful weight loss must also obviate the emotional and unconscious factors that prevent us from losing weight. Barker explained that using hypnotic drugs to reduce requires a special method than using hypnotic drugs in other situations—usually, it takes several times rather than only one to work out the individual's triggers. "Before hypnosis, I would like to find out whether are there snacks or people that enter the refrigerator between meals. Most are different. Everyone has their habits. It takes time to unravel them." The conversation starts with embedded commands, which may help customers control their eating ways. "After five or six bites, you shut your eyes and say to yourself 'enough,' or whenever you eat a plate of food, you shut your eyes and say, 'eat half the food.'"

Sleep Better

Lack of sleep can impair decision-making and memory and cause chronic health problems like heart condition, obesity, and depression. Although there are many treatments for insomnia, including medications, meditation, and cognitive-behavioral therapy, getting enough sleep isn't something you'll convince yourself to do. Mount Vernon, a hypnotist in Washington, explained that the unconscious mainly controls sleep. "Trying to unravel this type of problem with conscious thinking is like trying to make a corporation change with the receptionist—you got to get in-tuned with the CEO."

Worrying about snooze is additionally one of the key reasons why you cannot nod off. "Fear of insomnia is the explanation for insomnia," Buck said.

"When you eliminate anxiety and worry about not having the ability to urge an honest night's sleep, you'll get an honest night's sleep." To treat his patients, Barker first asked them to see the scene where they were sleeping all night, then he used hypnosis to put them in there. "I let people imagine their good sleep in the past, then allow them to remove the label 'I have insomnia' and replace it with 'I sleep a minimum of eight hours nightly.'"

Cure Phobia

The screaming of the drilling bit, the pinch of the needle, or the embarrassment of creating someone look in the mouth are just a few of the explanations people avoid getting to the dentist. Consistent with the British Dental Health Foundation, although the industry is functioning hard to use new dental technology to scale back the pressure to travel to the dentist's office, dental anxiety affects about 10% to twenty of the world's population.

Woods said: "For a few years, fear has kept many of my clients far away from the dentist's chair." "Fear may come from the dentist's negative experience, or it's going to be that somebody has experienced a negative experience."

To help her clients obviate the anxiety of getting to the dentist, she used neuro-linguistic programming (NLP), which may help the brain "reconnect" specific thinking processes and obtain obviate the automated thinking cycle. "When they begin to feel anxious about getting to the dentist, they will use NLP to eliminate anxiety and reconnect phobia on their own."

Relieve Chronic Pain

Woods said that pain might be a useful signal to us, but in the case of chronic pain, albeit the body has recovered, the nervous system may transmit pain signals. (There are several ways to make the pain worse). "We can use hypnosis to scale back pain." She recalled that patients with chronic low back pain couldn't sit on the chair. "He described this pain as a grizzly being on his spine." When she asked him what he required to do, he said he required to "put it to sleep." Woods worked with the customer to assist him to envision the bear crawling into a cave on a snowy day, curling back to sleep. Woods said: "Although hypnosis isn't magic, it sometimes seems like magic."

Manage Bereavement

Whether handling a national tragedy of losing loved ones, unfortunately, loss or grief may debilitate people, causing anxiety, insomnia, and depression. Losing yourself by crying can help your physical and psychological state.

Organizations like the American psychological state Organization and the American Psychological Association provide help to people affected by loss, including talking about a beloved's death, taking care of your health, handling injuries, and accepting your tribute to the emotions, and celebrating the lost people's lives. Barker explained that the coping mechanism to affect losses is personal.

Hypnosis can help you solve the symptoms of sadness by providing positive advice and finding an answer to the passage of your time. Buck puts a "timer" on the grief to assist people in dealing with the loss. "Normally, they're going to tell me once they are sick and uninterested in bereavement."

Reduce Anxiety

People with anxiety disorders can only be understood, like how frustrating and hopeless this example is often. Consistent with the American Psychiatric Association, nervousness sicknesses are the foremost mutual mental disturbance affecting 25 million Americans. Although anxiety disorders are usually treated with drugs or therapies or both, many of us also begin to hypnotize. The hypnotist's job is to work out the source of the stress or anxiety, whether it's situational, physical, or supported past problems.

Barker explained that sub-consciousness causes you to feel anxious and develop bad habits. Buck said: "When someone involves see me about nail-biting; nail-biting is typically not a drag, but anxiety." When an individual involves seeing Buck about speech disorders, he feels anxious for him.

Barker said: "His problems don't have anything to do with words, his problems are in his mind." During the meeting, Barker retreated the person to the age of six. Buck said: "He has climbed the roof of the house, and his father shouted due to the roof."

Although the American Stuttering Association doesn't support the claim that an emotional event causes stuttering, Buck believes that this is often the event (anxiety caused by his father's yelling and fear of being trapped on the roof) that contributed to his speech barrier. "During the meeting, I kept an equivalent memory, but from anger to an area. He held his arms hospitable to change his father's reaction, he loved him rather than yelling. When he was hypnotized, he stuttered missing."

Chapter 3 - How Powerful Is Our Subconscious

Grace's naturally magnificent charm and beauty brought her a complete scholarship to a prestigious modeling college. She fell out after six weeks because her weight ballooned to more than two hundred pounds, which stayed for another fifteen years regardless of persistent weight reduction attempts. Jack, fifty years older, was overweight since high school, even though playing sports, doing regular exercise, also creating many efforts at weight reduction. Whenever his weight starts to fall, he feels fearful until he regains the pounds.

Mary has won and gained the same twenty-five pounds throughout her adult life. She knows the routine and activates; however, she feels so helpless to alter them and shed the pounds once and for everyone. Alex is a successful executive in a competitive tech industry that always struggles with his burden.

He works hard, makes a higher income, and will multitask better than many, but cannot restrain the size of the waist. Ted has been CEO of a global source firm. His friends saw him as he moved from being a photograph of wellness to some health hazard due to excessive weight reduction. Grace, Jack, Mary, Alex, along with Ted, are actual cases we found in treatment for weight loss with hypnosis.

Like many other people, these folks once believed that food and eating were the issues causing their surplus fat. This chapter is all about what they discovered are the genuine culprit—the psychological mechanisms that affect or affect eating and weight reduction. We'll have a look at how inherent psychological problems are expressed in a way that triggers and keeps excess fat. We'll learn more about using hypnosis to discover the use of feelings and burdens. We're not likely to speak about eating disorders—like bulimia, anorexia, and pica—or even other hurtful behaviors. This chapter is about the most common methods by which our bodies can gain weight and keep it on.

The Mind-Body Mirror

Considering these are out of our mind-body medication practice, let's briefly examine a few of the standard methods that physical ailments are created by the mind-body. There are various examples where suppressed and repressed emotions locate saying by manifesting as physical symptoms and ailments.

Emotions and psychological conflicts that are not consciously acknowledged, voiced, or provided voice mayor will be voiced from the body. Here's a pervasive case. When anger isn't recognized and expressed, it can lead to muscles in your head, neck, and shoulders tightening up and stressed, which causes a pressure headache. It is the literal manifestation of something or somebody that's a pain in the throat. Another individual experiencing the very same feelings of anger may be burning over the circumstance, also expertise nausea, nausea, or an illness.

Your skin is the organ that's quite responsive to feelings. Also, a state of urticaria (hives) may erupt whenever somebody is getting under their skin or rubbing them the wrong manner or any time the individual is itching to say or do something, or even any emotion is erupting into the surface.

Your emotions are emotions, such as happy, sad, or mad. If feelings or emotions aren't expressed, the mind-body will reflect them in imaginative ways. Therapeutically, metaphors help us understand what the human body is expressing.

A figure of language or metaphor describing a psychological reaction like "a pain in the throat" is expressed through muscular strain and hassle, since the psychological frustration isn't being expressed differently. It can be a frequent encounter because, most times, it isn't okay or advisable to admit and convey anger or other emotions. For instance, if your boss embarrasses you or gets an unreasonable request, you can jeopardize your job if you have voiced your anger. Instead, you place it out of thoughts and go to another thing. Putting it from the mind doesn't place it from human anatomy.

Since you will notice from the hypnosis cases used in treatment, feelings and psychological conflicts could be placed out of thoughts, but not always from the body. You're able to suppress feelings or repress them. Suppressing feelings is if you intentionally decide not to consider them. Repressing emotions occurs whenever your subconscious does this without the advantage of choosing to perform it yourself. We'd love to spell out the difference between thoughts and feelings. Ideas are thoughts, beliefs, ideas, and conclusions on your own conscious or "thinking thoughts." Feelings or emotions are expressed in your entire body.

They arise in a crude place deep within the brain known as the limbic system. Both ideas and feelings are "items" in the meaning they're not only in your thoughts. They involve power and chemistry, and they're transmitted and energized throughout your nervous system along with other pathways inside the body.

The chemical compounds called hormones, like dopamine, serotonin, noradrenaline, and acetylcholine, would be the common ones included.

If someone experiences mental sluggishness, then he can notice more psychological acuity if he comprises nuts, oatmeal, along with other choline-rich foods within his everyday decisions. Choline affirms the purposes of acetylcholine, which subsequently promotes memory and mental sharpness. We would like to highlight that these psychological and cognitive reactions and routines are real and happen to be analyzed for our purposes.

Feelings or emotions comprise pain, anxiety, guilt, despair, joy, anger, pleasure, bliss, contentment, serene, stress, and isolation. Notice that "poor" and "good" aren't from the record of feelings. Though we may say "I feel awful" or "I'm great," these aren't emotions. These are conclusions about what you believe; however, they aren't feelings. More correctly, if you create these announcements, you believe "I feel sick" or even "I feel well," which are approaches to explain how you're feeling, maybe not what you're feeling.

Now, this is your only worth remembering: "Fat" isn't a feeling. Though folks say, "I feel fat," "fat" isn't a feeling. Whenever someone says they're "feeling fat, then" it's a declaration about a feeling, like feeling fulfilled, filled, complete, or outside full. You could be thinking, "Why the big deal on the selection of words? I understand what I mean when I state that." The reason why we emphasize that is your feelings, as well as your voice about your emotions, are part of your own beliefs about yourself, and if you maintain these in understanding or talk them aloud, they're direct messages to your subconscious mind. Your mind-body finds all of it, and also long after it's from the mind (consciousness), it isn't from your own body's mind. You are going to want to select carefully what your goal will be to think and anticipate about your weight loss and exactly what and how you are feeling about it, for it'll reflect it.

Saving Grace

One occurred to Grace that induced her to overlook her modeling college scholarship. She arrived at the office and expressed the desire to work with hypnosis to help her slim down. She clarified many trials of weight loss methods that had been ineffective. Whenever she didn't lose fat, it'd return. She believed that there was "something" keeping her out of losing weight. In carrying her background, we discovered she had been thirty-six years older, married with three kids, ages eight, seven, and five. Her weight was always over two hundred pounds for approximately fifteen decades. She grew up in the Midwest with a fantastic family and also had three sisters.

Grace explained herself as the only woman in her household having a weight issue. When asked regarding her weight record, she'd only say she "ate a lot." After finishing a thorough psychological and psychological evaluation, we proceeded to educate her about sculpting.

If she felt comfortable enough to move, we started with an induction method such as those on the sound with this publication. Grace relaxed readily into a trance country, wherein she had been absorbed in her thoughts and thoughts of a relaxing and enjoyable spectacle. As she pictured being on holiday with her loved ones, I provided hypnotic suggestions for her mind about letting her insight into the function or purpose of her extra body fat. In a couple of minutes, she seemed worried, and I asked her to explain what she was experiencing as she lasted.

She explained riding a train and also becoming the very first to arrive in the modeling school. The government office has been shut; however, a friendly janitor assisted her suitcases and unlocked the door to her delegated dining space. She was getting tearful and stressed as she continued talking. I assured her she would disrupt the squint at any moment or she would move more gradually and professionally. I informed her that she understood she had been at our office today as she recalled something which happened afterward, fifteen decades back. Through her tears, she clarified the favorable janitor returning after that night, allowing himself to her chamber and hammering her. The memory of the experience was rather exhausting and mentally draining for Grace. Discussing her following the trancework, I discovered it was nearly fifteen years since she'd thought about that adventure. She'd forgotten about it.

Initially, she opted to put this from her head, to curb this particular memory, but it had been put from her head so well that she'd forgotten that she forgot it. It had been repressed. She said this is the only real-time and location she had spoken to anybody about the encounter.

We spent a second session referring to her expertise in modeling faculty, and I requested her to earn some photos from this period. We used the photos to help her recall events so that she could chat about them at the security of treatment. She related that through the initial six months in school, her burden slowly improved, and she was anxious, fearful, embarrassed, depressed, and sleep-deprived. She didn't talk about the rape with anybody and moved home to wed her high school love.

He'd continuously accepted her for himself, and her burden was not a problem with him. Our counseling sessions demonstrated the goal of her excess body fat was a kind of defense. Her weight securely commanded her beauty, so that she had been shielded from becoming the target of the following sexual assault. After she confessed, voiced, and revived the experience and feelings (fear, pity), Grace's weight loss plan was quite robust in cutting her dimension to wherever she felt joyful and secure. In her situation, we realize that the subconscious had been working out a role, and also there was a reason for the surplus weight. It secured her and enabled her to feel secure. Though there was some time after she had been happy others found her appealing, the attack produced a panic that became linked to becoming captivating. After analyzing these feelings and eliminating this anxiety, she had been free to discharge her additional weight and feel secure when she felt appealing.

Chapter 4 - Losing Weight Fast and Easily

Forgiving Yourself for Your Dietary Mistakes

Forgiveness is an underrated and essential element of weight loss. Often, people that are within the position of wanting or not wanting to reduce and fail to acknowledge the very fact that they need been feeling incredibly frustrated with themselves. Anger, frustration, disappointment, and sadness directed at yourself once you are on this journey are all incredibly normal feelings to possess.

They can even be painful and overwhelming if you are doing not take the time to acknowledge them, forgive yourself, and heal them as you experience them. You may end up feeling angry, frustrated, disappointed, or sad that you simply let yourself gain such a lot of weight. You'll fail to acknowledge the very fact that it had been not intentional, or that it had causes that were beyond your control, mainly if your weight gain was associated with medical conditions or a scarcity of education around healthy eating.

Regardless of what causes you to gain weight, you'll feel contempt for yourself for "allowing" it to happen, which may make it difficult for you to plan to lose weight. When you sit in anger and frustration with yourself, it is often difficult to accept yourself as you're now and work toward improving your well-being through weight loss. Forgiving yourself for not knowing better or for not doing better, or maybe forgiving yourself for blaming yourself for something that was beyond your control, is vital.

The more you'll forgive yourself, the more likely you're to acknowledge that your weight is some things you would like to figure on. Through that, you'll be ready to work on weight loss from a peaceful frame of mind.

Studies have shown that those that accept themselves as they're and forgive their mistakes are more likely to lose the surplus weight and keep it off than those that refuse to forgive themselves. Refusing to forgive yourself can create a huge amount of stress inside you that creates it difficult for you to remain focused on exercising, eating healthy, and improving your wellness.

Many of us find that this difficulty in forgiving themselves worsens their self-esteem and self-confidence, which keeps them within the unhealthy cycle of behaviors and patterns that cause their weight gain in the first place. If you would like to beat these cycles, you would like to be willing to forgive yourself for your past choices, mistakes, and experiences, which may or may not be beyond your control.

Another area where you would like to master forgiveness is within the process of change. As you progress far away from old habits and behaviors and into a replacement way of taking care of your body, you're about bound to make mistakes. You are getting to have days or maybe weeks where you fall back to old patterns. Some people even fall back to old patterns and stay trapped in them for years. This fact happens because they're unwilling to forgive themselves for creating an error, then they fall back to the cycle of contempt and low self-esteem and self-worth.

If you would like to be ready to continue moving forward together with your wellness and to leap back on target as quickly as possible, you would like to be willing to forgive yourself for any mistakes you create.

This way means anytime you overeat, engage in an old eating pattern, choose an unhealthy food choice, or otherwise make a "mistake" in your diet, and you forgive yourself. Upon forgiving yourself, confirm that you also plan to take that have under consideration so that you'll make better choices. Make an honest effort to try to do better next time so that whenever you forgive yourself, you give yourself a reason to believe that your commitment to yourself genuinely means something.

When you can forgive yourself and believe that your commitment to bettering yourself and your life means something, you start to create your self-esteem. Through that, things like portion control begin to become easier, and you discover yourself naturally gravitating toward taking better care of yourself.

Meditation for Portion Control

The following may be a simple 5–10-minute meditation that you simply can do before you sit right down to eat a meal. Using the method will assist you in intentionally control portions so that you'll refrain from overeating.

Adding this meditation into the mixture will make sure that you're approaching your improved portion control from a deep subconscious level, allowing you to experience even more success in committing to moderation and healing your body through weight loss.

When you do that meditation, you ought to be actively sitting up with a straight spine. Laying down cause you to feel too tired or creating excess calmness in your day, which can cause you to struggle to take care of energy throughout the day.

The Meditation

I want you to start by intentionally taking one sweet deep breath into your belly, pressing your belly button and chest forward together with your breath. Then, once you exhale, let your belly button and chest drawback toward your spine. Feel the movement of your body because it naturally flows with each breath.

Do not attempt to control the speed at which you breathe, but instead feel how your body naturally breathes in and out for you. Feel your body intuitively drawing in and circulating oxygen throughout your body, and exhaling CO_2 from your body even as easily.

Notice how calm your body feels with each breath. Feel how breathing is so natural, so simple, so basic, and yet continues to be one of the strongest stress relievers we've. Meditate here together with your breath for a couple of moments as you sink deeply into this sense of trust in your body. In this way, your intuition will require you through each breath.

Now, I would like you to draw your awareness even deeper, into your stomach. Pause for a flash and see any hunger that arises in your body. Take into consideration what this hunger seems like and what cues your body is supplying you with that indicate that it's time to eat. Feel yourself acknowledging and becoming conscious of your own needs and trust that your intuition is providing you with the proper information about your body.

As you begin taking note of your intuition about your hunger, ask yourself: "How hungry am I?" Concentrate on the solution that rises. Are you hungry for a snack or a full meal? Be mindful of what proportion of food your body genuinely wants and the way much it needs.

Now, ask yourself, "What am I actually hungry for?" and pay close attention. Trust that whatever answer comes in is correct and be willing to figure alongside your body to seek out the simplest source of nutrition for you and your well-being. Trust that when you're done this meditation, you'll choose something healthier and more nutritious, which will help your body meet its needs.

As you still sit together with your intuition, develop a trust in your inner knowingness and your emotional ability to acknowledge your hunger cues. Ask your body to be honest about once you feel full and ask it to assist you to stop craving food naturally so that you'll stop eating when your body feels full.

Affirm that you simply want to require care of your body and earn its trust by serving it in the way that it truly must be served. Affirm that you deserve to enjoy healthy portions of food that nourish your body without overwhelming you. Feel yourself being fulfilled and satisfied by these affirmations. Trust that they're right, which your subconscious, unconscious, and conscious mind can all work together to assist you in managing your eating habits more effectively.

When you are able to awaken yourself from this meditation, bring your awareness back to your breath, then to your body. Feel yourself gently awakening from this moment of peace and permit yourself to acknowledge what your body told you it needed. Act thereon information and, to the simplest of your ability, follow your intuition and hunger cues to make sure that you simply feed yourself an appropriate amount of healthy, nutritious food.

If, during the meditation, your body informed you that it had been not hungry but instead required emotional support, make sure to avoid emotional eating and instead hunt down an alternate way for managing your emotions. The more you'll practice following these intuitive cues around feelings and other needs, additionally to your hunger cues, the higher you're getting to be ready to look out of yourself. Through this, you'll end up naturally engaging in portion control and taking care of your well-being through your diet. As a result, you'll reduce faster, easier, and healthier.

Affirmation to Cut Calories

Affirmations are an excellent tool to use alongside hypnosis to assist you in rewiring your brain and improving your weight loss abilities. Statements are essentially a tool that you use to remind you of your chosen "rewiring" and to encourage your mind to select your newer, healthier mindset over your old unhealthy one. Using affirmations is a crucial part of anchoring your hypnosis efforts into your lifestyle, so you must use them on a routine basis.

When using affirmations, it's important that you simply use relevant ones, which are getting to support you in anchoring your chosen reality into your present reality.

What Are Affirmations and How Do They Work?

Anytime you repeat something to yourself aloud, or in your thoughts, you're affirming something to yourself. We use affirmations consistently, whether we consciously know it or not. For instance, if you're on your weight loss journey and you repeat "I am never getting to lose the weight" to yourself daily, you're affirming to yourself that you only are never getting to succeed with weight loss. Likewise, if you're consistently saying, "I will always be fat" or "I am never getting to reach my goals," you're affirming those things to yourself, too.

When we use affirmations unintentionally, we frequently find ourselves using statements that will be hurtful and harmful to our psyche and our reality.

You might end up locking into becoming a mental bully toward yourself as you consistently repeat things to yourself that are unkind and even downright mean. As you are doing this, you affirm a lower sense of self-confidence, a scarcity of motivation, and a commitment to a body shape and wellness journey that you simply don't want to take care of.

Affirmations, whether positive or negative, conscious, or unconscious, are always creating or reinforcing the function of your brain and mindset. Each time you repeat something to yourself, your subconscious hears it and strives to form it, a neighborhood of your reality. This fact is often because your subconscious is liable for creating your truth and your sense of identity.

It creates both around your affirmations since these are what you perceive as being your absolute truth; therefore, they create a "concrete" foundation for your reality and identity to rest on.

If you would like to vary these two aspects of yourself and your experience, you're getting to got to change what you're routinely repeating to yourself so that you're not creating a reality and identity rooted in negativity.

To vary your subconscious experience, you would like to choose positive affirmations consciously and repeat them continuingly to assist you in achieving the truth and identity that you only genuinely want.

Chapter 5 - Focused Thinking, Meditation & Affirmations

If you think you will be happy when you reach your ideal weight but get stuck on a negative view of your body, it will not work.

Have you noticed that when you get up on the wrong foot, you are all day in a bad mood and you think that the spell is going on because you only get nasty things? On the contrary, with a cheerful mood people seem more pleasant to you, smiling, you feel light.

You have unknowingly emitted a vibration towards the universe, which sends your thoughts back to you. The positive attracts the positive. The negative brings you a negative result. This form of energy is transmitted to the universe, and it influences what you will get from your unconscious request.

Above all, do not focus on everything negative about weight, calories, fat, diet, suffering in an intensive sports practice. You just attract them with thought.

On the contrary, if you focus on the result you want to achieve, if you see this evolution step-by-step, you will modify your lifestyle to achieve this positive result for you. How can positive thinking be the most powerful solution for programming our brain and dictating that it makes us lose weight easily? Demons, get out of our head!

These demons (ideas, beliefs, emotions) build what we are by a very powerful influence, the law of coherence. Our obsessive desire to be and to appear consistent in our behavior sometimes pushes us to act contrary to our interests.

In other words, unconscious pressures force us to react in order to agree with what we choose to believe. This self-persuasion applies to all choices. It is impossible for us that our opinions are different from what we have already chosen, even if it means lying to us from time to time.

So choosing to think every day that one is overweight unconsciously leads to doing what it takes to be! So, great resolution, we are going to start losing weight by diet or any other method!

Yes but, as soon as we start to feel lighter, the brain panics because it is absolutely not consistent with the image of the choice that our mind makes daily (the fact that we think we are overweight).

This is when our demons come to tug at us. "I feel better slimmer but, strangely, I am pushed to crack and eat anything to feel better." Personally, the speech of my mind to allow me to make a gap (a big gap of sugar in general), was "you have made efforts, you can have fun, you will take things back seriously after." It was actually a big lie to return to an image consistent with my misconceptions about my physique.

Without understanding that the method we are choosing is not the right solution, we blame ourselves for not having succeeded. The snacking trend is reinstalling and so is the yo-yo. Making positive affirmations means talking to yourself, aloud (preferably when you are alone!) By telling yourself positive words, which boost. It may seem strange at first glance, but considering the incredible results, it doesn't cost anything to try!

It is a method of personal development that is used to reprogram your brain to think positively. You can make positive statements for your health, your work or your self-confidence, your relationships, etc.

The goal is to attract happiness by pronouncing it! At first, one does not believe frankly in what one says. The lyrics are even the opposite of what we really think but by dint of saying it, the brain will believe it and so will we! This is how they will have a real impact on our lives.

Some examples of statements to lose weight:

- I deserve to have the body I desire.

- I take care of myself and it makes me feel good.

- I feel better and better.

- I am proud not to give in to gluttony, bad for my health, each day brings me a little closer to my goal.

- I have a healthy life and I eliminate my bad habits I lose weight because I love myself (not because I don't like my body).

- I deserve to be happy and to have confidence in myself I can do it.

Mindset and Weight Loss

When you want to lose weight, you have to adopt good food hygiene and exercise. But also find a physical and psychological balance, learning to manage stress, and develop positive thoughts.

We will appreciate (also) the "good" foods Try to imagine that you are at the table in a "haven of peace," an idyllic place in which you feel comfortable, serene, and safe. In this dream location, we are well, the temperature is ideal. Right on a table, imagine "toxic" and fatty foods. Oily fries, gravy dishes, pasta drowned in grated cheese, cakes, anything that tempts us and makes us fat. On the left are the "good" foods. Fruits, vegetables, salads, grilled fish. Imagine eating them with pleasure. We feel calm, relaxed. We naturally choose foods rich in vitamins and minerals, feeling the benefits they provide, their freshness, their flavor. So you feel light, at peace with yourself, and full of vitality.

We already imagine with ideal weight. The purpose of this exercise is to visualize the silhouette of your dreams so that you feel perfectly good about yourself, as you wish to be. Inspire this new life, this new being to which we aspire. Expire negative experiences from the past. Expel unpleasant memories often associated with excess pounds from your body and mind. After several breaths through your stomach, you feel good, calm, relaxed. Imagine that you step on the scales to weigh yourself. Project on your mental screen, the ideal weight replacing the old one, which no longer suits us. Take a good look at the figures for this new weight, which are clearly displayed on the scale. See that we got there. Tense your body slightly by squeezing all the muscles from head to toe and holding your breath for 5 seconds. At the same time, bringing into your thoughts the new weight that you're will strive to achieve. Now, it is recorded, "programmed."

We Fill up But Calm

When you have a compulsive need for food, which in reality allows you to calm your anxiety, you have to be able to immediately tell the brain to stop. The goal: nourish your body with serenity and affection, rather than sugars and fats! To achieve this, adopt the "abdominal breathing" reflex. First, drink a glass of water to refocus. Breathing starting with the expiration: breathe first, and exhale by expelling this compulsive urge to throw yourself on food. Then inspire calm, relaxation. Try to take a step back, to see if this compulsion is not a way of running away from a negative emotion. Do a full breath: breath in the positive and calm and breath out the negative, stress.

We Pamper Our Body

Learning to love your body, to pamper it, is one of the keys to initiating weight loss. Put your hands on your body with love, including and especially on areas that are under tension, those that suffer or that do not like. This exercise can be done perfectly when taking a bath. Imagine then that the shower jet projects well-being on every part of the body. Massage slowly while lingering on the different parts that need to slim down to send them positive energy.

Law of Attraction

Be Aware

Be aware of your eating habits and what you have acquired since your childhood concerning food.

If these are negative thoughts, such as "I must finish my plate even if I am no longer hungry," especially do not force yourself to anything else, but enjoy eating your dish when you are hungry, learn to stop to feel satiated. Your relationship with food should become positive, a source of pleasure, not an obligation.

Likewise, your sport to lose weight must be done in all conscience so that your body takes pleasure in being in action. See it as fitness, a special time of the day. Be aware of its benefits for your body and keep in mind your weight loss goal.

Act as If...

Act like you have the ideal weight, the physical condition you want to have. If you focus on your current problems, which you do not like at home, you will receive the same thing, and you will not be able to lose weight.

You will perceive your body positively, you will learn to love it. You become aware of your needs; you get into the habit of seeing yourself as you want to be to get what you want, thanks to visualization.

Learn to Love Your Body

Believe in yourself, be confident. Learn to love your body. The positive energy will emit a vibration that the universe will receive to send you back what you want. Maintain this positivity, keep your goal in mind.

When you exercise, you must see this activity as a weight-loss tool and you must feel good. You are aware of and take care of the changes taking place in your body.

Of course, the sports sessions must be adapted to your physical condition and you must take pleasure in them.

Law of attraction techniques:

Address the Universe

Formulate a sentence to determine your objective and make your request clear and precise. Thus you will have a return following your objective.

Visualization

Visualize each part of your body with this 5 or 10 kg less. Take the time to do this visualization. Be specific and make your request humbly and positively.

A recommended technique for this exercise is drawing. Draw yourself with your slim body. Your visualization will be all the stronger. You can proceed in stages, within 30 days, for example. Then in 3 months, 6 months.

Gratitude

Thank the universe for the feedback you get. This gratitude means that you emit the energy of love, and this positive energy will come back to you. You can, for example, say thank you every evening for the good things obtained during the day: a good breakfast, your child's smile, the bright sun, a little less. These are simple everyday things that you enjoy and that allow you to emit positive energy.

This mindset will also encourage you to eat healthy, to do you good, and this will contribute to your weight loss. Sadness and negativity, on the contrary, push us to eat very high-calorie foods, too salty or sweet, which promote weight gain.

Meditation

Through meditation, you learn to nourish your soul, to find yourself in your interior. It allows you to refocus and will avoid the anxiety that pushes you to snack or eat too much. You no longer feel this lack or this emptiness within you. Regular practice is essential.

The Simplicity of the Law of Attraction in Your Life

In conclusion, the law of attraction is a natural phenomenon that we use in our lives often without being aware of it.

Your thoughts, your beliefs, your attitude influence your actions. You can decide your life with your thoughts, your beliefs, and your actions. You shape your life, and by doing so you express your desire to lose weight quickly, with positive thinking, and the universe conspires to offer it to you.

With the law of attraction, based on these steps and exercises, you will lose weight quickly and stay slim.

Chapter 6 - Hypnosis for Binge Eating

Hello and welcome to your hypnosis weight loss session "Binge eating" that will support your determination and install a mental gastric band so you can effortlessly follow through and stick to your diet plan. All sessions in this weight loss program are hypnotic in nature, and they can easily put you in a state of relaxation and absorb your conscious attention inside. Please do not listen to these sessions while driving or operating any machinery or at any other time, which requires your full, awaken attention.

I am the Hypnosis Guru, and I will guide you through this wonderfully relaxing experience and an amazing journey of discovering the inner strength and resources that will help you energize your inner willpower so you can naturally start losing weight while enjoying the process of change. You are here because you decided to be healthier, fitter, and feel good in your body.

Sometimes we allow ourselves to fill every hole in our belly, and typically we have many excuses for doing so. From classical excuses such as "I will start my diet tomorrow" all the way to "just one more bite." Whatever excuse we have, it is just our own permission to feel bad in the future about our weight and the way we look. The most common reason why we come up with any excuse is that we are trying to increase our sense of comfort. And that is perfectly fine if you want to increase your sense of comfort, but choose the strategy that will not make you feel bad about yourself in the future. Listening to this guided hypnosis is a good strategy to limit your food intake with the power of your mind, so you can stop binge eating, and certainly start feeling the benefits of sticking to a healthier lifestyle.

We will begin this guided hypnosis session by becoming consciously aware that we are always in control and always have a choice. At this moment the only choice you need to make now is to choose to go into a deep relaxation right now, or in a few moments when you make yourself more comfortable at ease and when you tell yourself, " I am going to relax now completely and effortlessly, while my subconscious mind learns everything that is needed to stop my binge eating."

Start inhaling purposefully, and a bit deeper than usual, then slowly push all the air out as much as you can, and once you push all the air out, pause for a second before you start inhaling again.

One more time, take another deep breath in and purposefully and slowly push all the air out completely and once all the air is out, pause for a second before you start inhaling again do not be surprised if you can already notice that the old compulsions are just starting to melt away as you inhale deeply and allow yourself to relax.

Continue breathing at a steady pace, just like you normally do, and allow the air to move in and out of your lungs and belly to deepen your relaxation. Imagine that each time you inhale, relaxation energy fills your head, neck, and chest, and as you exhale, that relaxation energy spreads through the rest of your body, just like a wave.

Filling your head, neck, and chest and as you inhale, and spreading that relaxation energy all over your body as it goes down, your arms and belly all the way down your legs and feet washing away your worries, concerns, and troubling thoughts.

Continue your relaxation by releasing everyday worries, concerns, and troubling thoughts by simply directing your focus to your body. Make yourself comfortable before you get completely absorbed by the sound of my voice that will lead you into a perfect state of mind to let go, release, and free yourself completely from binge eating and become more determined to limit your food intake.

As you make those final small adjustments. I would like you to mentally become aware of your feet. It doesn't matter if you are sitting or lying down, as long as you are aware of the sensation in your feet right now. At this moment, become aware of the sensation in your feet and imagine how light they would feel like, just after one week of stopping binge eating and consciously limiting your food intake.

Instruct all the small muscles in your feet to relax, and as your feet become even more relaxed, allow that relaxation to move upwards toward your calves and knees, making your muscles soften and become completely relaxed.

Fill that relaxation in your thighs, making you experience that pleasant heaviness of completely relaxed muscles in your legs. Relaxation and that inspiring image of limiting your food intake are moving up your torso lower back and wraps around your stomach and slowly start shrinking your stomach to a size that can match your consciously determined limit of food intake as you are becoming even more relaxed.

Each time you think of food and eating, you see this image wrapping around your stomach tightly, so it allows only a limited amount of food that is enough for you to stay healthy and become fit.

And naturally, as relaxation reaches your chest, you feel a strong desire to inhale deeply and fill your lungs with air, as your upper body evenly distributes that relaxation across your shoulders and arm all the way to your fingertips and that tingling sensation that you feel in your fingers and palms are there only to remind you that you are about to go into a wonderfully relaxed state of mind perfect for you to completely let go of all the worries, concerns and stop binge eating, but not just yet there is no rush, you will do this soon.

Before you go into a wonderfully relaxed state of mind, I would like you to imagine that you are standing in front of a staircase that is leading up. You can see ten steps in front of you and as I count from one to ten, you will imagine that you are climbing those stairs and with each and new step, your decision to limit your food intake becomes stronger. The moment you hear me say "ten" you will naturally go into a wonderfully relaxed state of mind and body and find yourself in a room with a dining table and a chair.

Starting to climb the stairs. One. Two. Feeling that familiar sense of determination. Three. Four. Increasing the willpower behind your intention to limit your food intake. Five. Six. Feeling deeply satisfied with the decision to stop binge eating. Seven. Eight. Choosing only to have 20 bites of fresh and healthier food for each meal. Nine. Ten. You are now at the top of the staircases in a room with a dining table, feeling completely relaxed and with a strong determination to limit your food intake to 20 bites per meal.

This will happen on its own. You don't have to do anything yet. Your body and your subconscious mind will know how to do that for you. Once you are ready to let go, release, and free yourself completely so that you can make more space for building a stronger intention and follow through with your decision to limit your food intake and choose food that is beneficial for your well-being.

Consciously imagine a big green number twenty and see it in your mind. Imagine that this is the number of bites that you are taking for each meal to eat. These twenty bites of carefully chosen healthier food are the perfect amount for the new size of your stomach that is wrapped up in that inviting image and the idea of limiting your food intake and stopping binge eating for good.

Each meal you are about to start, remember that big green number twenty and you instantly know that you have the opportunity to enjoy this healthy food meal as you make your determination to have a healthier lifestyle even stronger.

Give clear instructions to your subconscious mind to follow your lead and assist you in creating this habit and choices by visualizing yourself doing this. Visualize that you are sitting at the table covered with all kinds of food and even though that everything is available you are deciding to choose only healthy food that is good for your well-being and you are also deciding to have just a limited amount of that food. As you prepare yourself to start eating, a big green number twenty appears in front of you to remind you to completely enjoy these twenty bites of delicious healthy food. You take the first bite and start chewing very slowly so you can experience all the flavors and satisfy your senses.

Nineteen. You take another bite and you notice the fresh smells of your food as you chew slowly.

Eighteen. You are becoming more mindful when you are eating and you can notice all the soft sounds you make as you are slowly chewing your healthy food.

Seventeen. You are now aware of all the movements that your mouth, tongue, and jaw are making while you are eating.

Sixteen. Your awareness is following your food from the moment it touches your mouth, as it makes its way over the tongue down your throat into your stomach.

Fifteen. Your subconscious mind learns everything that is needed that will stop your binge eating disorder.

You continue to eat slowly and mindfully as you enjoy every bite. You are now at number ten, and you can notice that your stomach is becoming full. A few more delicious bites and you are now at the number five nearly there, but far away from old habits so far away from old compulsions far away from binge eating.

Now you have one more bite to complete your conscious food intake limit and when you eat this last bite you feel that your stomach is completely full and you feel very good about yourself. You know that this is the right choice for you to accomplish your diet goals.

The delicious and healthy meal is now finished. You stand up and move away from the table and as you are starting to make your way back to that staircase, the first thing you are starting to notice is that you are lighter and that your feet really relaxed and lighter than before so proud of yourself, because you are doing it, you are finally taking control.

In a moment I will ask you to start going down the stairs as I count down from ten to one and the moment you hear me say "one" you will allow your subconscious mind to take this vision of you happily enjoying twenty bites for each meal and make it into a new habit.

You will continue to do so, naturally and effortlessly until you are satisfied with the choices you are making to live a new and healthier way of life or until you find another strategy or a new behavior that will work even better than this for you to stop binge eating and achieve your diet goals.

Start going down the stairs as I do the countdown. Ten. Nine. Filling your subconscious mind with all the necessary information that it needs to support you in this important journey. Eight. Seven. Thinking about all the benefits that will come with your healthy lifestyle. Six. Five. Your decision to limit your food intake is getting stronger and stronger. Four. Three. You are following through with your plan. Two. You take only twenty bites per meal. One. Allowing your subconscious mind to create all the changes required to support your new habit and your healthy lifestyle.

You are now at the bottom of the stairs and you can see yourself integrating all of these learnings and useful insights as you prepare yourself to slowly come back to this present moment in time and whenever you are ready. Open your eyes and become fully awake and aware of your strong decision to make healthy choices.

Chapter 7 - Weight Reduction

Your weight is an activity in cautious control, and calories are a piece of that condition. Weight decrease reduces to burning through a bigger number of calories than you take in.

You can do that by reducing extra calories from sustenance and rewards, and extending calories burned through actual development. While that appears to be straightforward, it tends to be trying to actualize a useful, successful, and economical weight-reduction plan.

Be that as it may, you don't need to do only it. Converse with your PCP loved ones for help. Inquire if it is currently a decent time and in case you're prepared to roll out some important improvements. Likewise, plan brilliant: Anticipate how you'll deal with circumstances that challenge your purpose and the inescapable minor mishaps.

And because you have genuine medical issues due to your weight, your primary care physician may recommend weight reduction medical procedures or meds for you. In this situation, your PCP will talk about the potential advantages and the potential dangers with you.

In any case, remember the reality: The way to effective weight reduction is a pledge to making changes in your eating regimen and exercise propensities.

Weight Reduction—6 Procedures for Progress

Many crazy people abstain from food, health improvement plans, and inside and out tricks that guarantee brisk and simple weight reduction. Be that as it may, the establishment of effective weight reduction stays a solid, calorie-controlled eating regimen joined with expanded physical action. For effective, long-haul weight reduction, you should roll out lasting improvements in your way of life and well-being propensities.

How would you make those lasting changes? Consider following these six methodologies for weight reduction achievement.

Get Ready, Sure You Are

Long stretch weight decrease requires some venture and effort—and a long stretch duty. While you would not really like to put off weight decrease uncertainly, you ought to get ready sure you're to carry out constant upgrades to eating and activity penchants. Ask yourself the going with requests to help you with choosing your accessibility:

- Am I pushed to get more slender?

- Am I exorbitantly redirected by various loads?

- Do I utilize sustenance as an approach to adjust to pressure?

- Am I arranged to learn or use various techniques to adjust to pressure?

- Do I require other assistance—either from buddies or specialists—to manage the pressure?

- Am I prepared to change dietary examples?

- Am I prepared to change activity penchants?

Do I have the chance to spend on carrying out these upgrades?

Banter with your essential consideration doctor and because you need help watching out for stressors or sentiments that seem obstacles to your arrangement. Exactly when you're arranged, you'll see it more straightforward to set destinations, remain submitted, and change inclinations.

Find Your Internal Motivation

No one else can make you get fit as a fiddle. You should accept diet and exercise changes to fulfill yourself. What will give you the devouring drive to stick to your weight decrease plan?

Make a once-over of what's basic to you to help you with remaining prodded and focused, whether it's an exceptional outing or better all-around prosperity. By then, sort out some way to guarantee that you can move toward your helpful factors during previews of temptation. You should introduce an enabling note on yourself on the storeroom doorway or ice chest, for instance.

While you need to accept responsibility for your own lead for productive weight decrease, it has support—of the right kind. Pick people who will help you and allow you to have safe habits, without shame, disgrace, or damage.

Ideally, find people who will check out your inclinations and suppositions, contribute energy rehearsing with you or making strong menus, and offer the need you've set on developing a more profitable lifestyle. Your consideration gathering can similarly offer obligation, which can be a strong motivation for holding fast to your weight decrease goals.

What's more, since you need to keep your weight decrease plans hidden, be capable to yourself by having standard weigh-ins, recording your eating routine and exercise progress in a journal, or monitoring your improvement using progressed contraptions.

Set Reasonable Goals

It may show up incredibly clear to set sensible weight decrease targets. Nevertheless, do you really know what's sensible? As time goes on, it's splendid to target losing 1 to 2 pounds (0.5 to 1 kilogram) seven days. All around to lose 1 to 2 pounds each week, you need to burn through 500 to 1,000 calories more than you use each day, through a lower calorie diet and standard actual activity.

Dependent upon your weight, 5% of your current weight may be a down-to-earth level-headed, n any occasion for a basic goal. Furthermore, because you gauge 180 pounds (82 kilograms), that is 9 pounds (4 kilograms). Without a doubt, even this level of weight decrease can help cut down your risk of steady clinical issues, for instance, coronary ailment and type 2 diabetes.

Exactly when you're characterizing goals, consider both methodology and result destinations. "Walk every day for 30 minutes" is an instance of a system objective. "Shed 10 pounds" is an instance of an outcome objective. It isn't principal that you have an outcome objective, yet you should set system targets because changing your inclinations is a key to weight decrease.

Like More Invaluable Foods

Embracing another eating style that advances weight decrease should consolidate cutting down your total calorie utilization. However, reducing calories need not mean giving up taste, satisfaction, or even straightforwardness of supper status.

One way you can cut down your calorie confirmation is by eating more plant-based foods—natural items, vegetables, and whole grains. Gain ground toward variety to help you with achieving your destinations without giving up taste or sustenance.

Kick your weight decrease off with these tips:

• Eat on any occasion four servings of vegetables and three servings of natural items step-by-step.

• Supplant refined grains with whole grains.

- Utilize unassuming proportions of strong fats, for instance, olive oil, vegetable oils, avocados, nuts, nut spreads, and nut oils.

- Scale back sugar whatever amount as could sensibly be anticipated, besides the normal sugar in a natural item.

- Pick low-fat dairy things and lean meat and poultry in confined wholes.

Get Dynamic, Stay Dynamic

While you can shed pounds without work out, standard actual development notwithstanding calorie restriction can help give you the weight decrease edge. Exercise can help light with offing the bounty calories you can't cut through eating routine alone. Exercise moreover offers different clinical benefits, including boosting your mentality, sustaining your cardiovascular structure, and diminishing your circulatory strain. Exercise can in like manner help in keeping up weight decrease.

Studies show that people who keep up their weight decrease as time goes on achieve a real standard activity.

What number of calories you burn depends upon the repeat, term, and power of your activities. Likely the best way to deal with the loss of muscle to fat proportion is through tireless, energetic exercise—for instance, vivacious walking—for at any rate 30 minutes most days of the week. A couple of individuals may require more actual development than this to get more slender and keep up that weight decrease.

Any extra improvement burns through calories. Consider ways you can construct your actual activity for the span of the day and because you can't fit in proper exercise on a given day. For example, cheat a couple of times by walking down the steps instead of using the lift, or park further away when shopping.

Change Your Perspective

It's deficient to eat well foods and exercise for simply a large portion of a month or even a very long time in case you need a long stretch, successful weight the chiefs. These inclinations should transform into a way of life. Lifestyle changes start with examining your eating models and step-by-step plan.

Ensuing to assessing your own troubles to weight decrease, offer the opportunity to work out an approach to bit by bit change affinities and outlooks that have assaulted your previous undertakings. By then move past essentially seeing your troubles—plan for how you'll oversee them on the off chance that you will win for shedding pounds once and for all.

You probably will have a coincidental disaster. In any case, as opposed to giving up out and out after a setback, basically, start anew the next day. Review that you're aiming to change yourself. It will not happen simultaneously. Cling to your strong lifestyle and the results will be advocated, regardless of all the difficulty.

Chapter 8 - Diet Plans

With regards to weight reduction, there's no lack of diet plans. Check any magazine rack, and will undoubtedly observe the best in class diet plans. Be that as it may, how would you know whether an eating regimen plan meets your requirements and way of life?

Ask yourself these inquiries about any eating regimen plan you're thinking about:

• Does it incorporate different nourishments from the significant nutrition types: organic products, vegetables, grains, low-fat dairy items, lean protein sources, and nuts?

• Does it incorporate nourishments you like and that you would appreciate eating for a lifetime—not only for a little while or months?

• Can you effectively discover these nourishments in your neighborhood supermarket?

• Will you have the option to eat your preferred nourishments or, even better, all nourishments (regardless of whether some are in little amounts)?

• Does it fit your way of life and spending plan?

• Does it incorporate appropriate measures of supplements and calories to assist you with shedding pounds securely and successfully?

- Is ordinary physical action some portion of the arrangement?

On the off chance that the response to any of these inquiries is no, continue looking. There are better eating regimen designs out there for you.

Chapter 9 - The Secret to Getting Rid of Weight Problems

What is the key to disposing of weight issues? I will advise you. The stunt is breaking the old psyche blocks, creating new examples of thought, and blending the cognizant and subliminal brain. Spellbinding will assist you with overcoming the subliminal coalition impediments.

You'll feel much improved. They will feel in charge. You'll feel sure to have the option to control your weight in support and assurance to stay aware of your weight reduction objectives. Entrancing has none of the negative or hurtful symptoms of diet pills or medical procedures. If you pick an effective eating regimen and exercise plan and reinvent your psyche to make it done testing yet straightforward, lovely, and proficient to follow your food and wellness software engineer, you will surely succeed.

Have some good times practicing and practicing good eating habits, so you can quit causing self-instigated strain, stress, and debilitation. You will begin doing the things that will help you in your point of being protected and getting more fit, clearly. You need to dispose of the unfortunate propensities for felt that make you overweight. These idea designs, which are put away in your psyche mind, should be supplanted with better considerations and solid practices so you can naturally do what you are generally anticipated to manage while never mulling over it.

Does that sound interesting? In actuality, it's significantly less convoluted than you would envision. All you need is 10 to 20 minutes per day for a sum of 21 days (the measure of time it takes to fabricate a propensity). You would now be able to have the stuff to rapidly program your psyche to get thinner. Spellbinding is one of the present world's generally disregarded and incredible techniques for self-change.

At the point when you say "entrancing," the vast majority consider sorcery shows in Vegas or idiotic follows up on stage. Those dramatic were picked particularly in light of their defenselessness to the idea. They wouldn't do whatever they regularly wouldn't do in front of an audience. For the exposure they get, they truly "wouldn't fret" acting moronically in front of an audience. In the event that they don't perform, they realize they will be removed from the stage and back to the seat. There couldn't be anything further from current realities. In principle, spellbinding is a truly agreeable perspective wherein you become more open to ideas. During the day, you typically go through spellbinding ordinarily.

If the utilization of entrancing for treating disease has been acknowledged by significant clinical social orders, envision how incredibly effective and valuable it is when adapting to thought designs that hold up traffic of the sound body you merit.

The utilization of entrancing has been utilized for the greater part of a century to treat disease. Likewise, in 1955, the British Medical Association supported hypnotherapy use. Its utilization was endorsed in 1958 by the American Medical Association.

In a 9-week preliminary weight the board bunch study (one utilizing spellbinding and one not utilizing it), the entrancing gathering has kept on getting brings about the two-year follow-up, while the non-spellbinding gathering didn't show any further outcomes (Journal of Consulting and Clinical Psychology, 1985). The gatherings utilizing spellbinding lost a normal of 16 pounds in an example of 60 members, while the other gathering lost a normal of simply 0.5 pounds (Journal of Consulting and Clinical Psychology, 1986). Numerous investigations showed that the expansion of entrancing expanded the weight reduction by a normal of 97% during treatment and, all the more significantly, the adequacy expanded by over 146% after treatment. Spellbinding is known to perform much better over the long run (Journal of Consulting and Clinical Psychology, 1996). "The most ideal approach to bring an end to negative routines is by spellbinding," even Newsweek Magazine said.

Regardless of whether you need to utilize sound tapes or CDs for spellbinding, assess the content used to decide whether the ideas sound good to you. Ensure there are no regrettable ideas. The psyche won't hear "no" or "don't," so the idea's accentuation would be: "I don't devour stuffing food varieties." This will give you your goal the other way. Simply utilize useful input. "I simply eat new food varieties that cause me to feel strong, safe, and cheerful" is vastly improved.

How you see the ideas is critical. If somebody said, "That entryway ought to be shut," you get up and close the entryway or simply think, possibly it ought to be shut and another person should close it. At the point when you get up and close the entryway, it implies you've "construed" you should close your entryway. Some groups do not like to be told what to do (direct ideas).

You might be making your own sound more compelling. You may play an alleviating sound and afterward, peruse or compose your ideas.

At the point when you get up toward the beginning of the day and before going to bed at night is the best opportunity for your psyche to acknowledge these positive ideas. You need a calm room where nothing pesters you. At the point when you're getting a ton of activity in your home, you may have to discover a room where you can close the entryway and get undisturbed. It just endures from 10 to 20 minutes. Entrancing is definitely not a one-time fix for the vast majority, the outcomes are aggregate.

The more post-mesmerizing ideas are applied to the spellbinding, the more perpetual the outcomes become. In this way, scarcely any individuals are probably going to get entranced once to abstain from smoking or get in shape. We normally make another propensity on the off chance that they do, to supplant the one they just quit. The vast majority who quit smoking start gorging. We were supplanting just a single unwanted propensity with another. Except if the root(s) of the issue is found, there would be no compelling reason to add another propensity.

Having an expert talented in entrancing and the weight reduction battles could demonstrate helpfully. Working with an expert will assist you with understanding the previous programming and eliminate it. Particularly with weight reduction, utilize the unwinding and self-spellbinding each day and evening to be viable, changing and culminating your ideas while you get thinner. After arriving at the weight you are alright with, you should add different objectives alongside fortifying your smart dieting and practicing propensities.

You should begin with full unwinding from the outset, yet following a week or thereabouts, you will actually want to go rapidly into the modified loosened upstate by tallying down from 10 to 1. Continuously end your meeting with an idea that causes you to feel better, better than anyone might have expected, loose and either ready, perceptive, invigorated, and loaded with morning energy or loose and ready to adequately rest when you hit the hay around evening time.

Keep a pen and paper nearby to record any bits of knowledge that ring a bell while tuning in to your ideas or understanding them. You can review things that you were told as a youngster that presently impact your conduct. As far as I might be concerned, I began to recall a ton of things I was told when I was a kid that I never thought had irritated me until I was a lot more established. I simply didn't interface with those things that I recalled with my conduct. I turned out to be truly distraught when I reviewed. I understood the existence I missed by having faith in what these individuals had said or shown me as a kid and built up during that time by others and occasions.

Weight Reduction Affirmations
Are They Enough and How to Practice Them?

Weight reduction claims would say that one of the numerous daily insistences that individuals are rehearsing to develop themselves, yet would they say they are barely enough to roll out an improvement, and how would you rehearse them successfully? This article talks about what to incorporate with your positive weight-reduction certifications just as approaches to make them work.

As a matter of first importance, while rehearsing confirmations of weight reduction or some other attestations of confidence, recall that you're "working from the back to front." What that implies is that to roll out any improvement in your life, regardless of whether it's centered on your actual body or your funds, you need to change your outlook and inward brain (your inner mind) before any external change shows up.

While numerous individuals definitely think about this idea, it isn't constantly drilled so that positive cases for weight reduction or different certifications of confidence function just as they would. You should truly "accept" that you are meager to "be slender," and that is the place where the vast majority "tumble off the cart" and try not to make their ordinary confirmations because the external shift isn't adequately fast.

Thus, when you start, you choose to permit yourself sufficient opportunity to roll out the inward improvement with no "assumption" of seeing any outer changes.

Then, you will need to remember other positive affirmations for a regular routine, like self-esteem crowds, otherworldly confirmations, and confidence affirmations that are more assertive. Why? For what? Since when you're attempting to gain ground, particularly when it's about your own meaning of yourself, you simply need to "pour on affection" to yourself and introduce so much "certainty" in the process as could be expected, and in yourself.

Truth be told, expanding your confidence and the capacity to believe the cycle is basic for any self-certifications to deal with your rundown of insistences since when you can build your self-esteem, you have raised your "vibration" to the degree of affection that shows things faster. Regularly, you are bound to see yourself better because you have more noteworthy fearlessness, and before you know it, you have shed pounds easily.

It is likewise critical to confide in the system because the vibration of certainty is totally important to draw in what you need, which for this situation is to be thin. Also, incidentally, it's fundamental that you don't utilize words like "don't" or "weight" when rehearsing weight reduction insistences since they center your psyche on "what you "don't need."

"I would prefer not to indulge," for instance, centers on "gorging." On the other hand, insistence on weight reduction that contain terms like thin, alluring, fit, and safe are better alternatives as they "depend" on being slender, appealing, fit, and solid.

Inventive Visualization

When you track down the correct weight-reduction certifications that cause you to feel incredible, get a picture of the "ideal for your body" and spot it somewhere near your bed so when you get up in the first part of the day you quickly see your objective resulting you. At that point, close

81

your eyes and truly "feel" when your body resembles that, and say your good insistences for weight reduction and confidence certifications.

The primary concern to note toward the start is that you need the inward change to happen first and assertions are an extraordinary beginning move; however, self-entrancing might be a superior alternative to change your internal psyche. Notwithstanding, self-spellbinding for weight reduction is extremely regular, essentially because it first attempts to change your internal brain, which makes it ready for an external change to follow.

When you allow yourself to roll out the inward improvement of seeing yourself more slender with no assumptions for seeing the external change really getting more slender, and you get the hang of picturing your attestations of weight reduction that incorporate assertions of self-esteem and the ones of confidence and trust, you'll be amazed how rapidly you'll witness the external change.

Chapter 10 - Guidance

This is a nighttime contemplation, so before proceeding to tune in to this book recording, expel the ringtone from your cell phone, ensure you rest in a spot where nobody can trouble you, and rests in the most agreeable position you find, on a tangle or inside your bed. For an ideal consequence of the strategy, it is prescribed to likewise purchase the daytime contemplation and rehash them, exchanging them for in any event 21 continuous days.

By purchasing this book you have the chance to truly transform your life and that each time you stop one day it will be accurately a direct result of your oblivious, so when you rest in bed and feel that you are too worn out to even consider getting up and take the earphones, or it appears to be senseless to you to do it is at that exact second that you will have the option to perceive how your subconscious is working against you.

You should not battle it, you should essentially twist it to their will, rule it, educate it. At the point when your partner is nothing or nothing, it will be outlandish for you. Also, opposing before a doughnut or another burger or not having any desire to find a workable pace to the exercise center will be a breeze.

And since there is no partnership between the different sides, the subliminal personality will consistently win and in the face of that pie-cutting "you won't have the option to stand up to."

Chapter 11 - Techniques to Execute Gastric Band Hypnosis

Placing

In this meditation, you will learn how to walk along a beautiful beach walk, allowing you a deeply relax. Follow me on this mental vacation as we place an emotional and mental gastric band around your stomach, which will allow you to feel full as soon as you eat exactly as much food as you need.

So, get into a comfortable sitting position, on your favorite spot, so that you are undisturbed for the rest of this session. As you relax, the gastric band will become more powerful and influential in your life. Take a big deep breath, relax, and then exhale the tension and worry as you close your eyes. Feel your body already slowing down. Take another breath and let it go with a sigh of relief. This moment is for you to practice your new lifestyle, of being full, at the perfect time. Now say to you with faith, "overeating is impossible for me."

Now breathe into the truth of these words as you breathe them out into reality. You are creating a smaller stomach. Relax and breathe and then use the power of your imagination to visualize a beautiful beach with white sand reflecting in the sunlight. It looks like snow. You can see the turquoise waters fading to a deep blue as the ocean goes deeper.

Look down into the sand where you stand, and notice the beautiful bits of shells with all different colors and textures as you see dried seaweed scattered about something that catches your eye buried into the sand. It is your preferred color. So as you get closer, you will see that it is a small yet thick band that is as big around as your fist, and it just so happens that it is the most vivid version of your favorite color. The brightness of this hue brings you joy. The curious, round band, flashing of your most beloved color choice is called the gastric band.

It is placed around the top of your stomach, cinching down the amount your stomach can hold. So, it makes your stomach feel smaller, which gives you that feeling of fullness that you've had enough to eat. This band only exists in the medical world. But, you can get the same results, using the power of your mind, by placing the band within and around your stomach in this relaxing session.

Feel your feet entering the sand and allow yourself on each step to relax more and more. Notice the powdery texture, dispersing under your feet, and allow it to soothe deeply. Feel the ocean breeze, and smell the salty air. As you walk, you will get tired. A perfect chair has appeared just for you, facing the ocean. So have a seat and recline backward with your gastric band in your hand. Familiarize yourself with its shape and size. It is like a small belt that can be tightened and loosened. This relaxing gastric band session brings you to perfect health and weight through the power of your mind. It brings about a new and improved positive attitude to life with intention, positivity, and knowing when enough is enough. Now bring your hands into the mode of prayer and notice how you feel. Notice your mind and body going back on track, firmly ready to eat the healthy amount.

Take a few calming, relaxing moments before coming back to the present moment. Take a long breath in and feel the gastric band as it's limiting your ability to overeat. Feel the band affecting the weight throughout your body. When you are ready, just gently open your eyes. And then seal this in with a grateful smile.

Tightening

Welcome to this relaxing meditation. This meditation will guide you to a pristine lake that is surrounded by mountains and help you to tighten your gastric band, making for an even smaller stomach that will fill up quickly. Get yourself into a nice seated position where you can easily fully let go, and you will not be disturbed by the surrounding world.

As you get into a powerful state of relaxation, begin to imagine that you are tightening this gastric band, and as you do so, you will find that weight loss becomes easier and easier by the day. Now begin to breathe deeply while allowing your body to expand. Exhale all of your stress out and take another deep breath in, and as you exhale and allow, let your eyes gently closed.

Now notice how you feel. Notice how your body is settling down, and as it becomes relaxed as we go along. Let go of any current worries or obligations.

Enjoying for yourself, and you begin your health and wellness journey from the first session by placing a gastric band near your stomach with the power of your mind. So, appreciate yourself for taking on this amazing opportunity.

Now say to yourself, "I will eat only as much food as I need. I need less food to feel full."

Breathe in and allow these words to become part of every level of your awareness. Breathe out any doubt and breathe in any truth that you are capable of eating just the right amount to have the perfect shape, size, and overall wellness. Now relax, calm down, and be at complete ease. Let your body slow down just a little bit more. Activate your imagination by bringing into your mind the eye, the site of a magnificent lake that is surrounded by mountains. And the sky, which is a crisp turquoise blue dappled with the cloud. And the sun is shining all around you. The waters of this lake are crystal clear, and it's reflecting the blueness of the sky. The water is acting as a mirror for the mountain range.

Now become aware of your stomach and notice it becoming smaller from your wonderful session on the beach when you first found your gastric band. Feel how your stomach is comfortable and happy about its new size and wants to become even smaller.

As you walk toward the lake, notice the soil under your feet, becoming smooth and supportive. As you go near the water edge, dip your toes in the cool and fresh aqua. Even though your feet are submerged, the waters of this mystical lake relax your entire body.

Notice beside you the small red canoe waiting for you. Enter into this canoe and pick up the beautiful hand-carved oar. The oar signifies the ability to be able to tighten your gastric band. Dip the oar into the water, moving to the bottom of the lake, and push off the shore. Feel as this simple movement helps to tighten your gastric band by a millimeter.

Also, visualize yourself in your kitchen now, preparing your next meal. You will find that when you put the plate on your food, all of your choices are healthy. You will notice that you will only scoop a small amount of each item because you have a good ability to put the right amount of food that you need on your plate, now with your gastric band supporting you. You don't want to waste a bite of food. You should only eat the perfect amount.

See yourself eating this healthy meal, and shocked at the small food that it took for you to feel satisfied. Now, when you rise from this wonderful meditation, allow the image of the canoe and the see-through water to fade away from your mind, as well as the great mountains and the vision of your next meal.

Right now, bring yourself back from this experience into reality. Breathe deeply and become aware of your surroundings in the present moment. Wiggle around your toes and fingers a little bit and feel the fresh new energy and wisdom coming into you. And then whenever you are ready, open your eyes.

Removal

So far, you have placed this band around your stomach while walking on the relaxing beach and tightening the band while rowing your canoe on a crystal-clear lake. Right now, we will visit an ancient Japanese castle to be able to remove this band and discard it during the beautiful ceremony. Now make sure that you're in a comfortable position, in a place that you can enjoy practicing this relaxing session. This is the final step in your gastric band experience. So take a nice deep breath in and then breathe out while closing your eyes. Relax your body. Feel it sinking into the chair or bed, soft and supportive underneath you.

Breathe in and then breathe out while noticing the gentle rise and fall of your chest as you breathe in. Now start becoming aware of your abdomen and feel how slim it is as you're eating less food. You are becoming fuller and making hunger outdated. You know that you're supposed to eat, but eating doesn't consume your day or your mind. You only eat when you should eat and refuse to eat when you don't should eat. It's as simple as that.

Activate your creative mind again. Now imagine that you are standing in a beautiful field with tall grass blowing in your wind. Now imagine that there's a path in front of you, and that path is made up of smooth stones. As you walk along this path, see yourself coming towards a magnificent Japanese temple that was built hundreds of years ago.

The building is well maintained, with a fresh coat made of red paint as well as gold trim surrounding the windows and doors. Now make your way up to the front door and feel like the iron handle in your hand on this door is massive as you open it.

So as you step inside the temple, feel the cool air around you. Also, imagine that the interior of this structure is a work of art, crafted by sheer genius. Now notice that there is a large golden bowl in the center of the room that is set atop a marble column. Now, as you move away from this bowl, it will appear to be illuminated with a ray of sunlight, which is cast down through the window on the rooftop.

As you see the reflecting the light like a diamond. Now, you easily remove the gastric band and place it inside the sacred water. So you can see that it is your favorite color, yet it's a bit worn and tired from all the work that it did for your health. Now imagine as the ray of light beaming down and see it begin to dissolve the gastric band until the water is pure. Start to feel lighter than ever, and your stomach smaller, along with your figure, shrinking every day.

Feel the sensations of touch at your fingertips. Move your focus to your abdomen and all your vital organs. Notice how your belly feels and how it is digesting. Notice your pelvis and hips, and the sensations of your weight as it's pressing it down. This should take you into a deeper state of relaxation.

Your awareness should go down on each leg, over your knees, move down all the way to your feet, and touch each toe.

Chapter 12 - Simply Practicing Hypnosis for Extreme Weight Loss

We overall essentially need time to loosen up, to dream, and to envision. It is revitalizing the physical body and reestablishing the spirit. When we practice our enchanting, it offers us a unique opportunity to invigorate and improve our mind and body. The preparation is done just. You do not need anything more than a pleasant and safe spot.

A Few Simple Rules

There are a couple of guidelines for daze. They ensure that your preparation is the most profitable and yields the best focal points. Exactly when you are set up to begin using the sound, find a pleasant and safe spot in your home or office where you can sit in a seat, recline, or even rest. Guarantee, you are free and in a place where you do not have to zero in on whatever else. Do whatever it takes not to check out your daze work while driving a vehicle or working such a device. It is helpful to choose a customary time each day or night to practice your self-entrancing. Rest time is an excellent opportunity to capitalize on your shock work. Practicing starting now can be a brilliant strategy to enter a peaceful rest.

Interferences and impedances are inevitable. Instead of allowing them to upset you and eliminate you from your daze work, use them. Use the sounds in nature around you to update your shock understanding. For example, while doing your hypnotizing, you may see a sound and start accepting that this sound is redirecting you. You by then become more based on this interference than on your entrancing. You may be allured to fight against it—which eliminates essentialness from the hypnotizing. Alternatively, maybe, when you notice a sound that seems to occupy or aggravating from the beginning, accept accountability for it by giving it your approval to be there as an establishment sound. Give it an errand, for instance, thinking about inside that "the sound of the gabbing dog is helping me go further and more significant inside" or "the fan motor appears to be a course that is a quieting establishment sound." At our private practice in Tucson, a day school unquestionably lets the youths out to play during one of our fascinating gatherings. That is where we suggest, "The sound of adolescents can be an establishment sound that discharges you more significant and more significant inside yourself now." This is a bit of our "usage everything" hypothesis. Interferences in like manner fuse the sensations you may understand inside you. For example, you may end up observing a bit of your body that shivers. The more you base on the shivering or scratching the shiver, the less you focus your mindfulness on the surprise.

At those events, you prompt yourself that you have the approval to move your thought back to your daze or dream and let the shiver go unscratched. When working with patients who have torture issues, we train them to focus thought away from the "interference" of torture like this. In light of everything, we cannot control nature around us or the sensations inside us, yet we can pick where we concentrate. Confine yourself from anything that is fighting with your thought concerning your daze. Surrender any fight with nature. Just let it be there, and eventually, you will never again observe it.

Exactly when you make sense of how to recognize a sensation, fuss, or another part that interferes with your daze, you never also license it to have control over you.

Essential Techniques

Being ingested in your examinations and contemplations is that fragile journey into the point of convergence of yourself called "going into a daze."

The fundamental frameworks of self-hypnosis fuse going into shock, building up the surprise, using that surprised state to give messages and proposals to the mind-body, and leaving surprise.

Going Into Trance

Exactly when you are using the daze, deal with the sound; I will be your guide as you go into a trance. I will use a daze enrollment procedure that you will find calming and focusing on. You have no doubt watched the swinging watch method in movies, 35 years of preparation I have never watched anybody use. Yet, there are different ways to deal with the pack to go into surprise. You may look at a spot on the divider, use a breathing system, or use dynamic body loosening up. You will hear an arrangement of selection methodologies in the sound of the daze work.

They are essentially the prompts or the signs that you are accommodating yourself to state, "I am going into a daze" or "I will do my daze by and by." Going into surprise can similarly be thought of as "allowing yourself to dream deliberately." You are letting yourself become acclimatized in your examinations and contemplations, ingested, and allowing yourself to envision or imagine what you need as refined and authentic. There is no "going under." Instead, there is a breathtaking experience of heading inside.

Expanding the Trance

By expanding your daze energizes, you become progressively expansive in your contemplations, musings, and experience. This is done with dynamic loosening up: going "further and more significant inside" with pictures or scenes, or by checking a number gathering, for example. We like to suggest that as you hear the counting from ten down to zero, you make vertical connected with going further, a path driving down a mountain or into a grand green valley. As you hear me checking, you can picture or imagine going even more significantly into a scene or detect that is much progressively lovely and pleasing to you. This we mean by "expanding the shock."

Leaving Trance

Around the completion of the daze work gatherings, you will hear me looking at letting your body mix with a slant of reward, flourishing, and conveying that reward with you to the front surface of your mind, so you leave daze feeling effortlessly revived and alert. Then again, while doing your entrancing at rest time, you may coast into a significant, peaceful rest. After you are ready, it is necessary to address it.

This is an ideal chance to make a note or two for yourself if contemplations or considerations ring a bell that would be important to you. Habitually during daze, notwithstanding the way that you are offering messages to your body, yet your body is speaking with you, and you will listen to the mind of your body. Your body may share supportive information, and you may need to record it. For instance, let us state you have particular nutrition that you cannot dodge, food like French fries that have been your "ruin" in eating fewer carbs. During the daze work, you may get a piece of information that unveils why French fries transformed into an obstruction or even a "comfort" to you deep down.

That information allows you to pick what you need. The previous model was set up, possibly a very long time earlier, and imagined out of some energetic experience by and by long past and not, at this point, considerable in your life.

Jennifer was diligent and enduring in each aspect of her life and practically all aspects of her get-solid arrangement. She rehearsed every day, ate many dirt results, drank a ton of water, had a great time grain, and even bought usually when she was able. Then made incredibly smart choices for prosperity yet remained twenty pounds over her optimal weight. As she sat wretchedly in our office, she described her insatiable need for solidified yogurt every night and at every social open entryway that presented itself.

97

We asked about whether there was a bit of her that knew why she seemed to throb for solidified yogurt during her daze work. She hushed up for a couple of moments, and after that underscored the sometime in the past articulations of her mindful granddad: "Jenny, dear, solidified yogurt is the best pay for troublesome work, so eat up while it suffers, it may be gone tomorrow, many equivalents to me." Once she uncovered the wellspring of her pastry craving, she had the choice to value it anyway, not eat it so commonly.

The Time Has Come

The open door has shown up for you to tune in and make the most of your first taste of self-hypnosis. The sound associated with this redesigned eBook contains the tracks of daze work. You will begin your contribution in self-hypnotizing by checking out channels 1 and 2. Way 1 is a short introduction and instructional sound regarding the rules of practicing self-hypnotizing.

Track 2 is a preamble to self-daze, the "mind hors d'oeuvre" of the Self-Hypnosis Diet. You may value this little model on the way two similar numbers of times as you wish. So fundamentally tune in and appreciate. As you tune in, I may need you to consider me if I were in a comparative remain with you. Imagine me as your guide. Right when you close your eyes, I am in that spot with you. Delivery my voice with you as you practice your self-enchanting. This is just for you. By and by is the ideal time for your first taste of the self-hypnosis diet.

How Was the Experience for You?

Since you have had a contribution to self-enchanting, what did you experience? Is it precise to state that you were "entranced"? Did you go into a rest actuating surprise? A large portion of individuals who are new to hypnotizing will address whether they genuinely experienced it. You may feel a comparable way. In case you were envisioning an essentially changed state of insight, by then, you have discovered that there genuinely is no "going under" and no loss of mindfulness. Honestly, you thought about where you were and what you were doing most, if not all, of the time. We hear a minor takeoff from a comparative point when people have completed their first contribution in self-hypnotizing: "That was dazzling (or incomprehensible, or sensational, or amazing)." When I am asked what I experience in a daze, I am reminded of a model from my school years: I was looking out the window during a discussion. I understood the teacher was tending to. I could hear his voice, yet I did not know what he was expressing during those minutes.

Being in surprise is like being in a dream. When in a trance, you have a desire to outfit your cerebrum body with considerations or recommendations about what you need it to achieve for you.

Utilizing Self-Hypnosis

Indeed, the ordinary act of brief episodes of self-hypnosis makes significant upgrades in an individual's perspective and naturally supports the arrival of unwanted, abundant weight. In any case, we can likewise use

99

these "breaks" during our life to make positive inward recommendations that advance enhancement for an assortment of levels. I utilize a basic strategy that will enact the Relaxation Response and afterward add something unique to it.

When we disclose to a customer that moving into these self-coordinated conditions, it turns out to be evident to them that they can likewise utilize this chance to include positive proposals. Auto Suggestion, Most customers know about certifications. They may even say that they have had a go at using them, and they did not work. I will recognize their endeavors and state, "Amazing! Presently you will realize why that did not work so well." And afterward, disclose to them how increasing direct admittance to the psyche is so significant. The greatest constraint to utilizing assertions is that they generally include cognizant goals and neglect to have the subliminal domain.

Chapter 13 - Hypnosis and Meditation

If you wonder whether hypnosis and meditation really mean the same thing, you should understand the similarities and differences in their definitions. Anyway, both offer a deeply relaxing, calming, and extremely beneficial state of mind that plays a significant role in helping you get through the day.

Besides, hypnosis and meditation are keys to calmness and positivity as you address underlying psychological, physical, and social issues. The distinction between meditation and hypnosis is blurred, for they are wrapped around the same state of mind but have different belief systems in their purest form.

Hypnosis is a common natural state of mind where you concentrate on a single thought while meditation is a means to enter a hypnotic state. Meditation is often characterized by relaxation and visualization, especially when you aim to find tranquility, reconnecting with your personality, or seeking guidance on an issue. Notably, when this form of meditation has a purpose, structure, uses visualization, and tries to shape your life, then it can also be referred to as self-hypnosis.

A combination of the two states offers incredible results as they take control of your mind and perception. Meditation is most effective in emptying the mind and freeing it of all thoughts while hypnosis has a goal in mind to either overcome an obstacle, develop confidence, or rediscover your potential. It does not matter whether what you do today is meditation or hypnosis, as long as it is pleasant and offers a positive experience. The two states are vital if you wish to lead a fulfilled and happier life.

How They Work

Normally, your conscious mind makes you aware of your thought processes. As a result, you only think about the situations that you are facing and make the right choice of words and actions. Also, the subconscious mind is a critical aspect of your thinking as it functions "behind the scenes" and works hand in hand with the conscious mind.

For instance, as you consciously try to remember where you placed your keys, the subconscious mind accesses the information reservoir to solve the problem and finds the information of where you placed the keys. Similarly, the subconscious mind helps achieve tasks that seem automatic, such as constructing sentences and breathing. Hypnosis and meditation are the most natural way that you can directly access your subconscious mind and enhance the thought process and act as the brain behind every operation. The conscious mind is most active only when you are awake, as it evaluates your thoughts and decides to put most of your ideas into action. It is also responsible for processing acquired information to the subconscious mind.

On the contrary, the subconscious mind reigns whenever you fall asleep, rendering the conscious mind ineffective in the thinking process. Hypnosis and meditation are characterized by focused exercises and deep relaxation, which subdue and calm the conscious mind to a less active role, as in the sleep state. Although you remain aware of the happenings in the environment, hypnotizing and meditating deactivates the conscious mind, thus working directly with the subconscious mind. This state of mind enables you to control the brain and gain access to the information reservoir where you could change the perception about an impending task ahead.

In addition, you become more creative and free as the subconscious mind induces impulse and imagination. Hypnosis and meditation work through a combination of different mechanisms that include body awareness, change in self-perspective, emotion, and attention regulation. These components are essential in helping with various aspects of your life, and when combined, the cumulative process lends an enhanced self-regulation capacity. Lack of this capacity on a personal level is known to cause psychological suffering and distress. For that reason, practicing meditation plays a significant role in developing command over the mind machinery, making you capable of controlling your thoughts even after you finish meditating. The main aim of practicing hypnosis and meditation is to control your thoughts and achieve things that seem impossible through the conscious mind.

The Best Time for Hypnosis and Meditation

To succeed in these practices, you should have a routine to keep you on track and practice often. The practices are similar to other things in life that require daily commitment as one of the most about parts of achieving your results. The more you hypnotize and meditate, the more you take charge of yourself. Daily practices are recommended where you choose the best time depending on your schedule and lifestyle. For most people, meditation and hypnosis are best upon waking, during the lunchtime break, or before sleep.

Similarly, the practice is suitable during the morning break or immediately after work. Whatever your preference, ensure that the time you settle on works into your lifestyle. You do not have to take long meditating, as you are likely to lose interest or fall asleep. In general, it is advisable to practice sessions of around 15–20 minutes twice or thrice daily in a quiet and comfortable place. Initially, you may not notice significant results, as everything in life gets better with practice.

There are different ways of learning when meditating, and what is important is the ability to imagine and think about the changes you expect in your life. Therefore, it does not matter whether you are able to visualize or not. Making it a routine is a major step towards transforming your consciousness and addressing issues that appear complex.

For instance, hypnosis and meditation greatly enhance your emotional feelings, making it easy for you to deal with psychological problems such as anxiety, stress, and depression. Besides, if you want to experience a drastic weight loss and control your eating habits, you should incorporate hypnosis and meditation in your plan as one of your regular practices. You can practice meditation at any time and place as long as you remain inactive and with no interruptions.

Practical Guide to Hypnosis for Weight Loss

It is worth noting that your unconscious thoughts are shaped by your experiences, expectations, and memories. These aspects drive your conscious actions without even realizing it. Simply, it is your subconscious that sets you up to fail, thus the inability to address many of your bad habits. Hypnosis though is critical in updating and altering the negative thoughts, making it possible to address conditions such as substance abuse, chronic pain, and weight loss. When you train your mind to think differently about goals and challenges, you are able to get rid of thoughts that led to self-sabotage. Your mind becomes suggestible when in a trance state, enabling you to access and influence your powerful subconscious assumptions. By following this guide, you will find that you have taken some new and positive actions towards the new changes in your own life that you have successfully set for yourself.

Hypnosis Session for Weight Loss

So now you can relax and just take this time to wind yourself down and to let all of that tension start to flow out and disappear, and just bring to mind the remembrance that all hypnosis is self-hypnosis, and even as I am speaking to you now this is not something I can do either to you or for you but rather hypnosis is a state of deep relaxation which successfully bypasses your own critical factors so that suggestions which are all beneficial to our true self are more readily received and accepted by our deeper unconscious mind, and after all, trance is an everyday natural calming experience and I am helping you enter the experience easier and effortlessly now, and you can start by asking yourself, have I ever deliberately put myself in a calm and relaxing state before this moment now, and if so, you can just bring to mind any of those calm and relaxing states that you have previously experienced whether that be via a favorite hobby or an activity or a journey a holiday.

The most important thing is that you bring to mind now that relaxation and thinking of protective magical practices each day in your waking state because you know that practice makes it imprinted in your mind more and more, so as time goes by it becomes easier and easier to achieve these benefits of these experiences which promote self-acceptance and more importantly each time they become permanently fixed in your mind you know that they become active, increasing positive changes for you, and they become active in creating positive changes in your life that are all to your benefit and lead you forward towards a real realization of those changes, and as you talk directly to the deeper part of your own self that has full control of your own eating habits and your own weight, you realize that you have been eating much more than your body wants or needs and you know that a mind controls your own eating almost as if you are in your own control room, now just seeing all those controls and levers that you can adjust; however, you choose because you know you have the power over your own weight and eating.

And you know whatever you eat exactly when and how much you choose to eat is controlled now by you in this place with this deeper part of your authentic self and it is not your stomach or your appetite that controls what you eat because really it is your own mind and you can ask that deeper part of you beginning today now to develop new habits for yourself and set new positive goals because you are lying a mental foundation for the new you a cheerful ad attractive positive you, the authentic true you and of great importance to this new you to your healthy active and attractive body is the fact that you eat so much less in the fact that the less that you eat the happier you feel and the more that you smile and the more relaxed you are and the better you look and the better you feel and now you find satisfaction in eating less and pride yourself in knowing that each time you do you are rewarding your slimmer healthier natural self and you know that the slimmer you exists deep within you and as you exercise this new strength you find that it grows and grows and as you eat healthily and sensibly you find yourself satisfied and you find that the exercise makes it reinforced and more natural in your authentic identity because you know it is like using your muscles which become stronger and stronger now eating sensibly becomes easier and easier in a practical and positive way meaning that you mentally ask your body what foods it needs and then you take the time to quietly listen to your own body and always check in with your body on how much or how little your body needs from time to time and take time to integrate these ideas on that deeper level.

If you are listening to these and choosing to drift to a night of deeper sleep, you can just do so feeling good allowing your body to drift down and let go into the true deeper sound and restful sleep if you need to get up and continue with your activities then am going to count from one to five and when I reach five you, can open your eyes and come back to full conscious reality and so on, allowing yourself to come back to full conscious reality with ease and relaxation and two coming back slowly to full conscious reality, and three, taking nice deep relaxing breath, and four letting your eyes open as if they've been bathed with fresh water and now five open eyes completely and adjusting yourself to the environment ready to carry on with your day or night activity thanks for listening and talk to you soon.

Chapter 14 - Stop Food Addiction and Eat Healthy for Fast Weight Loss

Losing weight has long been the goal of many, enough that researchers, scientists, and experts have created countless diet plans. In addition to diet plans, exercise routines are also taught in gyms to promote weight loss.

Supplements have also been developed for the same purpose. Ultimately, a lifestyle change was suggested, stating that weight management is a long-term plan and should include not only diet or exercise or supplements alone but also efforts in all three or more aspects.

In the middle of all, this is a technique that includes control of the mind. This technique was called hypnotherapy. Hypnotherapy is based on the fact that the mind plays a very important role in many areas of life, including weight loss. For starters, losing weight begins with a decision. And decisions are made by the mind. This approach, in which the mind is involved, can be summarized through a process. Weight loss through hypnotherapy enables people to see and accept reality.

Many people who have to lose weight were not fully aware of the severity of their circumstances. At this stage, a person realizes that there is a weight problem, and something needs to be done.

The next part involves creating hope. For a person to act according to their circumstances, it is important to emphasize that besides something that needs to be done, something can be done. A hopeful disposition must be developed before proceeding with a program.

Then the part where the person sets out their action plan is as follows. With a clear mind (which can be achieved through hypnotherapy), a person who needs to lose weight can rationally weigh up their options. Now you can create specific weight loss plans that are challenging enough and, at the same time, achievable. This planning phase is important because it can also affect or interrupt the weight loss process. A goal that is too high can be daunting. And a goal that is too low is the same as not having a goal.

During the weight loss process or program, hypnotherapy helps a person avoid stressful activities and habits. Losing weight is a stressful reality. And this can be exacerbated if it is not handled properly.

Hypnotherapy for weight loss is not a completely independent approach. This aims to facilitate the successful implementation of any weight-loss program using. The feature of the approach is to condition the mind so that the subscribed weight loss program's potential is not wasted.

Chapter 15 - Eat Less for Healthy Weight Loss

Eating less for healthy weight loss may seem natural, but it is also true that many of us eat too much for our daily needs. Here are some healthy eating tips to help you convince yourself that you can reduce your food intake and eat less to lose weight healthily. One thing to understand is that it is possible to drink a coffee or a cup of tea without a plate full of different items. It's easy to do! Almost as a reflex action, many people add cookies or even a piece of cake with a cup of coffee. Stop it is not necessary, only eat comfortably.

Most health professionals suggest that all adults benefit from at least five fresh fruits and vegetables every day. Even the government participates in the law and encourages us all to go "five a day." No wonder if it is filled with vitamins, minerals, and fiber. The reasons are correct, as most fruits and vegetables contain about 75%–80%–80% water, which means that you can eat as much as you want. Water content has an added benefit because it hydrates the body and helps you feel satisfied, and certainly helps you eat less to lose weight healthily.

Another helpful tip concerns the presentation of meals. Many people tend to have large plates about 30 cm in size that can look a little sparse if left uncovered. All foods with reasonable and reasonable proportions easily fit on a 9-inch plate. The same principle applies to coffee and teacup and cup sizes. There is no doubt that the larger the container, the more people will eat or drink. So be careful and reduce the portions and eat less for healthy weight loss.

Another helpful tip is how often each bite is chewed since digestion begins as soon as the food gets into your mouth. Chewing is an important part of food digestion as it supports vital nutrients on their way to the stomach. It is a good idea to chew every bite about twenty times to ensure that your food is digested properly.

Water is a critical part of the formula in any healthy weight loss plan. When we feel like we need something, we often take a snack as a quick fix. It could be that a glass of water is sufficient. Water is necessary to keep us hydrated, and it also helps with this feeling of satiety. Most doctors recommend at least six glasses of water a day.

Don't be addicted to certain snacks. There are all kinds of addictions these days, but food obsession is rarely mentioned, although it should be. Most supermarkets offer plenty of seductive canned drinks and delicious snacks that guarantee your resolution. Many of them are remarkably addictive with their high salt and sugar content and are best avoided. If you want a snack and there is nothing wrong with it, take fruit and cereal bars. But read the label first. Now that you have it, six healthy eating tips will ensure that you eat less for healthy weight loss.

Knowing how not to eat helps a person control their weight. It also helps reduce body fat and maintain a perfect shape. Healthy eating is part of the plan, suggesting different types of foods and supplements. If you send the right message to the brain, you are in control of the eating trends. Keeping your weight under control largely depends on your eating habits. An individual has to judge the right amount of food his body needs, depending on health, activity, and the presence of special nutritional needs.

This will make you aware of what you need to eat and what you should avoid when you are losing weight. Serving food in small portions will reduce your desire to consume more because you know you have emptied the plate. It is not advisable to eat more servings.

Creating a meal plan has helped many people control their eating habits. It ensures that the body only needs food at the right time of the day. The temptation to have a snack is due to a lack of mealtimes. With the food discipline, you lose weight faster. When the time comes, and you are not so hungry, we recommend a snack.

Breakfast and lunch should include most of the calories for the day and not for dinner. Your activity during the day uses up most of the energy generated. This means that you can eat more at lunchtime. You will feel half-full at dinner and serve a snack or light meal. It is worth noting that little energy is needed during sleep. There is no chance that you will feel hungry.

Take your time to enjoy the food by chewing it completely. The mind uses the tasting mechanism to feel full and ensure that you eat less. If chewed properly, food can be digested easily and absorbed more quickly. This ensures that no fat accumulates, as the body cannot eliminate what it has eaten. Keep your food nutritious and healthy. You will continue to be healthier if you eat more vegetables and fruits than fat-burning foods in the main course.

However, this excludes sauces and heavy spices as they cancel out the value of fruits and vegetables. Be honest with yourself by avoiding food when you are not hungry. Treat yourself to occasionally banned foods such as candy bars and fast foods to reduce cravings. Essentially, avoid being too hard or strict when on a diet.

To maintain the dynamism in dealing with body fat, it is important to focus on the goal. This means making a conscious effort to keep an eye on your fat-burning diet and professionally prepared schedules. Drink a glass of water or a bowl of soup before eating. You eat less by feeling full. The mind helps implement the strategy of how not to eat. Smaller cups and saucers are misleading as to how much is consumed. Everything can be deleted, but it's never that much. Chewing gum and eating outside without television are other strategies.

How to Develop Healthy Eating Habits

A healthy diet will aid you in maintaining a healthy lifestyle. However, maintaining a healthy diet and exercise takes a lot of effort. Many people think they can eat what they want if they exercise regularly. But it's just a myth. Your diet is reflected in your body as well as in your physical and mental health. Neglecting your eating habits can prove fatal to you. Your bad eating habits or your tendency to overeat can lead to obesity and a propensity for various physical or psychological situations such as depression, cancer, diabetes, and poor digestion. Therefore, you must follow the guidelines below to maintain a healthy lifestyle:

Know Your Calorie Consumption

An average person should have at least 2,000 calories a day. However, this number should increase if you are an athlete or go to the gym to meet your energy needs. Your exact calorie intake depends directly on your gender, weight, height, and physical activity.

Eat Different Types of Food

Eat different types of foods, including whole grains, protein, fruits, and vegetables. The inability to have the right amount of fruits and vegetables in your diet can cause several shortcomings.

Be a Careful Buyer

Remember to check the food labels carefully when buying staples. If the food is low in fat or sugar, it doesn't mean it's a healthier option. Many food manufacturers add various unhealthy ingredients to reduce fat, carbohydrates, or sugar. Even healthy food may have been made with a less healthy ingredient. For example, you need to check whether wholemeal flour is the first ingredient in wholemeal bread. Also, you can request the nutritional information of your food when ordering food in a restaurant.

Eat Smaller Meals

If you eat 2-3 larger meals a day, your blood sugar level will rise, which will probably result in weight gain. On the other hand, eating 5 to 6 smaller meals a day will help boost your metabolism and maintain the energy and nutrients needed to meet your energy needs.

Avoid Junk Food

Junk food is bad for physical and mental health. People who have junk food feel depressed. Aside from that, you are likely to face many health problems in your life. Avoid junk food just for the taste. If you're struggling to curb your temptation to eat junk food, you can enjoy it occasionally, but never make it a habit!

You will find tips on creating a more sustainable regime on the Internet, in addition to these five tips. You can even get medical advice online to create healthier eating plans. Let your family and friends know and seek support to help them eat healthier. Your eating habits will surely be reflected in your health. So plan your diet carefully.

Feel Fuller with Fewer Calories

Weight loss needs more calories than you consume. However, it is not easy to feel full while eating less of the types of foods that have led to obesity.

Instead, you should start eating foods that allow you to feel fuller with fewer calories. Without this, long-term nutrition is almost impossible.

Chapter 16 - The Foundation of Hypnosis for Weight Loss

Brief History of Hypnosis

In 1765, Franz Anton Mesmer made miraculous remedies using magnets. Most analysts later said Mesmer achieved results because of the Force of persuasion of a Scottish doctor and physician, James Braid; So-called Hypnosis. Despite Braid's effort to change it, this word continued.

The term came from the discovery made under the Mesmer's power appeared to reach a state of "nervous sleep." Decided that this condition was more properly defined by the word monotheism.

One theory created the phenomenon proven by Magnet. Others have used fiction and imitation to develop an altered state of mind, and so chronically healed, Braid dismissed magnets altogether.

History revolves. Science deals with beliefs. The best part under which hypnosis and magnets were accepted as miracles of the moment of Mesmer. Mesmer and his disciples recovered for years from most people with multiple conditions using his techniques. Over time, Hypnotic Interior.

Fat Loss vs. Weight Loss

First, why do I distinguish between loss of fat and loss of weight? Ok, weight loss accounts for both losses of weight and loss of fat. Two different subjects.

You will lose weight without losing fat so that the distinction is important to note, particularly when you take the first step on your fat loss journey. You can first lose water weight when you start to reduce calories, particularly by limiting your carbohydrate intake. When you head further into the path of weight loss, fat loss continues happening.

The overall distinction between loss of weight and loss of fat is that while the loss of weight may be any form of mass or loss of water, loss of fat is purely a loss of fat.

How to Restrict Calories for Weight Loss (Calories in Vs. Calories Out)

In order to minimize calories and lose weight, you must first know how many calories are required (estimated) to sustain your body weight. When you know, you eat fewer calories than your body wants and lose weight.

Per week or so, you want to change your calories accordingly, based on the pace at which you lose weight. Reduce calories, so you don't lose weight. Hold your calories the same as you lose weight.

Depending on how long you have reduced your calories, whether you are plateauing if you want to take a diet break or reduce your calories. Bear in mind the loss of weight is not sequential. You could lose weight one week, and gain weight the next week so your success in weight loss will not improve for a while. In this case, by calorie reduction, you want to concentrate on your weight loss targets.

Diet Periodization for Weight Loss & Sustained Fat Loss

When you see that your weight loss is on a plateau, this could be an indication that your body metabolically adapts to your sustained calorie restriction time. When your body adapts to your gains in weight loss, you will gradually feel frustrated. Many individuals seem to be taking eating cycles entirely out. It is the secret not only to lasting weight loss but to persistent lifetime fat loss.

I see people cutting their calories without rhyme or explanation, so either they eat binge and eat more or get so blindly limited that they end up putting their bodies into hunger mode that their bodies have accumulated energy as fat for survival. This inability to schedule sabotages their success in weight loss. The trick to weight loss/loss of fat is to count and track the calories by macronutrients! Many people are too stubborn to do this or feel it is not important to lose weight.

When you lose weight sometimes, or you get a little chub, check the diet and lose fat that way. If you are overweight or obese, you can "tell" when the eye is balling. At this point, though, you have to shrink down and take monitoring seriously because you have a long way to go towards your weight loss goals.

In addition, many overweight or obese individuals need a lifestyle change. In other words, monitoring can be boring, but it gets the work done. It also facilitates your life, believes it or not.

And how are we regularizing our diet? This is an easy method and must not be so complex. The last thing I want to do is make your weight loss experience more difficult.

Concerning the 'how' for nutritional periodization, what you have to remember to prevent metabolic modification is:

• Track your calories and macronutrients and eliminate the cardio activity. After 6–8 weeks of continuous caloric weight control, you want the calories to be preserved. Thus, after your sixth or eighth week, you weigh as you regularly did count the calories for maintenance, and then eat the amount for about seven days.

Macronutrients and Body Composition for Fat Loss

You want to retain as much muscle as possible when aiming for fat loss, without too much weight loss. Make sure you choose the right macronutrient profile for your fat loss/weight loss objectives.

To retain muscle tissue, this ensures that the protein absorbs about 1.0 grams to 1.2 grams per pound of body weight. The other macro-nutrients for which you would potentially play. That's unless you are a bodybuilder or something physical.

It is really important to watch the macros for fat loss and muscle regeneration. If your macros are not monitored, and you have optimistic fitness targets, you are clearly lazy.

Micronutrients

Be sure to eat a suitable amount of your favorite fruits and vegetables, particularly when reducing calories, to fulfill your micronutrient profile. By reducing calories, you restrict the number of nutrients you ingest. This ensures you must be mindful of the consumption of fruit and vegetables.

Key Foundations of Weight Loss

The combined results of many strategies are required to achieve a rapid and successful fat loss. Employ these 12 main causes of successful weight loss performance.

Achieving quick and efficient fat loss involves the cumulative benefits of multiple strategies, which allow one to sustain their fat loss efforts to hold pounds off if used correctly for excess weight directly and indirectly. Quick shot methods like the "lose 10 kilos in 10 days" technique very rarely used, even if not permanent, since they are basically easy solutions intended to diminish fat via intense diet and workout techniques quickly, and may harm individuals if they stay longer than prescribed.

By targeting weight reduction by cutting off those nutrients or exercising on a certain area of the body/relying on only one fitness form, you may be in danger of compromising your well-being in many ways: a broad range of nutrients is required to handle the multiple functions of the body. Those that undergo successful physical transition have usually made their health and wellness a priority, which has rapidly become a lifestyle by reaping the rewards and promoting their preservation.

And this lays the secret to the progress of your long-term corporal transformation: successfully prepare and relate your training targets to your daily life. The following 4 main factors have proved to be a strong, realistic, and reliable basis for sustained progress in weight loss. Use them, and for many years to come, you can still experience better health and enviable physical growth.

Set Goals

Without a strong roadmap, very little is in place, whatever health and well-being goals you intend to accomplish. So, before you step foot in the gym and enjoy the first strength meal when you prepare to change your body, set aside some time to determine where you are today and equate it with, say, where you hope to be in one year. Be particular about your timeframes and have a good sense of what you want to look like and how you want to feel after your transition (be mindful that after you have reached your goals on health and well-being, you need additional goals to sustain or improve on what you have already accomplished).

Record your targets and make them readily available—to verify your results, you need to review them. In addition, these targets must be practical and achievable: developing muscles to rival Mr. Olympia with a fat ratio of 3 percent would certainly never happen in this lifetime or more. Consider your body shape and design your priorities accordingly. If you are severely overweight, be comfortable with gradual weight loss and are not disappointed if you don't manage to lose fat quickly enough. If you follow the instructions below, you will get the results you expect. Taking your priorities into account, and do not hesitate until you hit your perfect physique.

Train with Weights

This sounds very simple, but it is interesting how many people concentrate on physical workouts while striving to lose their weight when relegating weights to incidental status. To lose body weight, aerobic conditioning techniques must never be used at the cost of strength exercise. Owing to the sheer existence of muscle tissue, it is smart to construct the metabolic rate as frequently as possible even when we are restful so that mitochondrial activity is increased as much as possible. By motivating our metabolic rate, how quickly our bodies can absorb energy to function faster during rest (a total inactivity state where energy is required only for our vital organs), we will begin the process of fat burning long after our exercise.

Data from several success stories of transition have proven that anaerobic workouts, one type being weight lifting, are much preferable to aerobic workouts, such that we may raise our simple metabolic pace (or the pace we use while fully rested). Although exercise training eliminates fat while used, weight training improves metabolic rates and creates muscle to boost our metabolic rate. Being a metabolically active organ, muscle takes more energy than fat, which is excessive.

Do Cardio

Although weight lifting is important to improve the metabolic rate, aerobic exercise also helps fat loss efforts when used in combination with weights. The greatest concern is, it seems cardio is always overused. Many that are desperate for fat loss are quickly associated with weight loss exercise. When you look at the physics of those that exercise aerobically alone, while usually thin, they are soft in a very low tone.

You can see a huge change in physical appearance from these 'athletes' to bodybuilders, usually with lower levels of fat and almost always greater muscle growth. The explanation is that the bodybuilder combines his/her cardiovascular practice with weight lifting, which is a priority before aerobic exercises. For the effectiveness of corporal transformation, cardiovascular levels must be included that target body fat without interfering with weight training rehabilitation and muscle development.

Three 45 minutes of moderate strength production (approximately 70% of the full heart rate) is a decent start every week, first in the morning on an empty stomach. Make sure to track your progress to decide whether this level is appropriate for your particular needs—this number will have to be raised or reduced accordingly. As long as your body fat levels decrease and your body appears closer and no visible lack of muscle, you're on the right track.

Maintain a Well-Balanced Diet

The stable, persistent fat loss is more likely than any other predictor to generate attentive feeding. As stated, we need to create muscle and weight trains to stimulate it and direct the metabolism to increase the metabolic rate to promote a fat-burning effect around the clock. However, to attain the necessary energy levels to sustain adequate strength of training and recover from our rigorous training and development, we need high-quality nutrients interspersed all day. A large range of vitamins and minerals and calcium, carbohydrates, and fats are to be ingested, and a reasonable mix is to be prepared with each.

Chapter 17 - Eating Out and Still Losing Weight

Controlling your weight and eating at home can be kept under control because you can pick what you eat, what you eat, portion size, and all. If you've done a gastric banding procedure or imagine it as a hypnotic gastric banding procedure, you can monitor it at home.

Yet what happens when you leave. There are so many places to go and shop. You seemed to lose control of your diet, when you eat, and when you eat. This need not be the case; however, if you do some forward planning.

When I mean dining out, I'm not thinking about fast food establishments. I'm referring to those restaurants where you socialize, chat, have fun and enjoy food for either breakfast, lunch, or dinner.

So here are tips for dining out at these restaurants and still managing your weight and being comfortable at night.

Tip 1—Know the Restaurant

If you've been to a specific restaurant before, you'll probably know the type of food, the amount served, and the duration. Because you know this, you should intend to go there when you know you'll be hungry. If they feed you slowly, you can decide whether you have a meal entrance or dessert. If they feed you quickly, you can want to go to the main meal.

For a restaurant you don't recognize, go online and read the reviews of people who've eaten there. You'll find a lot of details that will help with preparation.

Tip 2—Watch How Much You Eat

Sometimes in Chinese, Indian, and other restaurants, they have banquets. They look good but typically have too much food. So skip the banquet tab, go to the main courses.

Tip 3—Choose Food to Please You When You Eat It Will Cost You Money

And you should make sure you buy what you want to please you, rather than what you think you need to eat. In the first scenario, if you're full, you'll find you don't want to eat. If you eat what you think you need to lose weight, you probably won't be happy and order more food.

Tip 4—Beverages and Food

If you want to have an alcoholic drink with your meal, note that it is handled equivalently to eating as though you are not hungry. To avoid drinking when you're not hungry, I recommend two things:

1.   Have water on the table and drink water before eating any course so you're not thirsty while dining.

2.   Drink slowly, enjoy. As you enjoy it, you'll find yourself more relaxed and will be able to stop when you're whole. Dining out isn't something you need to skip while trying to manage or lose weight; just prepare ahead.

Chapter 18 - Gastric Mind Band (GMB) Treatment

Hypnotherapy alone proved not to be the solution, but a likely innovative approach was built over the next twelve months, cleverly incorporating cognitive-behavioral therapy, NLP, hypnotherapy, and directed imaging, and the client's wish was granted.

The gastric mind band (GmB) treatment is not just a therapeutic approach focused on a single diet; as well as using the idea of having a "mentally" tailored gastric band to help you minimize portion sizes, the treatments also involve a mix of Cognitive-Behavior Therapy and NLP to motivate you to reconsider your whole attitude about food and nutrition and step away from the whole diet.

The GmB treatment shows you how to end your battle with food and introduces you to a new, lifelong lifestyle of healthier eating habits that will not only help you reach and sustain your ideal weight quickly but also improve your self-esteem in the process so that you feel much more optimistic and comfortable about yourself and overall life.

The human brain is divided into two parts: conscious and subconscious. The conscious mind accounts for just 10% of the overall consciousness; it deals with reasoning and decision-making.

The subconscious mind shapes the other 90 percent; it doesn't understand science, but it controls several things in your body that you don't have to consciously think about, including your breathing, heart rate, body temperature, and metabolism.

Sometimes, the subconscious works like a machine, storing all the information you've ever learned, and it regulates everything from your self-confidence and self-image to your emotions and behaviors. If an action is replicated repeatedly over time, a pattern is formed: it essentially produces a certain chain cycle in our brain, and the more frequently the action is replicated, the stronger the chain becomes.

And, if, for example, you regularly turn to food to fill a void when you feel lonely or stressed out, then your subconscious mind gradually sees this as your usual behavior, and you develop a pattern of eating automatically whenever you need any emotional support.

When there is often some tension between your consciousness and your subconscious mind, such as when you try to change a habit, then while your conscious mind will often win small battles along the way, the much more dominant subconscious mind will still triumph at the end, which means you ultimately go back to whatever behaviors your subconscious mind considers "natural" for you.

Therefore, diets based on willpower alone are still doomed to fail. This has nothing to do with being frail, this shows how strong the human mind is. The typical way to change our habits is by continuously repeating the new habit before the subconscious then embraces it: this can be a long, complicated process.

Nevertheless, since your subconscious mind readily absorbs new knowledge while you're in a comfortable state, we can speed up the process of changing behaviors by communicating directly to and reprogramming your subconscious mind using hypnosis. When you've spent a long time eating for emotional purposes, rather than real physical appetite, so you lose the ability to recognize and respond to the cues the body sends you when you're hungry and you've had plenty to eat.

Hypnosis helps you return to the natural reflexes of your own body, and CBT teaches you how to differentiate between hunger and cravings, so you can learn to eat only when you're hungry and not for any other reason, choose the right kind of food for your body to work efficiently, and eat just how much food you need to satisfy your hunger. This will then create a balanced eating habit that you will adopt for life, and you will never again have to struggle with diets and willpower.

In the hypnosis sessions, you are also told to imagine yourself looking thin, beautiful, safe, and happy, and your subconscious mind then embraces this vision as the current self-image you are working towards.

Once this new vision of yourself is deeply embedded in your subconscious mind, it becomes far more appealing to you than eating something that makes it harder for you to reach your goal. In other words, the long-term benefits of being slim and healthy far outweigh the short-term satisfaction, like eating a piece of chocolate cake. Unlike a diet, GmB's weight control system is an enjoyable experience. You'll be able to relax and stop being obsessed with food, and you'll never feel deprived or restricted about what you can or can't eat.

As the sessions progress, you will gradually be introduced to deep hypnotherapy, which will be used to ensure you have the feeling and sensation that your stomach is shrinking before the mental fitting of the band. Other therapy elements will be tailored based on knowledge collected during case conceptualization.

Chapter 19 - Emotional Eating and Eating Healthy

Mental eating satisfies your mental appetite. It's not about your kitchen, but the issue lies in your head. What are the most powerful emotional eating challenge strategies?

- List your food cravings to relax.

- Distracting yourself doesn't mean being lazy in this situation. It's not like texting while driving, or you're out of control. When you hide from your food cravings, it means you're turning your focus to something else. It's more purposeful.

- Do something or concentrate on another action or event. Whenever you feel like gorging on food, try getting a piece of paper and list five items from five categories of something like the names of five people whenever you feel upset, angry, or depressed.

- Perhaps you should mention five ways to relax. If you want to calm down, what are your five places?

- When anxious, what five feel-good phrases can you tell yourself? How about five things to stop eating? Place it on your fridge or kitchen cabinet after finishing this list. Next time you're overwhelmed by your persuasive food cravings, browse through your list and do one of the 25 things suggested there.

- Prepare ahead for future emotional issues.

- Over the weekend, grab a piece of paper and a pencil and take a path to your tasks in the days ahead. Your map reveals your expected exits and potential detours. Pick an emotionally consuming picture.

- Place the icon over an event or activity that could cause your food cravings, like early lunch with your in-laws. Prepare ahead for that case. Search for the restaurant menu online to order something delicious and nutritious.

- Drop the concerns inside.

- Whenever anxious, taking a deep breath helps. Another thing to detoxify yourself from stress is to do a visual trick. Breathe deeply and imagine a squeegee (that piece of cloth you use to clean your window or windshield) near your eyes. Slowly breathe out, picture the squeegee wiping clean inside.

- Delete all your concerns. Do it three times.

- Self-talk like you're royalty. Self-criticism is usually emotional. Toxic words you say to yourself, such as "I'm such a loser" or "I can never seem to do anything right," force you to drive to the nearest. Don't be fooled by these claims though brief.

Such feelings, like acid rain, slowly erode your well-being. The next time you're caught telling yourself these negative things, overcome by moving to the third-person perspective.

If you think "I'm such a mess," tell yourself then that "Janice is such a mess, but Janice will do what it takes to get things done and make herself happy." This approach will get you out of the negative self-talk loop and have some perspective. Pull up and be positive and have the strength and avoid emotional eating. Over-food is still not given enough consideration. It's always seen as not a serious problem to laugh at.

This is a totally incorrect view as a horrific condition needing urgent treatment. The positive thing is that you take action to help you avoid emotional eating forever. I know because I did it myself.

Step 1—Recognize Triggers

For each person, emotional eating is triggered differently. Some people get cravings when stressed out, some when depressed or bored. You need to work out the emotional causes. When you know what they are, you'll get an early notice when the urge to feed comes on you.

Step 2—Eliminate Temptation

One thing most people don't realize about emotional eating is that desire is always for one specific food. It's always ice cream or candy for kids. It's always pizza for guys.

When you couldn't fulfill this lure, it won't bother you. Save your home from all of these temptations. Throw out any nearby pizza delivery locations. Again, you know your temptations, so get rid of them and make overeating difficult.

Step 3—Break Contact

It's instant and urgent when the craving hits. You're fed right now! To stop this, you must break this immediate bond by taking some time between the desires and eating.

- Call a friend.

- Count to sixty.

- Write down what you feel like.

- Do some exercises.

- Go out for a walk.

- Take a shower.

What you can do to make the urge subside works wonders. Take these three moves, and you'll soon take them better and conquer emotional eating for good.

Chapter 20 - Burning Fat and Blasting Calories with Self-Hypnosis

Self-hypnosis is a powerful tool that you can use in moments of weakness. When you can remind yourself of just how powerful it is to burn your fat, working out, and reminding yourself to exercise more often, you will realize that you are capable of succeeding. You can burn that fat by remembering that you need to move. But, if you aren't motivated to get exercising, how are you supposed to keep yourself on track? What are you going to do if you are always making excuses for yourself?

When you do this the right way, you will be able to keep yourself motivated and push yourself forward. By self-hypnotizing, you can motivate yourself to keep moving forward. You will be able to remind yourself of all the reasons that you will need to get through everything. You will help yourself figure out how you can stay on track with what you are doing and how you can continue to burn the fat to get the weight off.

Ultimately, losing weight is all about figuring out how to balance out burning calories with how much you consume. Losing weight is all about making sure that you have less in your diet than you need so that you are burning fat in your body to help continue to run your body. Maintaining weight is when you want to eat only the foods that you will need. However, if you are not exercising, you will not be getting the fully healthy body that you will need.

You have to make sure that you are burning calories one way or another, and you also have to make sure that you are providing yourself with time and energy for your body to move and be active as well. When you do this the right way, you should be able to figure out what you are doing, and you should be able to get the results you are looking for.

To use self-hypnosis, all you have to do is walk yourself through relaxing to the point that you will be able to get those results that you are looking for. You want to make sure that you are walking yourself through how you can get to that same state of relaxation that a hypnotist would normally do for you.

When it comes to trying to self-hypnotizing, you have a few options. Some people choose to read their own scripts, but they are typically more effective and passive when you are listening rather than reading. For this reason, you want to try to locate some prompts that will help you.

Within this script that you will be provided, you will find yourself becoming motivated to work out more. You will be finding yourself passively taught that what you need to do above all else is to figure out how you can better yourself. You will find that you are capable of achieving that weight loss, even if you think that you are not.

This prompt is all about maintaining your willpower and helping to keep you on track. If you want to lose weight, you need to have the drive to do so, and that requires you to work through these processes. Are you ready? As with the other meditation prompts, they should not be utilized during driving or other activities for maximum effect. Listening to them as you settle down is one of the best options for you. You want to ensure that you are somewhere that you can completely relax and allow the script to kick in and create the desired, intended effect, and when you figure out how to do that, you will find yourself succeeding.

Self-Hypnosis Prompt

Settle down on your bed or chair and get comfortable. You should be somewhere that is perfectly relaxing for you. You shouldn't have any distractions present, and you should feel at peace where you are. As you relax, allow your eyes to begin to close. You can be as comfortable as possible. Don't worry about relaxation and it will come. Allow yourself to sit completely passively. Don't try to force it or try to focus too hard. Simply sit and be comfortable.

Take in a deep breath, and then breathe it out. Breathe in through your nose, feeling the air chilling your nostrils as you pull it in, and then exhale it when you try to release it all. Breathe in and breathe out. In and out. In and out. As you breathe out, you should feel the air escaping your lips in an O shape, and as you do, you should feel yourself relaxing further.

With every breath in, you feel your body nourishing itself with oxygen, and with every breath out, you feel your body purifying itself, releasing the waste that it no longer needs. Sit there and enjoy the breathing process and watch as soon and it feels that your chest rises on its own and then exhales on its own.

Your body is capable of giving you what you need. Your body will breathe on its own. You trust your body to give you the air that you will need to live, and you trust it to breathe out the toxins that you need to remove. You allow your body to regulate itself, and you allow your breathing to run itself.

As you breathe, you imagine the stress and tension within yourself gathering in your lungs. It is carried through your blood and released into the lungs, just like the air that you breathe. The stress and tension arrive in your lungs, and you exhale it out, just like the carbon dioxide that your body tries to rid itself of.

You breathe in and out again. You feel stronger. You feel better. You feel more capable of success. You feel relaxed. You feel like you are at ease where you are. As you do this, breathing in and out, you realize that you are in complete control of your body. You can change your breathing if you want to, but your body will naturally gravitate toward what it knows that you need.

You know that if you breathe faster, you can—but you might start to feel lightheaded. If you breathe slower than you need, you might start to feel like you don't have enough oxygen. You know that you are in control of your breathing, but usually, you know that it is best to let your body control your breathing itself.

Your body controls a lot of needs by itself, working on its own to change how you think, feel, and breathe. It controls how it regulates itself. Your body is very aware of everything that you are going to need to do. It is capable of controlling itself in many ways. It is capable of making sure that you eat just enough and just the right foods if you listen to it. It is capable of ensuring that you are perfectly healthy. It is capable of ensuring that you are eating enough food and making sure that you get the right ones. It will drive you to get moving if you need to—it will make you want to get exercise if you know how to listen to it.

Your body naturally will tell you what you need, how you need it, and how to get it if you listen to it—but you have to listen. Just like with breathing, you can take control of your body's actions as well. You can choose to eat things that your body wasn't initially looking for. You can choose to drink things that may not be very healthy for you because you like them. You can choose to sit down instead of going out to enjoy nature and explore the outdoors.

You can choose to override those basic needs that you have so that you can be the healthiest that you can be. When you do this the right way, you should be capable of getting to that point of success. This means that you need to listen to your body.

You breathe in and out. And you can feel your body relaxing. You can feel your body wanting to naturally do what you will need to make sure that you are healthy. You will be able to figure out how best to listen to yourself.

You feel more relaxed than ever right now. You feel like you are entirely capable of getting through the processes that you need. You feel like you are able to drift more and more. You feel like you are sinking into your bed where you sit, and you feel ready to stay there.

You imagine yourself looking in a mirror. As you are there, you can see yourself. That part of you is yourself. That person that you see right there is the part of you that wants you to listen. You see yourself there, and you can see the look of defeat on your face. You can see the look of depression. You can see the look of being stuck right there. You do this and see that you have been silencing this part of your body. You do this and see that you have been telling yourself not to listen to the part of you that knows best. You do this and see that you are in a position to not be able to get what you need. You are actively hurting yourself by not listening to what your body is trying to tell you.

You can see that reflection of you, and you realize that it is the part of you that you needed to listen to more than ever. That is the part of you that wanted to be healthy—the part of you that wanted to ensure that you would be comfortable in your body. You find yourself gazing into your sad eyes, wondering what happened. What caused you to bury this part of you behind so much? What made you step away from the person that you were before, and what made you decide to suppress this person? The answer is there if you know what to listen for. You were indulgent.

Your indulgence was harmful. Your indulgence buried a part of you away so far that you felt like you would never be able to get it back. Your indulgence buried yourself behind the person that you became: Unhealthy and unable to get through everything. That's right, there is a part of you that was actively sabotaging yourself. That part of you wanted to indulge in whatever made you happy—it wanted you to be the person that it wanted you to be without looking at what you would need.

And now, you have the opportunity to confront that part of yourself. You look down at yourself, and you realize that you are the part that has pushed that healthy part away. You are the part of yourself that caused your problems, and that means that you are the part of yourself that caused your problems, and that means that you are the only one that can fix the problem.

You must make sure that you are taking the time to better yourself. You must be willing to let go of those long-lost desires. You must be willing to get past that person that you were so that you can still lose the weight.

Chapter 21 - Using Self-Hypnosis to Improve Your Habits

Bad habits have a funny way of sneaking upon us. From biting nails to smoking and drinking, or even struggling to eat healthily, bad habits can range from being mildly annoying to incredibly harmful. You need to be able to see what kinds of bad habits you have so you can help yourself to remain as healthy as possible.

In particular, we are taking a look at self-hypnosis in the context of defeating bad habits. By being able to create habits that are going to be more beneficial to you, you will have a way that you can help yourself to stay healthier than you were before. By knowing what you are doing, you can ensure that you are on track to being the healthiest version of yourself that you can be.

By going into a trance state, you can start to directly alter the habits that you have. Whether those habits are good or bad, you can directly change them. This means that if you are working hard to better yourself by defeating bad habits, one of the best starting points is to make sure that you are doing so effectively by ensuring that you use self-hypnosis. You will be able to directly start new habits and maintain them. This is primarily because the method that you are using to do so involves self-control. Hypnosis is primarily an act of intense self-control that you can use. While it might seem like it is a moment of lacking focus, it is actually a state in which you are so focused that all the outside distractions simply do not matter to you. You do not register them at all, and that gives you immense power over yourself.

That kind of self-control that is required to entirely stop paying attention to everything else around you is intense, but you can learn to master it yourself as well.

Learning to hypnotize yourself might sound simple in theory, but you also must allow yourself to develop the skills in action as well. You need to ensure that you learn the different tactics that can go into learning those new habits. Really, it is just a matter of practice. The more that you practice creating this state for yourself, the more often that you will find it actually working for you. This means that the more that you use it, the more likely you are to find that success in triggering that state of mind.

While zoning out while you are waiting for something is a form of trance, it is not quite the same as hypnotizing yourself. It is like a less skilled version of it. It is doing so accidentally and creating that effect of hypnosis unintentionally. However, you can tap into those skills and see just how beneficial they can become for you. Within this chapter, we have a few key goals that you will need to follow.

First, we will discuss the act of preparing yourself for self-hypnosis. The mindset matters, after all, and ensuring that you get the right one is the perfect way to trigger the state that you need. From there, we will start addressing different ways that you can start hypnotizing yourself. These are just a few of the most common self-hypnosis techniques that are used, and you may find that you prefer very different ones. We will be considering the technique of breathing, body scanning, and visualizing. All of these play their own part in ensuring that you trigger that state and get the effect you intended to achieve.

This chapter essentially provides you with techniques that you will use to help yourself. They are techniques that you may or may not enjoy using, but at the end of the day, they are there to help you achieve success in controlling your mind to control your body. So, are you ready to get started? Are you ready to start seeing the different methods that you can use?

Preparing Yourself for Self-Hypnosis

Before we dive in, let's first talk about the right mindset. Having the right mindset for hypnosis means knowing what it is that you have to do with yourself to trigger the hypnosis in the first place. Being able to achieve that state is all about having the right frame of reference as well, and when you manage to do that, you should also find that you are more successful in triggering that state that you would like.

Being able to see what you can do and how you can influence yourself will help you to defeat those bad habits that you want to cut out. They will help you to change your mindset and ensure that you do take care of yourself the way that you deserve to be. After all, remember: You are deserving of love from yourself. You deserve to love the body that you have, and your body deserves to be cherished by you as well. So, how do you make that happen, you may ask? Simple! You have to prepare yourself for the hypnosis that you will use.

Preparing for hypnosis means having somewhere peaceful that you can use for it in the first place. You must have somewhere suitable for the hypnosis that you will be using if you want to hope to be treated as well as you can be.

If you want to be certain that you've mastered the hypnosis state, you must first make sure that you have the setting right. Then, you have to start shifting your mind as well.

The Right Environment

First, let's address the environment that you will be in. Because you can choose where you want to self-hypnotize, you should take time to consider the setting that you are choosing. It should be somewhere that is peaceful and comfortable for you to ensure that you do not feel like you are distracted by general discomfort. Because discomfort can cause so many issues, it will simply keep you from getting to that state that you need.

This means that the right environment will look different for every single person. However, one thing is true—the right environment should be somewhere that is calm, quiet and relaxing for you. Many people love to lounge in bed when they do this because it is easy for them to get comfortable and relax somewhere that they would usually do so.

Make sure the location is quiet, so you know that you are not going to be distracted constantly. You want to ensure that wherever you choose; it is peaceful and quiet. This will help you to ensure that you can keep that focus for yourself. Close the curtains, keep the sound low, and make sure that anything that could distract you, such as a phone or a tablet, or a computer that might beep at you. If you have kids, make sure they are not going to disturb you while you hypnotize yourself and find somewhere that you can be quiet.

Then, ensure that you are comfortable as well. You should not be hungry, thirsty, or have to use the restroom. Make sure that all of your immediate needs are met and ensure that your clothes are comfortable and the position that you will use is comfortable as well. Then, settle on in and close your eyes.

The Right Position

When your setting is right, then it is time to settle in. Get as comfortable as you can, remembering that you will be in this position for a while, and close your eyes. You can be in any position for this—some people prefer to stand while others sit, and others still lay down. Choose whatever is the most comfortable for you. After all, no one is going to see you, and you are setting yourself up to be in a position that no one else will be around. As long as it works for you, it is just right. Breathe deeply and start focusing.

The Right Mindset

Next comes the mindset. When you are ready to start the act of hypnosis, remember that it does require your utter focus and attention. You are not simply sitting there and passively relaxing—rather you are focusing intently.

You must approach hypnosis with acceptance. You need to remind yourself that you are allowing yourself to accept what is happening around you. Accept the power of the hypnosis that you are using and let it influence and guide you. Calmly accept what you are doing and do not resist.

The Right Way to Regroup

Finally, you must be ready for what will happen if you notice that your mind is wandering. If your mind starts to drift away from where it is supposed to be, you should simply return it to the focus that you had. You would slowly redirect your mind. The slow and calm part is the most important here—you are not trying to shame yourself into feeling hurt or into feeling betrayed. You should not make yourself feel like a failure. You are simply allowing yourself to relax and accept that as a human, sometimes you get distracted. Returning your focus back to what it is supposed to be on will help you to focus entirely. Simply allowing yourself to do this should ensure that you are kept on track.

Often, the point of focus during hypnosis, especially in the beginning processes, is breathing. You would simply listen to your breath, in and out, as you are falling into a trance. As soon as your mind wanders away, you shift it back to your breath without any judgment.

Keep in mind that hypnosis is not meant to be done when you are in your car or while you are doing something that requires your attention. Hypnosis should be an action that fully entrances you at the moment. You should not have to do anything else at the moment while you are using it. This means that you should dedicate some time just to hypnosis when you use it. This will ensure that you can get the fullest effect.

The Stages of Hypnosis

The relaxed state of hypnosis is not just turned on. You have to slowly ease yourself into it. Think about it—when you exercise your body, you are told to slowly warm yourself up to working out. You shouldn't just dive right into sprinting or lifting heavyweights. You have to work into it to ensure that your muscles warm up along the way. Likewise, hypnosis involves a sort of "warm-up" position in which you are slowly acclimating yourself to the state of mind that you are using.

Chapter 22 - Subconscious Relationship with Food and Weight Loss

Can real and long-lasting change in weight loss efforts be achieved through the subconscious mind?

This post will discuss the answer to the problem.

How Big a Nuisance Is That Extra Waistline Fat?

According to the NHANES data (National Health and Nutrition Examination Survey), over one in three adults were deemed to be overweight for 2013–2014. About one in six children and teenagers between the ages of two and nineteen were also considered obese. And being overweight and obese is one of the major causes of most diseases.

Of those diseases that cause overweight are type 2 diabetes, sleep apnea, heart failure and stroke, certain cancer types, just to name a few. The issues posed by excess fat in the body cannot be ignored, from the most serious cases of obesity to the natural weight gain due to higher calorie intake.

Being slightly overweight can lead to tiredness, and this, in turn, increases the levels of cortisol in the body, which increases stress. Apart from the physical health threats presented by being overweight, psychological side-effects are also present. Often our self-image and self-appreciation are tied in with how we feel. You won't look in shape when you're overweight, and that can have detrimental effects on your level of confidence.

Some clothes are not going to fit, you are not going to feel comfortable in your own skin, and you are not going to be happy with your body. If excess weight is a national crisis, why are most people overweight, anyway?

What's, do we still have that extra doughnut when we know the effects that this extra waistline fat can have on our lives?

We Are Programmed to Become Food Addicts

We are anatomically programmed to crave food, for the continuity of our species. Food is a natural strengthener for us.

Most of it all has to do with what our core programming is. We have to feed and copulate for our species to continue living. Otherwise, we'd have starved out of life ourselves. Each time we feel or consume food, there is a spike of dopamine in the brain's reward circuit. This is a chemical pleasure-giving that is supposed to act as a reward for feeding. It was all right back then when there was no McDonalds, KFCs, Nando's pizza, and food-on-demand with inexhaustible variety varieties.

We prefer to gorge on these various assortments. It's very difficult to say no to what we should be wanting. The kicker we are currently in this 21st century is that much of the food we consume from these sources has been genetically modified, and is riddled with weight-gaining substances such as trans-fat, HFCs, sodium, preservatives, and so on.

Such kinds of foods have a way of hijacking the brain's reward circuit, and that leaves us wanting more, although we know better. If it begins to get out of control I'm afraid that the train has already left the station about the overweight epidemic that ravaged our society.

The fast-food chains have become successful in making people addicted to their products through aggressive marketing and the convenience that they offer.

Apart from the fact that some weight gains are due to medical conditions such as an underactive thyroid and Cushing syndrome, most waistline gains are due to over-eating junk and lifestyle decisions. And both are primarily due to the individual's weak willpower.

Even people who are genetically predisposed to overweight can STILL take care of their weight with the proper attitude towards the food they eat and the rate at which they exercise.

Every Eating Disorder Is Emotional

If it's over-eating, or eating junk, or eating mentally, or eating tension, or eating bulimia, or anorexia, they're all bound into our feelings. The feelings may be negative or positive, but at the end of the day, our eating patterns are influenced by how we feel.

For example, some people start gaining weight after experiencing a major trauma, such as losing a person close to them. After childbirth, some women start gaining weight. Some people begin to gain weight after they have been successful; maybe they have not had enough to grow up to eat.

Regardless of their education, several people have been taught that they can never waste food. And, no matter how good the food is, they consume it all on their plate. After a bad day at work, some people binge on junks, and some binge on junks after a nice, productive day at work.

Many over-eat when happy, and some over-eat when sad. The list is endless and could fill in the entire book. What I am really trying to convince you is that all eating disorders are linked to our emotions.

Our Lifestyle in the 21st Century

We are living in a "sitting" environment right now. The majority of people drive to work, get to work, and sit for nearly 8 hours. When they get home, they stay for the rest of the day glued to their laptops, smartphones, and T.V., and finally, go to bed.

Most people don't regularly do exercise. Nowadays, the majority of people lead a sedentary lifestyle.

We don't go to shopping malls anymore today. The magnitude of the physical activity of some people is the path that they make from bed to screen. Why most traditional weight-loss approaches don't work. Only typing the sentence "weight loss services" into Google returned 171,000,000 tests.

There are countless plans for fantasy weight loss out there. The list is endless from diet plans to exercise services, herbs, vitamins, apps, bracelets (I'm not sure how this works), and personal trainers. Why is it that there are still a lot of people fighting their weight? Why is it that most people use it for two days after buying any of these programs, and after that, the software is left in the dust never to be seen or heard of again?

What's the problem with beginning and quitting a weight loss regimen halfway through? The reality is most of those systems are successful. And they work only for a limited percentage of people.

Such services often address the physical aspect of weight loss. They do not take the psychological and emotional aspects of the whole process into consideration. These programs do not see to it that the subconscious mind is on board.

When you are overweight subconsciously, and you're trying to lose weight, it'll be like trying to beat the water into submission. When you're doing a lot of things to lose weight, and your subconscious mind isn't aboard, success would be hard to achieve. When it comes to overweight, true and lasting improvement comes from inside.

I am a big believer in changing the outside from the inside. When your subconscious isn't on board with your choices, which is just because you are going backward.

The Subconscious Mind's Relationship to Weight Loss

If you want to lose weight at the end of the day, you should develop weight-losing habits to get rid of the additional fat. So, permit me to ask you this; do you have patterns of weight loss or weight gain? It is either one of these or the other.

Will you eat well, or do you regularly indulge in sodas and trans-fats? Were you sleeping properly, or are you a night owl? Should you do routine exercise, or are you a sitter?

Note, each of these is one or the other. The subconscious guides 90 percent of what you do every day. We do not make rational choices. The subconscious mind is the origin of all our religions and customs. And, if you've got a subconscious conviction that you're the sort of person who loses extra fat, you'll be able to pick up weight loss habits, and they'll stick.

It does not really matter what you do. If you can hack your subconscious and make it believe you're able to lose weight, everything you do will be backed up by a belief that makes it easier to execute everything else.

Ways to reprogram the subconscious mind to weight loss:

Weight-Loss-Related Affirmations

A very strong and efficient way to reach the subconscious is to use accurate affirmations. While it needs constant reinforcement, it can be a very good way to persuade the subconscious mind to gear you shed those extra pounds, if done correctly.

Below are ten statements that can be used to lose weight:

- In my life right now, I accept the qualities of fulfillment, happiness, and contentment.

- I enjoy eating healthy foods that put my body in very good shape.

- Exercising daily is something I would want to do.

- I'm handsome. And I'm a self-assured individual.

- I understand who I'm for.

- I love my working body parts every day. I'm grateful for all the good things my life has to offer.

- I respect one another so much. This helps me to give and receive affection.

- I continue to make good choices that will get me closer to my weight loss goals.

- Life is an adventure and a wonderful day to live.

- I am my corporeal lord. I can just lose weight.

Hypnotherapy

The idea of dealing with hypnotherapy has been around for a long time now. This includes using hypnosis as a way to reach out to the subconscious.

Hypnotherapy therapies are used in different areas of life where people can modify their views about a particular matter. This is used to stop smoking habits, eating disorders, weight loss, etc. Something about hypnotherapy is that it'll require guidance from a hypnosis specialist who will guide the patient into a relaxed realm where it is easy to reach the subconscious mind.

Inertia to Win the Weight Loss Game

If it comes to training the subconscious to learn weight-loss behaviors, this is the best plan out there. First, you have to reassure yourself that you will lose weight before beginning any weight-loss plan. It is just as simple as this. We spoke about why more people are gaining weight, and I'm sure you see that this is mainly emotional and internal.

So, it stands to reason that first, the subconscious mind needs to be tackled for meaningful change to occur. First of all, the subconscious mind needs to be conditioned to lose weight. By doing this, there will be observable lasting change.

What Is a Relationship with Food?

If you're unfamiliar with this term, referring to our link with food as a relationship may seem a little foreign. Many people don't even think they're food-related but believe me, you do. The dictionary defines the word 'relationship' as 'the link between two or more individuals or things.'

Essentially, if you fill your body with healthy foods and goodness, you'll be thanked in exchange for that. All are linked. Let's put it this way; you would not want to invite a friend you don't get along with or make you feel good at home, just as the food you eat needs to be beneficial and enhance your body. Perhaps even more so, because you're not only inviting food into your home but accepting it inside your body.

You may not be aware of this, but you and your life will affect both the food you consume and how you feel about it. If you eat something that does not agree with you, we all know it can ruin your day. Ever indulged in a big piece of chocolate cake, for example, and felt ten times worse afterward? Sugary foods could leave you feeling tired and stop productive operations. On the flip side, if you lovingly spend time preparing food for yourself and others, this tends to show up well in your body. For instance, if you feel tired and opt for a green juice as opposed to a milkshake, it will improve the way you feel right at that moment.

Chapter 23 - Hypnosis for Weight Loss

Until dealing with whether hypnosis works for weight loss, it is important to consider hypnosis as a whole subject or technique. Hypnosis is characterized as a trance-like mental state induced by enticing techniques and methodologies, typically a verbal guidance method and beginning with relaxation suggestions. A hypnotist can cause hypnosis, or sometimes even self-induced.

How does hypnosis contribute to weight loss? Hypnosis is something we usually see as entertainment, but have you ever considered weight loss hypnosis? Trying to use hypnosis to cope with an issue as extreme as obesity is easy to be cynical, but maybe it's not as crazy as it sounds. Hypnosis for weight loss is definitely an interesting concept—it offers people a fairly simple way out of their weight issue by avoiding food cravings at the source.

One weight-loss problem with hypnosis is the same problem that plagues most weight-loss remedies. There are plenty of scams out there, and those behind them won't think twice about trying to steal your money for a product that doesn't do anything. Hypnosis has the same problem. You may be able to trust certain statements about weight loss therapy for hypnosis, but many are full of lies.

In such cases, the old adage typically holds true: if anything seems too good to be true, it probably is. When hypnosis for weight loss treatment promises to help you shed some insane pounds in a couple of weeks or similar exaggerations, it's pretty safe to say it's a scam. If you find reports claiming that hypnosis can fully alter the way the mind works to avoid feeding, they're probably false.

The truth remains that hypnosis will help you lose weight. It's just that it won't make love handles melt away overnight. Hypnosis is more science than magic-all; it is when a person enters a state of intense, relaxed focus where they become more suggestive. This means thoughts put into a person's head during a session of hypnosis are much more likely to stick.

A hypnosis session won't turn you into a robot that's immune to cravings and programmed not to over-eat. What it can do is make a person more likely to adopt a proper dietary plan. The effects are solely emotional. Hypnosis can't "convince" your body to promote weight loss, and it can just implant the idea in your brain that you don't need to eat the second piece of cake.

Individuals pursuing hypnotic weight-loss approaches should be especially cautious about group hypnosis sessions. To function, hypnosis must be personalized specifically to the person receiving it. Community sessions obviously won't work because the hypnotist can't communicate with someone on his/her own. You should be cautioned against hypnosis cassettes or videos, as they share the same problem.

Hypnosis of weight loss is very enticing. If you can train your mind to reduce your cravings and improve your willpower, you're on your way to weight loss. Be vigilant and research all the choices before you purchase a drug or see a hypnotist, or else you may end up with nothing at all.

Every overweight person in the world seeks weight loss techniques. Many people are also willing to do something to make those extra kilos look appealing. The weight loss industry is making millions of dollars, and people cannot achieve what they want. Recently, studies have shown that hypnosis can assist in weight loss.

However, hypnosis is not a treatment that can help a person lose extra weight overnight. Weight loss hypnosis is a method used to concentrate people on their goals. It should be remembered that many people with disabilities and addiction issues were able to overcome their problems through hypnosis, and the same concepts apply to weight loss.

For a weight loss hypnosis program, a hypnotherapist first recognizes the goals a person needs to accomplish and analyzes the actual state of the person. You would also find eating habits and other factors that keep it from losing weight. Based on these findings, he/she will develop a system and reflect on his/her suggestions while in the hypnotic state.

It can take quite a several visits to produce results. The hypnotherapist can plant positive advice and ideas in the minds of the individual trying to lose weight. Hearing the same points and suggestions would improve his/her commitment and determination and make him/her do everything possible to lose weight and therefore stop all obstacles that hinder him/her from achieving his/her target.

How Hypnosis Works for Weight Loss

Diet, exercise, and loss of weight may be some of the most hated things that most people have to do in English and some of their most difficult things. When you are out of shape, it is a daunting struggle to get back into form.

Weight loss hypnosis is one method people are constantly using to get back into healthier lifestyles. This sounds like a brilliant idea for many people, but they don't really know how anything like this works. This is a short description of how weight loss hypnosis is working.

The goal is to alter how the subconscious works, like all the hypnosis plans. Training your subconscious will change your thoughts and actions and will catapult you toward meaningful changes in your life. I assume most people know hypnosis to avoid unhealthy habits such as alcohol and smoking. By changing the subconscious, your appetite, and your need for these things, you can regulate your pressures. For weight loss hypnosis, the same basic concepts are employed.

The purpose of the hypnosis of weight loss is to improve yourself over time; this is not an instant cure that can shed pounds within the first week. Rather, you stop eating fast food over time because you don't taste nearly as good, stop buying pizzas, stop eating when you are nervous or excited. After all, stop eating out of the habit. It is a tool to encourage you to turn to healthy eating by substituting good food for bad foods.

You learn how to eat well, and how to spend 20 minutes walking during your lunch break can improve your life's health. It won't instantly lose weight or change your life. It is possible to do this hypnosis in several different ways, including qualified individuals, DVDs, and even self-hypnosis. You will have to study the choice between these different choices to determine individually what is right for you.

In modern days, weight is a constant problem. Everybody tries to get in shape, they try, but success lags. There are so many items that treat the body. When you like most people, something is lacking in a weight-loss equation, you can try the sequence of "tested" diets and the most amazing exercises to get in shape, but if you don't care of giving the extra people a fight already lost, it doesn't take long before you regain it. The answer is to train the mind, and weight loss hypnosis is the best thing.

It helps you find new opportunities for achieving your target by using hypnosis for weight loss. Experts say there are four effective ways to achieve your goal. The first approach is to imagine the dream body with your inner eyes, how it feels, and how you walk around. Repeat these pictures every day, and your plans will be much easier to execute. The second approach is to listen to subliminal messages that are intended as weight loss hypnosis.

Listen to the tape or CD before going to bed. This works the following way, transmitting messages to the extremely sensitive subconscious mind. You will note any improvements when you wake up and do not forget to repeat the cycle every night.

Another effective hypnosis for weight loss is to overcome the stress problems; some studies indicate that people have great trouble losing weight if they cannot cope effectively with stress every day. The first step is to identify the key causes of stress and solve them by relaxation when coping with these issues and then concentrate on the weight problem.

And the final approach is by thinking positive motivational thoughts by using weight loss hypnosis. There is a basic universe rule that does what we want. The more we want it to be, the more easily it is real, be it good or bad. Therefore, the rational approach is not to use positive thought, so hypnosis for weight loss is a good idea for you.

Mastering the Magic of Hypnosis of Weight Loss

Hypnosis for weight loss has now become much more common. After the discovery, the brain plays a significant role in weight loss. It actually plays a greater role than most people expect or assume. People who haven't been on a weight loss plan will not understand this easily.

It is also said that the human fault is overweight. You may also have learned that you will stop eating and start exercising to lose weight. Most people who struggle with weight loss have done many things to lose their weight, but have obtained little to no positive results.

Although it is important to recognize certain factors that are responsible for weight gain and probably clarify the reasons why tentative weight loss attempts have failed, it does not go beyond this. Some claim that acquiring information and awareness about the cause of weight loss, and why efforts to lose weight failed, is part of the fight [of weight loss].

If you know this is half the fight for weight loss, you can definitely be considered the easiest part. Someone who wants to lose weight is already aware of what holds them off. What they don't know is how they would fix this.

Talk therapy has become very common these days, allowing people to change their minds and regulate their body weight better. There are various forms of speech therapy, but weight loss hypnosis has taken center stage.

While hypnosis can sound like an older term, it is one of the treatment methods frequently used by healthcare professionals and clinics for weight loss as it has proven to be highly successful in most patients.

Weight loss hypnosis is prescribed and favored due to the fast results that are long-term computer therapy or psychoanalysis. Hypnosis is a special technique, as it focuses primarily on positive factors that have changed the patient's body and mind.

Although most psychoanalytical approaches seek to explore the causes of weight loss issues, hypnosis easily works through and removes those barriers and thus provides an early road to weight loss. Hypnosis may simply be described as the ability to rewrite unconsciously and consciously the actions and the thoughts that go through your mind.

Weight loss hypnosis uses relaxation and repetition. The sessions typically consist of 20 to 30 minutes of guided and repeated meditation every day.

When administered for a continuous 30-day duration, the brain adopts a new style of thought or behaviors.

For most instances, the human brain consumes all that it experiences or sees through layers of consciousness. When a person hears or sees something, it is stored in the short memory of the brain. The data accumulated in the short memory will serve as a permanent influence on the mind, contributing to new patterns or beliefs.

Hypnosis for Weight Loss—Reasons to Use It

Have you thought about hypnosis to lose weight? For many people, the word hypnosis is associated with something magical and mysterious. It also often conjures up images of people falling asleep on stage and behaving in a funny or sometimes ridiculous way.

Fortunately, hypnosis, contrary to what it seems to see these shows, cannot get a person to do something against their will or who does not agree with its principles.

Chapter 24 - Heal Your Relation with Food

All too often, we eat well beyond what is needed, and this may lead to unwanted weight gain down the line. Mindful eating is important because it will help you appreciate food more.

Rather than eating large portions just to feel full, you will work on savoring every bite.

This will be helpful for those people who want to fast but need to do something to increase their willpower when they are elongating the periods in between their mealtimes. It will also be very helpful for individuals who struggle with binge eating.

Portion control alone can be enough for some people to see the physical results of their weight-loss plan. Do your best to incorporate mindful eating practices in your daily life so that you can control how much you are eating.

This meditation is going to be specific to eating an apple. You can practice mindful eating without meditation by sharing meals with others or sitting alone with nothing but a nice view out the window.

This meditation will still guide you so that you understand the kinds of thoughts that will be helpful while staying mindful during your meals.

Mindful Eating Meditation

You are now sitting down, completely relaxed. Find a comfortable spot where you can keep your feet on the ground and put as little strain throughout your body as possible. You are focused on breathing in as deeply as you can.

Close your eyes as we take you through this meditation. If you want to actually eat an apple as we go through this that is great. Alternatively, it can simply be an exercise that you can use to envision yourself eating an apple.

Let's start with a breathing exercise. Take your hand and make a fist. Point out your thumb and your pink. Now, place your right pinky on your left nostril. Breathe in through your right nostril.

Now, take your thumb and place it on your right nostril. Release your pink and breathe out through your nostrils. This is a great breathing exercise that will help to keep you focused. While you continue to do this, breathe in for one, two, three, four, and five.

Breathe out for six, seven, eight, nine, and ten. Breathe in for one, two, three, four, and five. Breathe out for six, seven, eight, nine, and ten. You can place your hand back down but ensure that you are keeping up with this breathing pattern to regulate the air inside your body. It will allow you to remain focused and centered now. Close your eyes and let yourself become more relaxed. Breathe in and then out.

In front of you, there is an apple and a glass of water. The apple has been perfectly sliced already because you want to be able to eat the fruit with ease. You do not need to cut it every time, but it is nice to change up the form and texture of the apple before eating it. Breathe in for one, two, three, four, and five. Breathe out for six, seven, eight, nine, and ten.

Now, you reach for the water and take a sip. You do not chug the water as it makes it hard for your body to process the liquid easily. You are sipping the water, taking in everything about it. You are made up of water, so you need to constantly replenish yourself with nature's nectar.

You are still focused on breathing and becoming more relaxed. Then, you reach for a slice of apple and slowly place it in your mouth. You let it sit there for a moment and then you take a bite.

It crunches between your teeth; the texture satisfying your craving. Amazingly, this apple came from nature. It always surprises you how delicious and sweet something that comes straight from the earth can be.

You chew the apple slowly, breaking it down as much as you can. You know how important it is for your food to be broken down as much as possible so that you can digest it. This will help your body absorb as many vitamins and minerals as possible.

This bit is making you feel healthy. Each time you take another bite, it fills you more and more with the good things that your body needs. Each time you take a bite, you are deciding in favor of your health. Each time you swallow a piece of the apple, you are becoming more centered on feeling and looking even better.

You are taking a break from eating now. You do not need to eat this apple fast. You know that it is more important to take your time. Look down at the apple now. It has an attractive skin on the outside. You wouldn't think by looking at it about what this sweet fruit might look like inside. Its skin was built to protect it. Its skin keeps everything good inside.

The inside is white, fresh, and very juicy. Think of all this apple could have been used for. Sauce, juice, and pie. Instead, it is going directly into your body. It is going to provide you with delicious fruit that can give you nourishment.

You reach for your glass of water and take a long drink. It is still okay to take big drinks. However, you are focused now on going back to small sips. You take a drink and allow the water to move through your mouth. You use this water not just to fill your body but to clean it. Water washes over you, and you can use it in your mouth to wash things out as well.

You swallow your water and feel it as it begins to travel through your body. You place the water down now and reach for another apple slice. You take a bite, feeling the apple crunch between your teeth once again. You feel this apple slice travel from your mouth throughout the rest of your body.

Your body is going to work to break down every part of the apple and use it for nourishment. Your body knows how to take the good things that you are feeding it and use that for something good. Your body is smart. Your body is strong. Your body understands what needs to be done to become as healthy as possible.

You are eating until you are full. You do not need to eat any more than what is necessary to keep your body healthy. You are only eating things that are good for it.

You continue to drink water. You feel how it awakens you. You are like a plant that starts to sag once you don't have enough water. You are energized, hydrated, and filled with everything needed to live a happy and healthy life.

You are still focused on your breathing. We will now finish the meditation, and you can move on either finishing the apple or doing something relaxing. You are centered on your health. You are keeping track of your breathing. You feel the air come into your body. You also feel it as it leaves. When we reach zero, you will be out of the meditation.

Twenty, nineteen, eighteen, seventeen, sixteen, fifteen, fourteen, thirteen, twelve, eleven, ten, nine, eight, seven, six, five, four, three, two, one.

You should work and invest time and effort into reaching your desired body weight, not because of some thin body ideal circling around and not because of other people around you, but because weight gain in addition to helping you be more satisfied with your body image also brings numerous health benefits which are crucial on top of all other weight loss effects on your life.

The truth is that you do not have to lose some excess amount of weight to experience weight loss health benefits as losing only several pounds can make a huge difference.

For instance, losing ten pounds for a person weighing two hundred pounds improves his/her overall health state, makes him/her feel better, more energized, and much more.

Losing only ten pounds can rapidly ease up on your joints, remove some pressure off your knees as well as remove pressure off your other lower body joints, which can wear out easily when you have to carry around those additional pounds.

Additional fat accumulated in the body can also cause various types of chronic inflammatory disorders as chemicals contained in the body, which tend to do tissue damage while damaging your joints as well.

Therefore, losing weight can prevent this from happening as well as reduce your risk for developing arthritis at some point later in life due to your weight.

Losing those extra pounds also can decrease your chances of developing some types of cancers. In fact, there is one study showing that a female who lost at least five percent of her body weight lowered her chances of developing breast cancer by twelve percent. There is no clear proof that losing weight can protect you from other types of cancer, but even the slightest weight loss progress decreases the chances of developing breast cancer.

For instance, overweight females who lose extra pounds also tend to lower their hormone levels, which are linked to the development of cancer cells including androgens, insulin, and estrogens.

If you are more likely to develop type 2 diabetes, weight loss is absolutely your way to go to delay or even prevent it from occurring. Moreover, in addition to losing weight in these cases, moderate exercise for at least thirty minutes per day is also highly recommended.

On the other hand, if you have already been diagnosed with diabetes, losing those additional pounds can help you in many ways such as keeping your blood sugar levels in control, lowering your odds of the condition causing some other health issues, and lowering your need for taking all of those medications.

By losing additional pounds, you can also lower your levels of bad LDL cholesterol just by embracing healthy dieting options. Unlike balancing those LDL cholesterol levels, balancing those levels of good HDL cholesterol is harder, but not impossible by losing body fat and by exercising regularly.

Just as you can balance your cholesterol levels, by losing those additional pounds, you can also bring down your triglyceride levels that are responsible for transporting energy and fat storage throughout the body. High triglyceride levels mean you are more likely to have a stroke or heart attack, so moving closer to those healthy triglyceride levels is crucial for maintaining an optimal health state.

Those who are overweight and struggle with high blood pressure can absolutely make a huge change by losing those additional pounds. As you know, having excess body weight puts the body under more stress so the blood starts pushing harder against the artery walls.

In these cases, the heart needs to work harder as well. To avoid suffering complications related to high blood pressure, trimming only five percent of your total body mass can make a massive change. Another dieting tip for lowering high blood pressure includes eating plenty of low-fat dairy products, plenty of foods and veggies, and cutting down on salty foods.

Individuals who struggle with excessive weight are at much greater risk for developing sleep apnea due to the excess fat situated in their throat tissue. When the body relaxes when sleeping, that throat tissue can slightly drop down blocking the airway which can make people stop breathing periodically over the night.

Fortunately, shedding only several pounds of your overall body mass is in some cases enough to prevent sleep apnea and avoid the health issues which it brings.

Chapter 25 - Hypnosis and Power of Mind

Have you surveyed your life to find out how satisfied you're with the outcomes?

Are there unsuitable regions in your day-to-day existence, as relational connections, funds, well-being, or work? Does one need to know why? It is safe to say that you are obliterating yourself or developing your fantasies and wants? What extent of time did you spend to comprehend the self-sufficient cycles and modern instruments of your reasoning? Your answer is straightforwardly connected with the norm of life.

Shrewdness lies in dominating contemplations. To totally get a handle on the wide force that your idea's creation wants, we'd prefer to consider a free substance of self-care and self-realization. Through goal, an individual is completely equipped for planning his preferred reality. Thinking deals with three unique levels: cognizant, subliminal, and oblivious.

Cognizant reasoning is a part of reasoning and is responsible for all insightful, normal data, STM, thinking, and addressing, which intentionally empowers us to absorb different assignments and make obvious end results.

The inner mind is a kind of ownership, everything being equal, convictions, mental self-view, and information. It's related to LTM. The inner mind is commonly customized intentionally or automatically by our essential guardian, culture, culture, and religion. Yet we don't comprehend the inner mind, it generally exists and influences how we carry on every day.

The psyche mind is a locale where our bodies work naturally. For example, squinting happens consequently without stress. The subconscious psyche is impacted by the feelings we hold in the inner mind. We add "default mode" or "self-sufficient driving." If you find yourself in an upset state, it will influence the body's actual capacity straightforwardly.

As you'll see, the vast majority of the exercises of the brain occur in the psyche. Looking at our souls' profundities is significant for understanding what drives us or triggers us in certain life circumstances.

To perceive our considerations' basic part in our lives, we'd prefer to know the office of dreams. To start with, all pieces of the brain are significant and dynamic. Our mental self-portrait stores in our minds and the most convincing idea a great many people battle with is the "I am" feeling. The feeling of "I'm," or because the savant Alan Watts put it: "The skin-wrapped self" is essentially an idea that every last one of the people is compelled to receive in our youth to coordinate into family and private to be a piece of the incorporating local area. The improvement of "I'm" is predicated on a progression of subliminal modes that decide the person's character and the capacity to exact themselves. To address some of our more significant issues, we'd prefer to deliver the "be that as it may, the voice of awareness and investigate the clarifications.

At the degree of awareness, a considerable lot of us are applying toward joy, well-being, and satisfaction. Be that as it may, in the psyche, they'll

182

convey interior shortage, uncertain injury, passionate problems, and mental limitations. At the phone level, our DNA records karma buildups, generational data, previous existence encounters, uncertain feelings, and each kind of information that we unconsciously consumed during adolescence. The amount of information put away in the psyche is faltering, and it's a major effect on both positive cognizance and negative reasoning.

The initial phase in a significant individual change is to talk with the psyche. As referenced before, the psyche is the root clarification for the matter. However long individuals actually treat manifestations of passionate and actual difficulties or infections rather than the premise cause, they will wind up in an endless loop. How about we take the occasion of someone engaging in food habit? People may intentionally pick a solid eating regimen and exercise more; in the best case, urgent eaters will endeavor to stay with their new propensities in a brief timeframe until some enthusiastic issues show up.

By and large, people will recover their propensities and fall under old propensities. It is because the extreme, passionate, mental, and actual preparation requires a profound shadow of the characters hiding at the inner mind level. A strategy to inclination and work with the psyche is to utilize spellbinding.

Spellbinding is frequently misconstrued as a condition of obviousness when an individual nods off and doesn't have the foggiest idea of what's going on. It's a condition of focus, a condition of expanded awareness, and at a comparable time, knowledge into interior cycles that are likewise improved.

Entrancing treatment was endorsed by the British Medical Association in 1955 furthermore, supported by the American Medical Association in 1958, and has been joined with psychotherapy since its commencement. Dr. Milton H. Erickson is an American therapist who represents considerable authority in spellbinding and private cures. He added to the numerous changes of contemporary psychotherapy. In 1957, Dr. Erickson and bunches of associates established the American Society of Clinical Hypnosis. Regardless of this current, it's as yet a method of exceptional discussion and is considered to need viability or is utilized as a stunt in the receiving area. Notwithstanding these errors, spellbinding treatment is typically a popular and successful technique used to manage conduct changes and passionate contentions and has enduring impacts.

Entrancing might be a recuperating device that will straightforwardly enter the inner mind and sidestep fundamental pieces of cognizance. On the cognizant level, it's hard to get the most seasoned experience that an individual has, which is of impressive importance to feelings on the grounds that cognizant reasoning can frustrate individuals' turn of events. It regularly tells the best way to monitor people against recollecting and mitigating antagonistic feelings and unattractive recollections; however, it likewise can keep individuals from defeating these recollections and awful encounters.

Utilizing hypnotherapy and psychotherapy procedures, the essential clarification for the matter is frequently straightforwardly found and settled. Under the direction of a hypnotic specialist and utilizing psychotherapy and entrancing treatment methods, clients can follow the essential clarification for their unique awful mishap, along these lines impeding their advancement.

For instance, I worked with a customer who is ceaselessly needing desserts. My yearning returns to my adolescence. At the point when the customer was just five years of age, she saw different children eating desserts; however, her dad said that they had no money to look for sweets. During that piece of the classification, she felt pitiful and began crying. By watching the occurrence with a grown-up's understanding, she will forsake trouble, shortage, and supplanting it with placated wants, fulfilling feelings, and truly getting things. We took her back to this while supplanting every single negative inclination, convictions, and feelings related to that occasion with new, good, glad, and fulfilled sentiments, realizing that she will appreciate every one of the treats she needs whenever and anyplace. A long time later, she shared her long-term want to eat desserts.

Another model is the point at which somebody battles with self-esteem. When dealing with a critical injury, the customer will coordinate the essential clarification for the matter.

When the underlying stun that caused him/her to feel awkward or improper is settled, the customer accepts the path of confidence and acknowledgment. Consequently, changing the view from "I'm not good enough," "Nobody loves me," "Life is inane" to "I'm adored," "I'm commendable," "I'm freed." The difficult occasions that caused this sense should be settled; something else, it's useless to disentangle this issue from a cognizant viewpoint.

Spellbinding treatment widens the patient's frame of reference by assisting patients with delivering their previous encounters and impact. By initiating a self-tour, clients will be presented to their normal potential. All through the human experience, this limitless development and furthermore the potential for co-creation stays unaltered. Opening the entrance key to the flood of cognizant creation is to explain the oblivious and subliminal limitations that we are brought into the world with or have collected in the course of our life. When light streams in the estimation of our clouded side, our awareness will be cleaned, and that we can emanate in through the opened entryways of festivity and acknowledgment.

There is proof to demonstrate the proficiency of spellbinding. A progression of studies led in the course of recent years has shown that entrancing treatment can help take care of different medical conditions. It was found to decidedly influence asthma, joint inflammation, breaks, torment, a disorder of the fractious bowels, and migraines. It's found to help ladies who conceive offspring and lessen agonizing encounters. It's likewise identified with better and quicker mending and improved recuperation after medical procedures.

Spellbinding can utilize the brain's office on the oblivious' significant perspectives, which may hugely affect the psyche and body. It is frequently more straightforwardly associated with people's inborn mending power yet may be prevented by cognizant convictions, questions, and contemplations. It's a fast compromise technique, bypassing those perspectives that hurt a person's capacity to determine their enthusiastic problems.

Spellbinding is as of now recuperating because more examination shows that it's compelling. There are schools and focuses devoted to the investigation and educating of entrancing treatment and patients' treatment.

With everything taken into account, entrancing treatment is an appropriate treatment instrument used to deliver curbed feelings and influence clashes inside and out to search out the wellspring of the matter. It can initiate the office of thought and utilize individual assets to disentangle issues that may reflect physical or enthusiastic restoration. Our mind has two sections—the cognizant part and what we call "subliminal." The jobs in those two sections are totally different. For example, when you cut your finger, you'll intentionally plan to clean the injury and apply the mortar. In any case, all work to recuperate wounds is constrained by the inner mind. The development of aroused regions shields the rest of the body from contaminations; the framework's inclusion will eliminate microbes. Hence, the body will frame a substitution skin to trade the lost skin—all of which can occur with no cognizant info!

At the point when we notice spellbinding and entrancing treatment, we regularly notice the inner mind. There's little inquiry of the office of our "imperceptible" part. The psyche controls each snapshot of our balance, figures out who we like, how we respond to other people, how we carry on in explicit circumstances, "excruciating expenses," diversion approaches to appreciate, and sexual perspectives. If the psyche interaction gives us a base tone with no control, we will do anything.

The Subconscious Does Not Think

The inner mind is finished without reason or rationale, judgment or analysis, capability, or resilience. Subliminally, everything is dark or white, regardless of the weather. It's only the responsive, enthusiastic focus where our intuitive assets dwell, be it normal assets or the assets we've procured throughout life.

It's an assessment framework that ceaselessly gauges each contribution to each snapshot of life through our faculties. The inner mind speaks with cognizant contemplations just through sentiments and utilizations this correspondence to chase approaches to make us stay safe.

It is by all accounts prepared to assess each new contribution from our five detects that upheld all that we've encountered in life so far. Assume the principal data matches what has effectively been capable. Around there, the reaction we saw will rely on the outcome, regardless of whether it's a legitimate reaction (likely a satisfying response) or a deficient reaction (maybe a dread reaction). Subliminal work is completely undetectable.

The Subconscious Is Entirely Invisible Consciousness

Nobody can feel their subliminal at work, so we've no chance to get of realizing that it contrasts and new info, which clarifies why we may abruptly

Disdain a particular individual or even frightened of something moderately little. Obviously, it additionally can rapidly invert. Have you at any point experienced such a circumstance, though you wish it yourself, befuddling you? Eventually, you'll say:

"God realizes why I'm so fascinated," it will be an improper accomplice, or it will be a touch of garments or nearly anything.

The Subconscious Processing Power Is Incredibly Fast

Presently, this is regularly a convoluted touch. In any case, the very certainty is that once you are intentionally aware of an upgrade, contribution from any of your faculties, including your point of view. When you are intentionally aware of the boost, the psyche has effectively been aware of the improvement.

Chapter 26 - Hypnotherapy and Insomnia/Sleep Problems

To limit or treat a sleep disorder, hypnotherapy might be extremely powerful, albeit not all types of sleep disorders are defenseless against entrancing consideration.

Hypnotherapy may not react well to sleep deprivation instigated by organic issues, disorders, or medical impacts. Notwithstanding, assuming the vital reasons for your sleep deprivation are pressure and uneasiness, spellbinding, along with legitimate rest cleanliness, can well give a productive fix.

Sleep Hypnosis

What Is Insomnia?

Rest is something that everyone needs. In both our physical and mental prosperity, it has an urgent impact. Yet, resting messes, like sleep deprivation, can make having sufficient rest hard for specific individuals. Absence of rest, just as causing you to feel depleted, will prompt actual sickness, and increment the danger of coronary illness. Intellectually, not having sufficient rest will prompt uneasiness and make the center hard for you. A sleeping disorder is depicted as an inconvenience of attempting to rest or staying snoozing long enough for the following morning to feel invigorated.

At the point when you can't figure out how to nod off, the greater part of us will have encountered an evening of upset rest and will know how it feels. You might be stressed for the following day or you may have had a cup excessively near sleep time. You may think that it's simple to nod off, yet you keep awakening around evening time. An extreme rest will leave you feeling depleted and bad-tempered the following day, in any case. Numerous who experience the ill effects of a sleeping disorder will habitually feel these feelings. 33% of people in the UK are accounted to have episodes of a sleeping disorder for the duration of their lives. While it can impact anybody at whatever stage in life, it appears to be that people beyond 60 years old and ladies are more helpless.

Various Types of Insomnia

There are a few particular types of a sleeping disorder, yet they are generally assembled into two classes:

Transitory Insomnia

At the point when it keeps going between one evening and three to about a month, a sleeping disorder is known as transient or intense.

Fly slack, a shift of timetable or workspaces, stress, caffeine, and liquor are run-of-the-mill reasons for transient sleep deprivation.

Transient or inconsistent sleep deprivation is the name of specific instances of brief sleep deprivation. This is the place where the individual infrequently creates resting challenges over months or years.

Determined Insomnia

This is viewed as constant sleep deprivation as well. The issue would as a rule proceed practically daily, for a time of about a month. This may likewise happen as rest is upset by torment or therapy from ailments. This may incorporate joint pain, Parkinson's sickness, asthma, sensitivities, synthetics that change, or worries with psychological well-being.

Side Effects of Insomnia

In light of explicit conditions, signs shift. There are basic manifestations, be that as it may, including:

- Keeping up around evening time for extended periods.

- Not being aware of nodding off.

- Awakening during the night a few times.

- Getting up right on time and being not able to rest once more.

- Feeling depleted the following morning and lethargic.

- Thinking that it's difficult to center or work accurately.

- The feeling of peevishness.

Reasons for Insomnia

The issue has various potential sources. In specific cases, restlessness might be brought about by just one reason, while others may go through a combination of factors.

Any of sleep deprivation's potential causes include:

Conditions in Physical Fitness

If you experience the ill effects of a medical problem that causes you uneasiness, you can discover nodding off troublesome.

Moreover, if you have an illness, similar to asthma, that influences your relaxation. It is expected that rest cycles can likewise be brought about by chemical issues and urinary conditions. There is a danger your rest will be upset by the medication you are taking.

Converse with the specialist on the off chance that you speculate an ailment or figure that your medication can trigger an issue with your rest.

Mental Health Conditions

Dozing issues might be made by such emotional well-being conditions. A person with outrageous misery, for example, is bound to experience the ill effects of a sleeping disorder. At the point when an individual loses rest, the discouraged dispositions that accompany despondency may likewise be exacerbated.

Another problem that is frequently connected with sleep deprivation is uneasiness. Nervousness may make a substance feel tense, stressed, and depleted. These feelings can think that it's hard to nod off. When attempting to rest, the psyche of the individual will consistently run, feeling like they can't "switch off." Sleep can likewise be upset by the worry and the individual may awaken in the evening. The uneasiness about not having sufficient rest will transform into an endless loop if this pattern proceeds.

Lifestyle

Dozing practices might be influenced by regular exercises and ways of life. First of all, if you drink liquor day by day, you can find that during the night you awaken. Liquor is an energizer and surprisingly after taking a couple of beverages, it can show up simple to nod off. It normally adds to awful rest generally.

Medications and caffeine can comparably prompt issues with rest. Any dependence on drugs will influence how you rest, so it is essential to look for help. It is informed that you limit the utilization of caffeine on the off chance that you experience the ill effects of a sleeping disorder.

Worked really hard into the night will think that it's difficult to kill the mind. For your inward clock, shift work will make a tumult and make dozing precarious. It very well may merit reevaluating your hours if your work (or business-related pressure) is influencing your sleeping disorder.

The Way Insomnia Works

Individuals with a sleeping disorder additionally say they are "restless people"; that is, hereditarily inclined to a sleeping disorder. There ought to be nothing far from current realities. There is a lethargic time in any living being, so rest is ordinary, so sleep deprivation is unnatural.

A sleeping disorder overall is brought about by a characteristic dread that might be about families, monetary issues, inquiries of confidence, and various different nerves. Each customer is unique. Be that as it may, we can sort out what's going on and fix the side effects at a psyche level by utilizing hypnotherapy for Insomnia, taking you back to a typical rest cycle.

"Just about 30% of the populace has a kind of restlessness. Nervousness quite often supports sleep deprivation, and this tension intrudes on the typical beat of rest. This dread is something people with sleep deprivation seem to ruminate on when resting, which is the thing that hypnotherapy focuses on with a sleeping disorder. This rumination produces raised degrees of tension and subsequently, inside the restless person, a raised level of readiness and hence rest escapes them. This tension is frequently poor to such an extent that the customer probably won't be truly aware of it and along these lines accepts that there is little reason for the deficiency of rest.

Paul White, the sleep deprivation expert at the Surrey Institute of Clinical Hypnotherapy.

Treatment for Insomnia

There are various techniques you may take when treating dozing issues. To eliminate every actual trigger, it is important to initially converse with the specialist.

To help you rest, your PCP can recommend that you take medicine. This might be a proficient treatment for specific people; however, it is important to attempt to sort out the main driver of the issue. Conduct treatments and voice treatments are additionally proposed.

Another treatment decision that numerous individuals find effective is hypnotherapy. Sleeping disorder hypnotherapy can resolve the potential triggers while assisting you with unwinding and rest. For instance, if the reason for your sleep deprivation is nervousness or melancholy, rest entrancing can enhance your treatment setting. It would then be able to assist with changing the resting routine by taking care of these issues.

On the other hand, hypnotherapy for sleep deprivation will attempt to end this propensity if a propensity causes a sleeping disorder (like liquor).

As the ideas made by spellbinding treatment permit your brain and body to unwind and get the rest you need, the concern, uneasiness, and dread that can keep you from nodding off disappear.

Hypnotherapy for Sleep

Although there might be a clear justification for some resting issues, others won't. If you are muddled whether you are experiencing difficulty dozing, hypnotherapy for sleep deprivation might be gainful. A subliminal specialist can venture into the psyche, utilizing various techniques to find what might have caused the issue. A customized treatment created by the subliminal specialist will start after the reason is recognized.

The propensities for rest aggravations will get instilled in the subliminal when experiencing a sleeping disorder for a significant time. The point of entrancing for sleep deprivation is to draw in with it and propose valuable changes. These ideas will expect to end the propensities for negative reasoning that trigger the issue.

Showing you how to unwind is a fundamental part of hypnotherapy for sleep deprivation. Physical or enthusiastic pressure can make dozing awkward for specific people. To help assuage tension, a trance inducer can utilize loosening up strategies, like progressive muscle unwinding.

A trance specialist will likewise show you self-spellbinding. It will assist you with making a timetable, just as figure out how to manage the issue that triggers the causes. Utilizing spellbinding at home for sleep deprivation will help you put into your day-by-day life the procedures you have acquired in the meeting room.

What Exactly Is Sleep Hypnosis?

If there was a simple and hazard-free tranquilizer that you may utilize every day, wouldn't it be a fantasy? Indeed, there is one, and it's called entrancing of rest! Spellbinding has been a notable quieting and understood idea technique for well longer than a century. The expanding utilization of this otherworldly personal growth approach has been lighted by the utilization of rest entrancing for halting cigarettes, treating constant torment, relieving a sleeping disorder, and that's just the beginning.

Rest spellbinding is utilized by specific people as a procedure to make them nod off. Rest spellbinding, basically, is a method that requires guided ideas to lead an individual into a condition of unwinding. This agreeable state could, indeed, make it simpler to nod off. A few sorts of rest spellbinding accessible can be downloaded to your telephone or gadget, although it isn't sure if they are precise. Peruse on for data about what it is, regardless of whether you are attempting rest entrancing, and discover different methods that might be more viable when you need to get a nice night's rest. Rest entrancing is a meeting through which a trance inducer guides a member by verbal motions to cause quiet and a daze that might be utilized to help you float to rest, either face to face or by a video.

Entrancing aides the beneficiary to effectively "rest" while still subliminally mindful. The following trancelike state occurs with the delta, theta, alpha conditions of lower-level brainwave enactment where cognizant action dies down, and subliminal movement rises. It is likewise conceivable to utilize rest entrancing to bring the audience into profound and remedial rest. Rest to tune in to a trance the audible signals of a trance specialist that are intended to bring you by the power of influence into a daze-like condition. Trance specialists utilize various procedures, like concentrated focus, control of side effects, and coordinated perception, to advance alleviation. An individual who is spellbound can hear phrases like "unwind," "profound," "simple," "and let go." These words should urge somebody to float off to rest.

A spellbinding meeting for rest incorporates:

- **Settling down:** The beneficiary rests and gets settled.

- **Giving up:** The audience is coordinated to put to the side any questions or concerns.

- **Acceptance:** By loosening up the cognizant brain and opening up the inner mind, it readies the audience to go further into unwinding.

- **Breathing:** This section requires intentional breathing that brings the beneficiary into balance much more seriously.

- **The idea:** This involves coordinated representation that plants the planned result into the psyche brain of the audience, the longest and last piece of the entrancing.

You might be interested whether living in fantasy land is entrancing or if it works. Luckily, there is an impressive examination regarding the matter of rest spellbinding.

Chapter 27 - Overcoming Mental Blocks to Lose Weight

What convictions are clutching your weight?

- I'm mediocre.

- I'm inadequate.

- I'm unimportant, so I even need to frame myself large to be seen losing weight is simply excessively troublesome.

- I will come up short and set the heap all back on once more.

- I should be so horrendous not to be prepared to control my eating I need to rebuff myself.

- It is too difficult to even think about beginning to slim down.

- My weight is familial, and that I can't change that my weight is hereditary and that I can't change that I am not adequate/I am sufficiently not.

- I self-harm myself.

- I'm useless.

- I severely dislike myself.

Healing Negative Beliefs

The most ideal approaches to improve negative convictions and assemble certainty are:

- Emotional freedom technique (EFTTM).

- Bach flower remedies.

- Assertions.

- Ask your aides and holy messengers to help and mend you.

An example might be a program that you basically have, which is a part of your character. For example, in your character may be the contemplations: I am not close to the same as individuals

This reality implies that you block your weight reduction as you feel that the undertaking is simply excessively overwhelming, and you'll fizzle. New examples are frequently handily introduced utilizing EFTTM.

A square is a few things that stop you from pushing ahead, and in this way the greatest one among these is fear. The contrary one is protected. If your psyche feels that it's undependable, it'll not permit you to abound in the roughage. Thus, if your inner mind imagines that getting in shape isn't protected, you'll not lose weight!

Additionally, if you imagine that you're useless, else you believe you are doing not merit, this may make you self-harm.

Healing Negative Patterns and Blocks

The most ideal approaches to treat negative examples and squares are:

- Emotional freedom technique.

- Bach flower remedies.

- Confirmations.

- Reflection.

Ask your aides and heavenly messengers to help and mend you.

What Is Self-Harm?

The term self-damage portrays our regularly oblivious capacity to keep ourselves from being, doing, or having, being the individual we might want to be, doing what we might want to encounter or accomplish, or having our objectives and wants to become a reality.

More often than not, we are absolutely uninformed that we are self-attacking because it occurs on a psyche level. In any case, now and again we are aware of that minuscule voice inside the rear of our head that says, "You can't become familiar with a language" or "don't be ludicrous, you can't get in shape."

Our inner mind might be an amazing asset and consistently imagines that it's acting to our greatest advantage. Halting us getting into a new area, deterring us from facing challenges guarantees that we don't get injured, we aren't embarrassed, and that we don't fall flat—that is the reason various ventures never get off the base.

Rather than playing to win, self-harm plays to stay away from rout. The reason for this part of the inner mind is self-insurance and endurance.

It can even adversely influence your well-being on the off chance that it imagines that this may shield you from more serious danger. Layers of abundance weight have for some time been perceived as security. Frequently the inner mind will utilize weight gain to watch you against saw perils you would perhaps be presented to as a slimmer individual. For example, where somebody has been mishandled as a baby, the psyche may add weight to frame them ugly (it suspects as much) that the maltreatment isn't rehashed.

Thus, individuals may make reference to self-harm about their weight since they ate genuinely and set on weight. Nonetheless, in some cases, self-harm will influence your chemicals and organs, causing weight acquisition in individuals who eat just a humble sum.

In some cases, individuals can decrease yet consistently set it back on simply one more technique for self-damage. When the apparent had the chance to ensure through self-damage has been mended and delivered, our ailments and weight may vanish.

My Experience of Self-Sabotage

In my journey to lose the heap and water I had gathered, I counseled a lady who represented considerable authority in 'muscle testing.' Once we posed the inquiry "Do I might want to be thin," the obvious answer was "no!" which took me out of nowhere. So then began the excursion of revelation on why my inner mind didn't need me to be thin.

For what reason would I say I was self-undermining?

During the long seventeen years during which I gradually cleared and recuperated the clarifications for my self-harm:

• I had discovered a self-discipline/fall to pieces program because of what I had cleared out previous existences.

• I had discovered security around me (weight and water) because of the rape, assault, and male consideration I had—I didn't feel it had been protected to be a woman.

• I had a few previous existence issues with starving to death and didn't have any desire to starve during this lifetime.

• I had a few previous existence issues with biting the dust of thirst, subsequently the excess water during this lifetime, to ensure that it didn't occur once more.

• I had an inconceivable measure of other karma I imagined that on the off chance that I turned into an advisor, I was unable to confide in myself not to damage, or trial on patients, as I had cut them before in previous existences, at that point I used to be just having the opportunity to be a specialist once I was 'thin.'

• I was scared to require spices, as I had seen various individuals bite the dust from them in previous existences.

• Since I had been aggrieved in previous existences for recuperating individuals, I accepted that I may be mishandled during this life; additionally, I used to be terrified of being amazing I was scared to attempt to work I used to be affirmed to do I was scared that the book would come up short.

• I identify with my self-harm with weight and well-being; however, there have been numerous parts of my life that influenced me.

• I was consistently underwater and won't ever take care of my charge cards I never got the work I merited and was sensibly regularly out of the work If I got business, there would consistently be somebody giving me an inconvenient time (karmic recompense!).

At the point when I had any medicines, similar to red vein treatment or corrective medical procedures, it may consistently fall flat.

In all honesty, my inner mind was making a reality where the entirety of the above happened—the mind is that solid, trust me. Indeed, even whenever I had delivered the connections and got forestall the impact of my mom, my psyche was all the while following their models, and as I strived to encourage better, my inner mind kicked in and aggravated it.

In this way, my inner mind was really influencing every one of my organs and making them wastefully work so I set on six stones and expand with water.

This reality was because my inner mind realized I could diminish, and it concluded this was the most straightforward arrangement of assault.

That is the reason a few groups lessen, then set it back on. To begin with, the psyche does not generally understand what is going on, so it is a misfortune of the heap. It at that point kicks in achievement in endurance mode, and subsequently, the weight backpedals on. You'd not lose six stones at that point, set it back on again—you would conceivably supplant a stone at that point get on-off. Individuals' fault eats less or losing it excessively fast; however, it's only your psyche disrupting you.

Emotional and Luxury Eating

At the point when you read magazine articles, they generally notice that people eat with passion and gain weight. A few groups eat for mental reasons and dreariness. A few groups gorge themselves and there are clarifications for this. You might want to recognize your passionate eating triggers and utilization of a way like EFTtm to dispense with them. In any case, if you might want to eat an endeavor to stand by 10 minutes breathing profoundly and you should track down that, at that point, the need to eat has gone.

In any case, I do know huge loads of thin individuals that indulge and drink an unnecessary measure of. They eat more for passionate reasons likewise—slight individuals aren't great or without their issues.

One of the clarifications I composed in this book is to call attention to that overweight individuals don't eat genuinely any more than thin/standard individuals. How frequently would you say you are on vacation and you watch individuals have a gigantic breakfast, trailed by an enormous lunch, then three courses for supper, in addition to alcohol, a day for about fourteen days?

How regularly does one see a thin individual eat a bundle of rolls or a bar of chocolate? Constantly!

You need to search out the clarifications why your psyche would not like to lessen and either discharge the portrayals if these are previous existences based or change your subliminal 'conviction framework' if they're greater character characteristics.

Removing the Self-Sabotage

At the point when I was going through a colossal measure of money with specialists and zip worked, I referenced that I'd act naturally undermining myself. A large portion of them surrendered with sickening dread and disclosed to me it had been recently a pardon to indulge (here we return, I thought).

I read tons about the Emotional Freedom Technique (EFTTM), and inside the absolute first passage, I read it referenced self-harm. This way was very incredible. In any case, my self-damage was so profoundly imbued that for an all-encompassing time, EFTTM just aggravated everything, as my psyche attempted to convey into its control of me.

I, hence, needed to burrow a lot further by clearing the connections, previous existences, and karma. At that point, I could utilize EFTTM and my different strategies to shift my subliminal discernment and its conviction framework that "I didn't merit."

Mental Inversion

I imagined that I needed to diminish, yet I didn't, and my inner mind was halting me. You might want to search out every one of the clarifications of why and deliver and recuperate them individually. For this, you utilize the EFTTM mental inversion strategies.

How are you self-attacking because my experience would persuade that you just are?

Propensity for Self-Harm

I had an otherworldly understanding meeting and was informed that the self-discipline had been recuperated; however, I actually had the 'propensity,' which should have been dealt with and not reproduced. I feel it's fundamental to consolidate it during this book since it would haven't happened to me that I had the propensity and was fit for reproducing the training whenever. Our body and the subliminal are so detrimental to us that a training program is scheduled. So in any event, when the principal improvements are recuperated, the propensity remains. In this way, make sure to check to determine whether there's a propensity at that point treat appropriately (regularly a comparative way you mended the primary example). Affirm you don't reproduce the training by echoing confirmations and if you are feeling yourself slipping once again to 'meriting the example 'quickly drop this sense and ensure that you hold mending it.

What Is the Secondary Gain?

In all honesty, each ailment and issue can have a huge advantage for the one that is encountering it. Experts utilize the term 'optional increase' for this notable wonder, and you'll begin to recognize this conduct in people that you perceive. Now and again, the upsides of getting the matter are so extraordinary they exceed the enduring the thing is causing.

This issue is made by the psyche, absolutely unbeknown to the individual. Frequently this individual propelling themselves excessively hard, and accordingly the oblivious, will think about how to influence what is going on there in the person's life, so making it an ailment or a drag that is not heavily influenced by them. A decent inquiry to pose to yourself is, "what benefits does this ailment bring to you, and for what reason would you say you are keeping it around?" All in all, what are the benefits of you clutching the excess weight? Examine this inquiry cautiously and burrow until you get to its absolute bottom.

Chapter 28 - Virtual Gastric Band for Eating Disorder

The utilization of spellbinding as an enhancement to a food rebalancing with a dietitian is an interest in solid increment. However, what are the conceivable outcomes of spellbinding that help you with pounds loss?

The most well-known apparatus is the respite of a virtual gastric band. By making the patient daydream, utilizing his/her creative mind, which goes through a careful activity, allowing him/her to lessen his/her craving and reconnect with the sensation of satiety.

The upside of this convention is that it stays away from medical procedures, which is impossible in individuals with heart conditions, who are sensitive to sedatives, or who fear activities. This is a fascinating instrument; however, is it reasonable for all individuals who need to lose weight?

Truth be told, all that will rely upon request because there are many dietary issues from one limit to the next, the most popular are anorexia and bulimia, yet you additionally have orthorexia, sugar reliance, 1 gorge, and so on Before explaining the commitment of spellbinding around here, let us check out the way to deal with follow because dietary problems are multifactorial.

Behind these issues are here and there covered up clinical causes known as diabetes or cholesterol, utilitarian colopathy, others still ineffectively referred to, for example, dysfunctions of the intestinal microbiota, candida albican and so on It is consequently fundamental to investigate the clinical causes before falling back on entrancing.

If no clinical reason is discovered, it is important to likewise counsel a dietician because over and over again individuals think they realize how to eat a fair eating regimen when they commit errors. This is the way a couple of years prior, I chose to quit treating weight reduction because there was a hole between the desires of the patients and the necessities of a reasonable eating routine. Schematically, individuals requested that I assist them with getting in shape yet without transforming anything in their eating regimen or figured they could eat because they were following a ladies' magazine diet. The plan to recall is that on the off chance that you eat ineffectively or excessively little, you won't get thinner. At the point when I say eating seriously, I'm not in any event, discussing modern food varieties but instead about mistakes in the decision of food. Take two models: Starchy food varieties are a wellspring of energy for the body. In fact, the association stores them to establish saves; however, they have a focal part in the sensation of satiety. So eliminating them totally implies facing the challenge of starving your body and breaking routinely by eating chocolates, cakes, and so forth

Natural products are useful for well-being given they are eaten with some restraint. They can be totally coordinated with regards to a nibble at 4 p.m. For instance, the basic blunder is to end a feast with a product of the soil yogurt when both contain sugar and that the mix of the two will unavoidably build glucose and along these lines cause the emission of insulin to corrupt this sugar and store it.

These are only two models that show that we regularly have confidence by some basic honesty about how to eat when our suppers are not adjusted. The last model is the eating regimen. This is to radically diminish the calorie admission of your suppers. Unquestionably, weight reduction can be quick; however, be careful with the yoyo impact by starving your body, generally storing in disparity. Likewise, it is hard to follow an eating routine both actually and mentally, so unavoidably, you will break consistently and you will lose inspiration.

It is subsequently critical to be joined by a wholesome observing proficient to track down the privileged healthful equilibrium that will help you arrive at your objective over the long-haul.

After this significant diversion, we go to the mental component of dietary problems by tending to the various tomahawks:

- **The psychological conduct recovery pivot:** today we invest less energy setting up our dinners, we eat in a short time and this adds to advancing food dysfunctions. Realize that the stomach-related framework is made out of 200 million neurons in association with the cerebrum and that satiety is gotten by an input circle between the mouth, the stomach, and the mind, thus the significance of eating gradually. I won't harp on the inquiry, you can discover more data on the weight reduction page and it is a subject examined during the meeting.

213

- **The enthusiastic pivot:** It is clearly the one that will intrigue you the most and that you know the least. The stomach has a neural knowledge interconnected with the cerebrum. Feelings in body memory can influence feelings of anxiety as a rule and the working of the gut specifically. A few groups will have stomachs tied by stress, tension, and dread and will, in general, get in shape, others actually will take asylum in food to discover a wellspring of brief mollification. As a decent clinician, I additionally realize that weight acquire is likewise a guard for some individuals whose beginning is regularly found in adolescence: following embarrassment we might need to be "solid" or then again not to if it's not too much trouble, to keep away from all threat from sexual viciousness, tribal connections and so forth.

In youth, there are likewise parental orders: "finish your plate to satisfy your mother," the youngster who needs acknowledgment comprehends that to get the blessings of his/her mom, he/she should fulfill him/her by completing his/her plate without tuning it on his/her body.

Likewise, along these lines, in the event of the absence of parental love, desserts regularly bring solace. These are only a couple of the components to assist you with understanding that sincerely charged occasions influence the equilibrium of the stomach-related and intestinal frameworks, causing dietary issues. This is the reason my weight reduction strategy depends on enthusiastic purifying work enhanced with explicit work: "Finish your plate to satisfy your mother," the kid who needs acknowledgment comprehends that to get the blessings of his/her mom, he/she should fulfill him/her by completing his/her plate without tuning it on his/her body. Additionally

214

along these lines, if there should be an occurrence of absence of parental love, desserts frequently bring solace.

This is the reason my weight reduction strategy depends on enthusiastic purging work enhanced with explicit: taking everything into account, the message I need to pass on is that the virtual gastric band is one choice among others which isn't really important because passionate work as of now normally improves supper the executives, conduct control and expands the inspiration. If you just have 10 to 15 kg to lose, this should be possible without the break of a ring. What's more, if you experience the ill effects of sugar dependence, the best is to treat it with another particular convention and not the ring which is primarily used to diminish craving yet not dependence on an item.

Recollect that weight reduction is fundamentally multifactorial, and that spellbinding is a decent instrument; however, notwithstanding a sound and adjusted eating regimen and that it works without clinical issues adding to this weight acquire.

Weigh Management and Hypnosis Changes

The dysfunctions of eating conduct are basically the same as reliance, particularly reliance on sugar, Coca-Cola, chocolate, and so forth Individuals who have issues with bulimia or food impulses stop their assaults after 1 or 2 meetings. Knowing the beginning of the weight gain deals with this issue adequately.

Very much joined by an advisor, the body permits admittance to the memory of the feelings of lived occasions.

Another inquiry emerges in the food impulse: there is a vacuum, an enthusiastic need, a food impulse, there is mental affliction: the misery of passionate void, guarding against an insufferable inside the real world, disillusionment involved with friends and family, absence of inner security, dejection, dread of desertion, and so forth. Physiological, mental, and passionate administration due to entry and Neurotherapy generally give excellent outcomes.

Rapidly the individual no longer has a similar relationship with food, he no longer feels a captive to food, much of the time the impulses stop after the primary meeting of entrancing. Spellbinding assists with finding and keeps a decent inspiration to get thinner successfully and reasonably. The virtual gastric band strategy was the subject of a similar report on 25 volunteers following a meeting of one hour every week for three weeks every one of the volunteers shed pounds and changed their dietary patterns. These meetings are to be incorporated into the general administration of weight issues with dietary suggestions and the guideline of neuromodulators.

Conclusion

A Gastric Band is a very effective tool in the world of weight loss. They can reduce the amount of food you can eat, which thereby helps your body feel satiated and satisfied for longer periods. This way, you will burn more calories throughout the day without even realizing it. Additionally, bands also help with portion control so you never end up binging on foods that might be bad for weight loss or putting yourself at risk for an eating disorder.

You simply pass a tube through an incision in your abdomen and attach it to a type of adjustable ring around your stomach. This ring will slowly decrease in size over time, which makes it so you feel hungry less often and your stomach can hold less food. It is a much safer alternative to gastric bypass surgery.

Who Is a Good Candidate for a Gastric Band?

To determine whether an adjustable gastric band may be the best option for you, your doctor will need to look at several factors. He or she will consider your current weight and BMI, any medical conditions that you have, whether you have failed with previous diets and weight loss attempts. If you have a medical condition, your doctor will want to know about any medications you are taking and whether they cause weight gain. Your doctor mustn't recommend a gastric band if you have a much higher BMI or a serious eating disorder since these patients may not be able to properly adjust their diet with the help of the band.

What Are the Advantages of Using an Adjustable Gastric Band?

There are many advantages to using an adjustable gastric band other than just gaining weight loss, such as:

- They are easy to use and can achieve quick results.

- There is a lower chance of incisional hernias since the band is placed around your stomach.

- They do not require general anesthesia.

- They are reversible and can be removed if something goes wrong.

- It takes roughly an hour to place and remove adjustable gastric bands.

Can You Get an Adjustable Gastric Band Offered by Many Doctors?

The answer to this question is a definite yes! However, this kind of surgery is not covered by insurance in most cases. It will be up to your insurance company to determine whether they will cover these procedures. However, several doctors offer them for free or at a very low cost. These doctors include Bariatric Centers, anesthesiology clinics, and even some Endocrinology groups in the country. You must find a doctor that you trust and feel comfortable with so he or she can understand what your specific needs are.

Gastric bands for weight loss are a popular choice for those who would like to control their portion sizes and lose weight. They are much easier to use than traditional methods of achieving weight loss, such as diet pills or supplements. You can also expect your doctor to be able to provide you with information about a gastric band through e-mail or another form of communication so that you know exactly what is going on.

The Gastric Band is designed to help you lose weight safely and effectively while also lowering the risk of injury during the procedure itself in comparison to bypass surgery. The Gastric Band is typically placed via Laparoscopic Surgery, which will require minimal downtime and complication following surgery.

It also helps people lose their weight safely without having to worry about their body rejecting surgery like gastric bypass.

How the Gastric Band Works

The Adjustable Gastric Band works by restricting the amount of food you can fit into your stomach. This way, you can feel full much more easily and steadily throughout the day. Think of it as a training belt that allows you to feel full with a small amount of food rather than eating three large meals per day. The material is flexible enough that it will not affect your daily routine or lifestyle negatively. You should be able to work, play and live your life as normal while using an adjustable band for weight loss.

The Benefits of the Gastric Band

There are several benefits to using a Gastric Band for weight loss. They include:

• You will not have to change your lifestyle drastically to lose the weight you want. In fact, many patients are still able to eat the foods they love while using an adjustable band for weight loss. You can also choose what types of foods you would like to eat and your body will still respond favorably.

• Those who use a gastric band typically have no trouble with portion control as they never feel too full or too empty. They are also able to eat the foods they love while still losing weight.

• It is a much safer alternative to gastric bypass surgery since it does not involve cutting your stomach in two like conventional bariatric surgeries. This method helps improve your overall health and lowers the risks of complications that can occur from gastric bypass surgery.

• It is a permanent device and will be removed once you have changed your eating habits or lost enough weight that you no longer need to use it. No more daily visits to the bathroom to check your band, no more worrying about losing too much weight or having another gastric bypass surgery because you simply did not follow the program correctly.

• It is a safe and natural way to lose weight that will help you keep the weight off longer than traditional methods.

How to Use the Gastric Band for Weight Loss

There are several ways in which you can use the gastric band for weight loss. These include:

• You can have a general medical checkup and get a band inserted as early as one or even two weeks after your surgery plan has been finalized. You will then be able to follow the plan for at least 3 months or until you reach your desired weight loss goals. After that, you can choose to remove the band completely, but there are no additional fees associated with this option. You will have to opt-out of insurance coverage.

• You can also choose to have your band removed after you have lost the weight you want to lose. This process takes approximately 5 minutes with no additional charges. You should expect to lose about 3 or 4 pounds per month for the first year, but then you will probably see a decrease in your rate of loss as the years go by.

The Gastric Band is completely reversible, which means that you will not have any permanent damage done to your body if you choose to remove it after using it for weight loss. If you need further assistance, all of our surgeons are capable and trained in bariatric surgery reversal procedures and would love to discuss options with you further at your consultation appointment.

What to Expect When Using the Gastric Band for Weight Loss

Here are some of the things that you can expect when using a gastric band:

- You will not have to change what you eat and how much you eat. Your body does not get any signals from your brain telling it when to eat more or less food. You just eat as much food as you normally would and your body will adjust accordingly. You must stick to the program or your weight loss efforts will be decreased and success may even be impossible to reach.

- You should check with your doctor before using a gastric band. It is a very complex procedure and is not an option for everyone. It may be a good option for someone that already suffers from Type II diabetes, hypertension, and heart disease. You will have to see if the band makes sense to you.

- The band does not have any detrimental health risks, which makes it one of the safest options for weight loss available today. However, the surgery itself can still lead to some complications such as infection or reactions to anesthesia. These are possible risks of any surgery, but you should speak with your doctor about how to keep these issues from becoming more serious problems during surgery.

- You will have a small port that is inserted into your abdomen through which the gastric band will be connected to your stomach pouch.

The port should be kept clean and free of food and fluid to avoid bacterial infection.

• You will also need to have a way to monitor the amount of food that you eat. The operation takes about three hours, so you should plan on staying at least four to six hours after eating or fasting before surgery.

After the surgery, your new pouch will stay there permanently, which requires a different diet than you may have been used to before surgery. You can eat as much as you want within reason for the first day or two post-ops. Just do not expect anything resembling your old diet after the procedure.

BOOK 2 :

HYPNOTIC GASTRIC BAND FOR EXTREME WEIGHT LOSS

A RAPID WAY TO STOP EMOTIONAL EATING FOR MEN AND WOMEN TO LOSE WEIGHT AND IMPROVE SELF-ESTEEM WITH POSITIVE AFFIRMATIONS AND MEDITATION

Introduction

This is an innovative, FDA-approved gastric band procedure that helps you lose weight more efficiently. The world's first hypnotherapeutic weight loss procedure

Have you ever experienced a difficult time losing fat? Have you had so much difficulty with your weight reduction regimen that it becomes impossible to continue? Do you often try new diets and workout plans but have little success with them, or they cause intolerable side effects?

The solution could be revolutionary, FDA-approved Gastric Banding. This long-term treatment option helps the body naturally reduce hunger and cravings while stimulating appetite suppression. It uses advanced psychotherapy techniques like hypnosis to help overcome food addiction by changing how food is seen in the mind. The HypnoGastric Band is a non-surgical procedure for weight loss that requires no downtime.

It is an FDA-approved procedure, so you don't need to go under the knife or have complications with general anesthesia. It can only be done once, but you can continue to eat and drink and lose your excess fat for up to five years.

The HypnoGastric Band treatment program starts with a consultation, and one of our qualified staff members will help to guide you every step of the way as we prepare for your individualized hypnotherapy sessions. The treatment generally takes about two hours, which includes instruction on food addiction, tracking body weight and measurements, body composition analysis, and a relaxation session. All of this takes place in our private office or hospital setting.

For this one session, the HypnoGastric Band will be fitted with a flexible silicone device. This allows you to fast for approximately 24 hours before the procedure. Approximately two weeks later, you will begin your one-hour hypnotherapy sessions. You will be required to see three hypnotherapists in total for your treatment plan and should expect to see them at least once a week after each 40-minutes session for a period of at least eight weeks.

Overall, the goal is to help you lose 30 pounds in the first six months and maintain that weight loss for years. Over time, you should begin to experience a renewed interest in healthy eating and regular exercise.

While Gastric Banding is a safe, effective treatment for extreme weight loss, there are a few things you should know:

• First and foremost, the procedure is only for people suffering from food addiction. It is designed to help them break their addiction and realize how much better they feel without it. While some people may lose more than 30 pounds in the first six months, others may take twice as long to reach their goal weight. This is normal as each person has unique body chemistry and different medical issues that contribute to their unique weight loss journey.

• You will need to maintain the weight loss after the procedure with regular exercise and healthy eating patterns. If you follow the recommended diet and exercise plan and lose weight, you may still keep it off. If you do not continue to eat right or do not exercise enough to maintain your weight, you will regain the weight within about six months.

• The band may cause some abdominal discomfort at first, but the discomfort usually disappears after a few days. In some cases, patients have reported experiencing bloating during their first few weeks of wearing the band. Some patients have had some sagging of their skin after wearing the band for a few months.

Chapter 1 - Managing Stress to Manage Your Weight

Welcome to your weight loss entrancing meeting. This one is designated "Managing Stress to Manage Your Weight." During this activity, I will direct you through a reflective excursion and help you wire your body to consume fat rapidly and easily. Similarly, as with most entrancing, you may wind up shipped into an alternate degree of harmony, a condition of total unwinding. Your psyche, body, and consideration will be totally ingested. Prior to starting, if it's not too much trouble, ensure you are in a protected, calm climate and not playing out any undertakings that require your consideration, like driving or working close to wellbeing dangers.

In a perfect world, you should give your full attention to this fascinating meeting to get the best results.

At the point when you are prepared, subside into a decent headspace, and unwind as I manage you through a delightful, extraordinary, and exceptionally groundbreaking experience. You will wind up in a condition of profound unwinding, stress-help, solace, serenity, and inward force. Beset up to have your whole outlook about weight loss adjusted and your resolve dramatically expanded. Before long, you will end up getting in shape normally and easily. This is the force of hypnosis. Try not to be amazed in the event that you start to appreciate shedding pounds and creating better propensities.

Take a full breath in through your nose and out through your mouth. Pick a speed that doesn't leave you short of breath a while later—pleasant sluggish quiet breaths.

Do this for a couple of moments to allow your framework to avoid a regression.

•   Interruption. Presently close your eyes, on the off chance that you have not as of now, and take another breath in through your nose, totally filling your lungs and breathing out through your mouth, letting the entirety of the air out.

•   Respite. You may decide to do this again, or you may now keep on breathing at a typical agreeable speed.

•   Respite. As you take your next breath, I need you to recall when you imagine that the air you breathe in resembles a thick haze. This thick haze that you are breathing in is a positive energy that is clearing into your body to purify you, to free you of any regrettable energy and pressure that you might be conveying.

•   Delay. As you breathe in, pause for a minute to imagine the white, thick haze as it enters your lungs

Imagine this positive energy clearing down into your arms, down to the tips of your fingers, and afterward back to your lungs and out of your mouth as you breathe out that breath.

•   Delay. This is clearing out the entirety of the pressures and stress and is leaving you feeling light and vaporous. Breathe in through your nose and imagine that positive white mist going all through your midsection, purging as it goes.

- Interruption. Imagine the positive energy going down every leg and touching each toe at that point going back up and out of your mouth as you breathe out.

- Interruption. You ought to feel extremely loose and quiet. Each muscle and joint in your body has been rubbed and feels light and loose.

- Respite. Your body feels lighter and unhindered at this point. You can, without much of a stretch, vibe yourself floating with every breath that you breathe in.

- Interruption. As you skim around in this state of complete unwinding, you are as yet mindful of the inward activities of your body. Truth be told, you may turn out to be more mindful of the inward activities of your body. You may hear your stomach snarl. You may feel a muscle or a quake.

- Respite. The entirety of this is ok, as it is extremely normal for you to feel and detect your inward body capacities as you investigate this trance-like state.

- Respite. You will, in the end, let the sounds and impressions of this room blur into the foundation of your psyche. The lone thing that you should zero in on is the sound of my voice and the quiet, consistent speed of your relaxation.

- Interruption. I need you currently to imagine that you are at the top of that wonderful flight of stairs once more, within a perfect home with numerous windows getting the splendid light. As I tally to 10, you will make a stride down the flight of stairs.

- Delay. With each progression down, you go further and more profound into this quiet trance. I will tally from 1 to 10, and with each progression you take and each number that I say, you will feel looser. Profoundly loose.

- Delay. One. You are extremely loose—two getting looser. Three, you are extending your unwinding. Four, getting further and more profound into this trance-like state. Five, you are so loose.

- Interruption. Six, Deeper, Seven, very loose. Eight, so really quiet.

- Interruption. Nine, you are in a total condition of rapture. Ten, you have arrived at the bottom of the steps, and now you can step onto the arrival. Feel the glow of the sun getting through the windows; the glow is perfect. Feel the breeze run over your body as the windows are open and the blinds are influencing by the breeze. You would now be able to stroll towards an open entryway.

- Respite. As you focus on your breathing and the sound of my voice, you will start to feel lighter. Permit you to buoy and float, maybe, into this condition of complete unwinding. You keep on breathing those tranquil breaths at the speed that you feel the most agreeable.

- Delay. Contemplations may crawl into your psyche, and that is ok. Just let them come in, recognize their reality, and let them blur directly back out. Simply continue zeroing in on the sensation of floating and the sensation of being light and breezy.

- Interruption. You are working really hard to zero in on your casual express, this tranquil inclination, with each agreeable breath that you take.

- Respite. Relish this serene inclination. Observe how your body feels, being at an equivalent condition of quietness. Keep your breathing at an ordinary speed. Beginning the way toward turning out to be more present is an illuminating one.

- Respite. Working with the five faculties should be possible regardless of whether you are deficient with regards to at least one of the five detects. Tailor it to work for you.

- Delay. Allow us to begin with one day, regardless of whether it is busy working or whether you are approaching your day at home. The assignment is to start with your feeling of sound. After you are awoken for the afternoon, sit briefly and tune in to the world. Are there birds trilling? Is the canine restlessly pacing, holding back to be gone for a stroll? Did the espresso producer automatically turn on and begin preparing? Would you be able to hear the ambitious people driving on the streets close to you? What do you hear?

- Delay. Attempt to push ahead with your day recognizing the sounds in your day-to-day existence.

You can exclude the irritating sounds, similar to the hints of somebody biting.

All things being equal, tune in for the great sounds, similar to somebody's giggling, and pause for a minute to see the value in how that sound occurred. Tune in to another person's talk. Don't simply hear them talk, however truly tune in to what they need to say.

- Delay. Set off to purposefully smell your morning espresso or tea. The fragrance can carry a grin to your face and cause you to stand by sufficiently long to taste and relish tenderly. Ordinarily, we race through our morning schedule and skirt directly over how astounding the least complex of scents are. Do this each time you cook or eat too. Take in the scents, tastes, and surfaces of the food. Sincerely attempt to be available at the time and see how your body is moving. Notice the speed and strength you are biting with. Notice the manner in which the food feels on your tongue.

• Delay. Past food and drink, be perceptive of your natural scents too. Embrace your partner, adored one or a friend, and take in their fragrance. Feel the solace of the commonality, and rather than a speedy hi and farewell, embrace them.

Take this on a more significant level when you head outside. Close your eyes and smell your general surroundings. Is it breezy and fresh? Do you smell the wood consuming in a close-by chimney? What do you smell?

• Interruption. Presently to chip away at your feeling of touch. The things that we touch frequently go undetected for quite a long time, the sensation of that new fluffy pullover. Feel it.

The glow of your mug toward the beginning of the day; allow the glow truly to enter your hands. The sensation of your pet's hide as you control your hand from head to tail. Feel it. Feel the paper that you touch when you read a book. Is it produced using quality paper? Feeling occurs with something other than your hands. Put your exposed feet straightforwardly on the Earth. Do you feel something beyond soil or grass? Do you feel a more profound vibration? What do you feel?

• Respite. Sight. Perhaps the most impressive faculties. Take in all that you see. Do the mists appear to be unique today? Does the sun sparkle more brilliant, projecting an entrancing orange gleam after everything? Notice everything. Sit in your number one room toward the beginning of the day or the end and "see" why it causes you to feel the way that it does. Is it the style of the room? The furnishings? The style? What do you see?

• Delay. At the point when you upgrade your capacity to be more present, you permit yourself to appreciate everything around you. Interior and outer stressors can totally disappear. You like the excellence of your common faculties, and you will be thankful for the chance to appreciate a single snapshot of being alive.

• Delay. Managing your stress is the way to managing your weight. You have made significant progress and created as an individual in manners that you don't understand. Weight loss presently comes simple for you. Weight loss is something that isn't a battle for you, nor is managing your stress. You are NOT characterized by your weight. You are characterized by the exertion that you put into yourself and into the world. You are stunning, and you are just improving.

Affirmations:

1. I don't allow stress to develop.

2. I have created sound approaches to handle stress.

3. I won't go to nourishment for solace.

4. I exercise to keep my stress levels low.

5. I'm in charge of my contemplations and feelings.

6.   I will resist the urge to panic, cool, and gathered.

7.   Stress doesn't influence my eating regimen and what I decide to eat.

8.   I can deal with stress adequately.

9.   I will just eat at assigned eating times.

10.   I will drink water on the off chance that I begin to feel overpowered.

Chapter 2 - Three Day Affirmation Challenge for Rapid Weight Loss

At long last, in this section, we'll list affirmations for three days of training.

Remember that affirmations are more kind of a guarantee, so consistently satisfy your revelation so it can work for you.

The Very Beginning

- I believe in my ability to love and recognize myself for who I am.

- I set myself freed from the entire fault I haul around about the food decisions I made before.

- I'm reliably rehearsing and dealing with my body.

- Patching goes on in both my body and brain.

- Each time I breathe in, new imperativeness fills my entire presence, and each time I breathe out, all toxins and muscle fat leave my body.

- My prosperity is improving progressively more reliably, just like my body.

- All that I eat retouches and supports my body, which rouses me to arrive at the correct weight.

- I'm reliably closer to my ideal weight each and every day.

- I'm so playful and appreciative that I shed kilograms/pounds. (Fill in the ideal number.)

- I can do that, I'm doing this, and my body is shedding pounds right away.

- I'm giving up any fault that I hold around food.

- Eating great food empowers my body to take every one of the enhancements it needs.

- I feel my searching for fat-rich food sources dissolving.

- I have a convincing drive to eat just quality food sources and desert any prepared food sources.

- I'm essentially the easiest form, and that I am endeavoring to be vastly improved. I will actually want to shed pounds since I need to and that I have the ability to do this.

- My body is my safe haven; I carefully influence it reliably by eating simply strong sustenances that retouch and backing me.

- I'm careful that my processing is working in my favored situation by assisting me with arriving at my optimal weight.

- I'm achieving and keeping up my optimal weight.

- I have the ability to successfully control my weight through a combination of an incredible eating routine and exercise.

- I'm appreciative to my body for every one of the things it achieves for the benefit of me.

- Every cell in my body is sound and fit, as I am.

- I feel my body shedding pounds in every preview of the day.

- I, for the most part, bite my food suitably so my body can deal with it and utilize the enhancements to shed pounds.

- I put stock in my ability to differ my affinities and make new positive ones.

- I never again need to fill my body with junk food; I can, without a very noticeable stretch, entice strangeness.

- I like life by staying fit and keeping up my ideal weight.

- I'm prepared to achieving my weight loss objectives and will not allow anything to switch my demeanor around to that point.

- I recognize my body accurately the manner in which it is and consistently work on improving it.

- I comprehend that undesirable food sources don't assist me with getting shape, so I simply eat stable and nutritious food.

- My assimilation rate is at its optimal level, which urges me to prevail in my ideal weight.

- I'm a specific person who is enjoyed by everyone around me.

- I'm a unique and excellent individual, and that I merit everyone's consideration.

- I recognize myself, and I love myself for who I am. It has little effect on what others say. What's critical to me is the manner in which I react and what I believe.

- My mind is stacked up with positive insights; I recognize and desert any regrettable contemplation.

- I breathe in for loosening up and breathe out pressure.

- I consider myself to be what others around me do.

- I such as myself simply the manner in which I am constantly content with my life.

- I invite everything I have in my life. I stay in bed out and amuse.

- I feel anxious when life brings me problems, and I recognize them quickly without guilt or effort.

- I supplant "I need to" and "I ought to" with "I will."

- I open dependent upon myself; I realize that I'm an excellent individual who everyone regards.

- Meeting new people is straightforward. I can make strong associations and make new friends without feeling jumpy.

- I perceive both my attributes and blemishes and that I, for the most part, try to improve them.

- I'm a drawn-in individual; I will not stop accomplishing something since I feel tried or violated.

Day Two

- I'm big-hearted, venerating, and mindful; I take care of the people around me.

- I breathe in boldness and breathe out fear and pressure.

- I gloat genuineness, just like a trustworthy individual, and by and large, do what I exactly say. Everybody can open dependent upon me.

- I trust and put confidence in myself; I surrender negative feelings.

- Being alive makes me a bright person.

- Acting normally is appropriate and satisfying; I, by and large, consider challenges to be opportunities to show my capacities.

- I merit all that is worthy in this world. I release any necessity for agony, and that I can feel euphoria, sureness, and love venturing into my body, mind, and soul.

- I'm energized and red hot, and conviction might be a critical piece of my inclination.

- I'm sound, solid and steady, and alluring; I perceive both my inside and outside greatness.

- I thrive with my incomparable boldness. My life is brilliant; I like every single depiction of it.

- I never come close to individuals, as I comprehend my uniqueness.

- Each time I breathe in, conviction fills my overall presence, and each time I breathe out all fault and humility escape.

- I recognize myself as I am and give indications of progress by and large in everything I do.

- I'm a person who adequately recognizes new requests.

- Change is certain; I recognize it wholeheartedly.

- Reliably all around, I'm advancing toward my ideal weight.

- I love being in great shape and losing sufficient weight with the objective that I have set as my ideal weight.

- My assimilation rate is correct, and it urges me to show up at my ideal weight.

- I like rehearsing every day, and it urges me to arrive at my ideal weight.

- I love eating great food, and it urges me to arrive at my ideal weight.

- I have confidence in my ability to love myself for who I am.

- I recognize my body shape and perceive the superbness it holds.

- I'm the producer of my future and the driver of my mind.

- I forsake terrible practices around food.

- I empower myself to pick choices and decisions for my own awesome.

- I bring the qualities of fulfillment, rapture, and joy into my life as I'm available.

- I forsake any fault that I hold around food choices.

- I recognize my body for the form I have been regarded with.

- I desert associations that are no longer for my own personal great.

- I have confidence in myself and perceive my immensity.

- I empower myself to feel extraordinary being me.

- I recognize myself for who I am.

- I bring the qualities of reverence into my heart.

- I have assumptions and sureness about what's to return.

- I'm grateful for the body I guarantee and all that it achieves for me.

- I immovably put stock in my ability to shed pounds.

- Shedding pounds becomes all-good easily for my benefit.

- I'm happily achieving my weight loss objectives.

- I get fit as a fiddle each day.

- I like to train ordinarily.

- I'm eating food sources that expand my prosperity and success.

- I possibly eat when I'm eager.

243

- I can see myself at my ideal weight.

- I love the kind of astounding food.

- I'm answerable for the amount I eat.

- I get a charge out of comprehension; it causes me to feel incredible.

Day Three

- I'm getting fitter and more grounded consistently through workouts.

- I'm adequately arriving at my ideal weight.

- I like and care for my body.

- I reserve the option to have a thin, strong, engaging body.

- I'm becoming progressively acceptable at customary eating fewer carbs.

- I get slimmer reliably.

- I look and feel phenomenal.

- I do whatever it takes to be strong.

- I'm cheerfully rediscovering my accomplishment.

- I intend to figure.

- I had the opportunity to eat food varieties that cause me to look and feel incredible.

244

- I'm at risk for my prosperity.

- I love my body.

- I rest to improve my body.

- I blissfully practice every morning once I'm alert by saying that I will arrive at my weight loss objective.

- I'm yielding to choose to get solid by changing my dietary propensities from undesirable to solid.

- I'm content with everything, and I kill my effort to be better.

- I get slimmer.

- I'm developing an engaging body.

- I'm developed of life loaded up with vigorous prosperity.

- I'm making a body that I like and appreciate.

- My progressions in dietary patterns are changing my body.

- I'm feeling staggering since I have shed 10 pounds.

- I have a level stomach.

- I praise my own special ability to pick choices around food.

- I'm euphorically gauging 20 pounds less.

- I like to walk 3 to several times a day and do wellness modeling several times a day.

- I drink eight glasses of water each day.

- I eat regular food varieties daily and eat the foremost piece of chicken and fish.

- I'm learning and using the mental, energetic, and other common aptitudes for progress. I will actually want to change!

- I will make new tests about myself and my body.

- I appreciate and esteem my body.

- It's empowering to search out my stand-out food and exercise system for weight loss.

- My weight loss is an illustration of conquering affliction.

- I'm captivated to be the correct weight for the benefit of me.

- It's basic for me to follow a strong eating regimen plan.

- I can make certain upgrades throughout my lifetime.

- It feels extraordinary to move my body. Exercise is agreeable!

- I use significant breathing to assist me with loosening up and taking care of pressing factors.

- I'm a staggering person.

- I reserve the option to be at my ideal weight.

- I am a charming person. I deserve credit for love. It is good for my benefit that I am better.

- I reject the need to rebuff my body.

- I recognize and make the foremost of my sexuality. It's alright to feel stimulated.

- My absorption is extraordinary.

Chapter 3 - Sleep Hypnosis

Insomnia

Sleep is something that everyone needs. In both our physical and mental prosperity, it has a vital influence. In either case, trouble sleeping, such as a sleep disorder, can make it difficult for some people to get enough sleep. In addition to making you feel depleted, sleep deprivation will cause you to become truly ill and increase the danger of coronary heart disease. Intellectually, not having sufficient sleep will prompt tension and makes it hard for you to concentrate.

A sleeping disorder is depicted as an inconvenience of attempting to sleep or staying asleep long enough for the following morning to feel invigorated.

At the point when you can't figure out how to nod off, like the vast majority of us, you will have encountered an evening of upset sleep and will know how it feels. You might be stressed for the following day, or you may have had a cup excessively near sleep time. You may think that it's simple to nod off; however, you keep awakening around evening time. An intense sleep will leave you feeling depleted and bad-tempered the following day, in any case. Many people who experience the ill effects of a sleeping disorder will regularly show these feelings. 33% of people in the UK are accounted to have episodes of sleep deprivation for the duration of their lives. While it can impact anybody at whatever stage in life, it appears to be that people beyond 60 years old and ladies are more susceptible.

Various Types of Insomnia

There are a few particular types of a sleeping disorder, yet they are usually assembled into two classes:

1. Impermanent Insomnia

At the point when it endures between one evening and three to about a month, sleep deprivation is known as transient or intense.

Stream slack, a shift of timetable or workspaces, stress, caffeine, and liquor are regular reasons for transient sleep deprivation.

Transient or inconsistent sleep deprivation is the name of specific instances of impermanent sleep deprivation. This is the place where the individual at times creates sleeping troubles over months or years.

2. Steady Insomnia

This is viewed as a constant sleeping disorder also. The issue would, as a rule, proceed practically daily, for a time of about a month. This may likewise happen as sleep is disturbed by agony or therapy from ailments. This may include joint inflammation, Parkinson's infection, asthma, hypersensitivities, synthetic compounds that change, or worries about psychological wellness.

Manifestations of Insomnia

In light of explicit conditions, signs change. There are regular side effects, in any case, including:

- Keep up around evening time for extended periods of time.

- Be unaware of sleeping.

- Wake up during the night a few times.

- Get up ahead of schedule and not being able to sleep once more.

- To feel exhausted the following morning and sluggish.

- The feeling of peevishness.

Reasons for Insomnia

The issue has various potential sources. In specific cases, sleeplessness might be brought about by just one reason, while others may go through a combination of factors.

Any of sleep deprivation's potential causes include:

Conditions in Physical Fitness

On the off chance that you experience the ill effects of a medical problem that causes you inconvenience, you can discover sleeping troubles.

There is a danger that your sleep will be disturbed by the medication you are taking.

Talk with the specialist in the event that you speculate on an ailment or figure that your medication can trigger an issue with your sleep.

Mental Health Conditions

Sleeping issues might be caused by such psychological wellbeing conditions. A person with extreme sadness, for example, is bound to experience the ill effects of a sleeping disorder. At the point when an individual loses sleep, the discouraged mindsets that accompany gloom may likewise be exacerbated.

Another issue that is frequently connected with a sleeping disorder is tension. Uneasiness may make a person feel tense, stressed, and depleted. These feelings can make it difficult to fall asleep. When attempting to sleep, the psyche of the individual will consistently run, feeling like they can't "switch off." Sleep can likewise be disturbed by the worry, and the individual may awaken in the evening.

The nervousness about not having enough sleep will transform into an endless loop if this pattern proceeds.

Lifestyle

Sleeping practices might be influenced by ordinary exercises and ways of life. First of all, if you drink liquor every day, you may find that you wake up during the night. Liquor is an energizer, and surprisingly, after taking a couple of drinks, it can be simple to doze off; it ordinarily adds to terrible sleep in general.

Medications and caffeine can likewise prompt issues with sleep. Any dependence on drugs will influence how you sleep, so it is imperative to look for help. It is mandatory that you limit the use of caffeine on the off chance that you experience the ill effects of sleep deprivation.

Those who work a lot at night will think it's hard to kill the brain. For your internal clock, shift work will wreak havoc and make sleep interesting. It may very well merit rethinking your schedule if your work (or business-related pressure) is affecting your sleep deprivation.

The Way Insomnia Works

Individuals with sleep deprivation additionally say they are "restless people"; that is, hereditarily inclined to a sleeping disorder.

There ought to be nothing farther from current realities. There is a lethargic time in any living organic entity, so sleep is ordinary, so a sleeping disorder is unnatural.

Overall, sleep deprivation is brought about by a characteristic dread that might be about families, monetary issues, inquiries of confidence, and various different nerves.

Each and every customer is unique. Nonetheless, we can sort out what's going on and fix the manifestations at an inner mind level by using hypnotherapy for Insomnia, taking you back to a typical sleep cycle.

"Right around 30% of the population has a kind of sleeplessness. Uneasiness quite often supports a sleeping disorder, and this tension intrudes on the ordinary beat of sleep. This dread is something people with a sleeping disorder seem to meditate on when resting, which is the thing that hypnotherapy focuses on with a sleeping disorder. This rumination produces raised degrees of tension, and subsequently, inside the light sleeper, a raised level of sharpness, and along these lines, sleep evades them. This uneasiness is regularly poor to such an extent that the customer probably won't be truly aware of it and subsequently expects that there is little reason for the deficiency of sleep." The sleeping disorder expert Paul White at the Surrey Institute of Clinical Hypnotherapy.

Treatment for Insomnia

There are various techniques you may take when treating sleeping issues; it is important to talk with the specialist initially to eliminate every single actual trigger.

To help you sleep, your PCP can recommend that you take medication. This might be a proficient treatment for specific people, yet it is important to attempt to sort out the underlying driver of the issue. Conduct treatments and voice treatments are additionally recommended.

Another treatment decision that numerous individuals find effective is hypnotherapy. Sleep deprivation hypnotherapy can resolve the potential triggers while assisting you with unwinding and rest. For instance, if the reason for your sleep deprivation is tension or melancholy, sleep hypnosis can enhance your setup treatment. It would then be able to assist with changing the everyday sleeping practice by taking care of these issues.

On the other hand, hypnotherapy for a sleeping disorder will attempt to end this propensity if a propensity causes you to have a sleeping disorder (like liquor).

"As the ideas made by hypnosis treatment permit your psyche and body to unwind and get the sleep you need, the concern, uneasiness, and dread that can keep you from nodding off disappear." Ogunyemi Biodun

Hypnotherapy for Sleep

In spite of the fact that there might be an obvious justification for some sleeping issues, others won't. On the off chance that you are hazy, whether you are experiencing difficulty sleeping, hypnotherapy for sleep deprivation might be gainful.

A hypnotist can venture into the psyche using various techniques to find what might have caused the issue. A customized treatment created by the subliminal specialist will start after the reason is distinguished.

The propensities for sleep aggravations will get imbued in the subliminal when experiencing a sleeping disorder for an extensive period of time. The point of hypnosis for sleep deprivation is to draw in with it and propose useful changes. These ideas will mean to end the propensities for negative reasoning that trigger the issue.

Showing you how to unwind is a fundamental part of hypnotherapy for a sleeping disorder. Physical or passionate pressure can make sleeping awkward for specific people. A trance inducer can use loosening up techniques, like slow muscle unwinding to help calm nervousness.

A subliminal specialist will likewise show you self-hypnosis. It will assist you with making a timetable, just as figure out how to manage the issue setting off the causes.

Using hypnosis at home for sleep deprivation will help you put into your everyday life the procedures you have acquired in the meeting room.

What Sleep Hypnosis Exactly Is

On the off chance that there was a simple and hazard-free sleep help that you may use every day, wouldn't it be a fantasy? All things considered, there is one, and it's called hypnosis of sleep! Hypnosis has been a notable quieting and understood idea strategy for well longer than a century. The expanding use of this supernatural personal development approach has been lighted by the use of sleep hypnosis for quit smoking, treating ongoing torment, relieving sleep deprivation, and that's only the tip of the iceberg.

Sleep hypnosis is used by specific people as a method to make them nod off. Sleep hypnosis, more or less, is a technique that requires guided ideas to lead an individual into a condition of unwinding.

This agreeable state could, indeed, make it simpler to nod off. A few sorts of sleep hypnosis accessible can be downloaded to your telephone or gadget, despite the fact that it isn't sure if they are exact. Check for data about what it is, regardless of whether you are attempting sleep hypnosis, and discover different procedures that might be more viable when you need to get a fair night's sleep.

Chapter 4 - Eating Healthily

Like yoga, empowering eating propensities are outlined by assumption and practice.

Have you followed this supported assessment and chosen to develop your, for the most part, changed, attainable relationship with food yet?

As a private who has never endeavored another eating regimen, you know it's definitely not hard to represent considerable authority in a good dieting plan—and fundamentally more straightforward to lose steam or self-control and dispose of your motivation following a large portion of a month or perhaps days. That is on the grounds that most of us don't give our new solid propensities the time and thought they should be customized.

A careful approach can help you move a charge toward outlining a good diet propensity, regardless of the fact that you will probably choose vegetables over refined carbohydrates to be leaner and back off to get dinner time or eliminate meat to organize your ethics. "Caring helps decay the effort people intuit in making changes. It seems to help us or associate us with all or none of the most amazing approaches to floating those old neural pathways that are really cut in the brain and work to get and make new ones to fortify."

The "going with a game plan" will help you set real longings for the length expected to carry out an enduring improvement while gradually melding Mindfulness practices, sharp food decisions, and more pleasure into each meal.

Zeroing in on occasion to a second eating experience can assist you with improving your eating routine, manage food longings, and even get fit as a fiddle. Here's the best approach to start eating carefully.

What Mindful Eating Is

Careful eating keeps an in-the-moment awareness of the food and drink you put into your body, looking against the choice of how the food makes you feel and, in this way, the signals your body sends about taste, satisfaction, and wholeness. Mindful eating expects you to recognize the considerable feelings, contemplations, and sensations you have and that you can come to modify the route to purchasing, preparing, and consuming food.

For a great part of people, our clamoring lives make eating times briskly attempted, or we wind up eating in the vehicle while driving, at the workplace before a PC screen, or left on the armchair sitting in front of the TV. We eat carelessly, scooping food down if we're so far enthusiastic. We routinely eat for reasons besides hunger—to satisfy eager necessities, soothe pressing factors, or adjust to unfortunate feelings, like pity, strain, melancholy, or exhaustion. Careful eating is here and there in opposition to the current sort of undesirable "thoughtless" eating.

Careful eating isn't connected to being extraordinary, continually eating the correct things, or never allowing yourself to eat in a hurry again. Besides, it isn't connected to fixing exacting standards for what number of calories you'll eat or which food you might want to consolidate or keep an essential separation from in your eating regimen. Or on the other hand, even connected to focusing the entirety of your resources and being accessible as you shop, cook, serve, and eat your food. While Mindfulness isn't for everybody, various individuals find that by eating thusly, regardless, for not exactly a couple of meals seven days, you'll end up being more responsive to your body. This will assist you with avoiding overeating and simplify it to fluctuate your dietary propensities to upgrade things and like the improved mental and actual thriving that goes with a better eating regimen.

Benefits of Mindful Eating

By giving close thought to how you feel as you eat—the surface and tastes of each huge piece, your body's longing, and all-out signals, how various food varieties impact your energy and perspective—you can discover how to appreciate both your food and furthermore the experience of eating. Being aware of the food you eat can progress better preparing, keep you full with less food, and effect more smart decisions about what you eat subsequently.

It can moreover help you with liberating yourself from undesirable propensities around food and eating. Eating carefully can push you to:

• Get abundant relief from the rushing around of your day, working with pressing factors and anxiety.

• Look at and adjust your relationship with food—helping you, for instance, to note once you go to nourishment for reasons besides hunger.

• Get more significant pleasure from the food you eat, as you work out the best approach to backtrack from everybody, the more esteemed your dinners and goodies become.

• Settle on better decisions about what you eat by focusing on how every food makes you feel in the wake of eating it.

- Improve your preparation by eating all the more gradually.

- Feel more satisfied sooner and by eating less food.

- Make an unmistakable relationship with where your food starts from, how it's conveyed, and the excursion it's taken to your plate.

- Try to eat in a better, logically changed way.

The Most Effective Method to Rehearse Mindfully

Eating

To practice Mindfulness, you might want to require an interest in a movement with hard and fast Mindfulness. Because of careful eating, it's fundamental to eat with the entirety of your thought as against on "modified pilot" or while you're checking, looking at your phone, sitting in front of the TV, fantasizing, or masterminding what you're doing later. When your thought strays, softly return it to your food and, furthermore, the experience of cooking, serving, and eating.

Have a go at practicing careful eating for brief five-minute ranges all along and consistently create from that time. Besides, remember, you'll start careful eating when you are doing your shopping once-over or checking the diner menu. Carefully assess everything to expand your summary or peruse the rundown.

Start by taking a couple of full breaths and consider the wellbeing assessment of each unique smidgen of food. Although nutrition experts talk endlessly about which varieties of foods are "good" and which are not, the least difficult rule of thumb is to eat foods that are as close as possible to the way nature made them.

Use the entirety of your resources while you're shopping, cooking, serving, and eating your food. How do various food varieties look, smell, and feel as you hack?

How might they sound as they're being cooked? How might they taste as you eat?

Be intrigued and notice target realities about yourself, even as the food you will eat. Notice how you're sitting; sit with a high position; be that as it may, stay loose. Perceive your ecological factors yet discover the best approach to shut them out. Focusing on what's going on around you will redirect from your methodology of eating and diminish the experience.

Tune into your longing; how eager, isn't that so? You might want to encourage each other when you're excited yet not eager in the wake of skipping suppers.

Acknowledge what your assumptions are in eating this particular dinner. Is it genuine that you are basically eating since you're truly ravenous, or is it that you're depleted, need a break, or trust it's what you need to do?

With the food before you, stop briefly to invite everybody you are imparting the food to prior to eating. Represent considerable authority in the surfaces, shapes, tints, and scents of the food. What reactions does one need from the food, and how do the aromas make you feel?

Take a snack, and perceive how it feels in your mouth. How might you depict the surface now? Plan to recognize everything on the side, every one of the different flavors. Chomp totally and perceive how you nibble and what that appears as.

Focus on how your experience shifts from one second to another. For example, does one feel yourself getting full? Is it exact in specifying that you are satisfied?

Take the greatest measure of time required, stay present, and don't flood the experience.

Put your utensils down between eats. Set aside some push to consider how you feel—anxious, fulfilled—prior to getting your utensils once more. Tune to your stomach, not your plate. Acknowledge when you're full and stopped eating.

Give appreciation and accept where this food began from, the plants or animals notwithstanding, and all individuals it took to deliver the food and pass on it onto your plate. Being dynamically careful about our food's beginning stages can help all people settle on more brilliant and progressively sensible decisions.

Keep continuously eating as you talk along with your eating partners, giving close consideration to your body's signs of satiety. In case you're eating alone, plan to remain present to the experience of eating up the feast.

Fitting Mindful Eating Into Your Life

It's absurd for most people who work; we will be aware of each snack or perhaps for each dinner we eat. The workloads and family now and then mean you're constrained to feast in a hurry or have quite recently an obliged window to eat something or the risk of going hungry for the rest of the day. This is because of the fact that once you can't hold close to a coldblooded careful eating practice, you can, regardless, swear off eating carelessly and dismissing your body's signs.

Perhaps you will take a couple of complete breaths before eating a feast or treat to consider inconspicuously what you will be putting into your body. Is it accurate to specify that you are basically eating in the light of signs of desire, or would you say you are eating because of a passionate sign? Perhaps you are exhausted, nervous, or discouraged? Likewise, would you say you are eating food that is invigorating and stable, or would you say you are eating food that is genuinely relieving? However, you may want to dismantle your workplace. For example, would you be willing to require a couple of moments to focus all your attention on your food instead of performing different tasks or being sidetracked by your PC or phone?

Consider careful eating like exercise, each piece counts. Concentrate only in the transit of eating to your body's tune; it is the more conspicuous fulfillment you'll experience from your food and the more noticeable.

Chapter 5 - Virtual Gastric Band for Eating Disorder

The use of entrancing as an enhancement to a food rebalancing with a dietitian is an interest in solid increment. Be that as it may, what are the potential outcomes of hypnosis in assisting you with getting in shape?

The most mainstream device is the interruption of a virtual gastric band. By making the patient daydream, using his creative mind, he goes through a careful activity, which permits him to diminish his cravings and reconnect with the sensation of satiety.

The benefit of this convention is that it dodges a medical procedure that is impossible on individuals with heart conditions, who are adversely affected by sedatives or who fear tasks. In this, it is a fascinating device, yet is it reasonable for all individuals who need to get thinner?

In fact, everything will be based on the premise that there are many eating disorders from one limit to another, the most popular being anorexia and bulimia, but you also have orthorexia, sugar addiction, gorging, and so on. Before explaining the commitment of enchantment over here, let's evaluate how to try to follow by the fact that eating disorders are multifactorial.

Behind these issues are in some cases covered up clinical causes known as diabetes or cholesterol, useful colopathy, others still ineffectively referred to, for example, dysfunctions of the intestinal microbiota, Candida Albicans, and so forth. It is therefore fundamental to investigate the clinical causes before depending on hypnosis.

In the event that no clinical reason is discovered, it is important to consult a nutritionist as well, as time and again, people think they know how to have a fair eating routine when they make mistakes. This is the manner by which a couple of years prior, I chose to quit treating weight reduction on the grounds that there was a hole between the desires of the patients and the prerequisites of a reasonable eating routine. Schematically, individuals requested that I assist them with getting thinner; however, without transforming anything in their eating regimen, or figured they could eat on the grounds that they were following a lady's magazine diet. The plan to remember is that on the off chance that you eat ineffectively or excessively little, you won't get thinner.

At the point when I say eating seriously, I'm not, in any event, discussing modern food varieties yet rather about mistakes in the decision of food. Take two models; Starchy food sources are a wellspring of energy for the body. Truly the association stores them to establish saves, yet they have a focal part in the sensation of satiety. So totally eliminating them implies facing the challenge of starving your body and breaking consistently by eating chocolates, cakes, and so on.

Natural products are useful for wellbeing, given they are eaten with some restraint. They can be entirely included with regards to a nibble at 4 p.m. for instance; however, the normal blunder is to end a supper with a leafy foods yogurt when both contain sugar and that the mix of the two will unavoidably expand glucose and therefore cause the discharge of insulin to break this sugar and store it.

These are only two models that show that we frequently trust in compliance with common decency on how to eat when our dinners are not adjusted. The last model is the eating regimen. This is to diminish the calorie admission of your suppers radically. Positively weight reduction can be quick; however, be careful with the yoyo impact on the grounds that starving your body will work in a general store at the principal error. What's more, it is hard to follow an eating routine both truly and mentally, so unavoidably you will break consistently, and you will lose inspiration.

Therefore, it is essential to be accompanied by an expert dietary control in the search for the privileged dietary balance that will help you reach your long-term goal.

After this important parenthesis, we turn to the mental component of eating disorders by looking at the different tomahawks:

• **The psychological conduct recovery pivot:** Today, we invest less energy setting up our suppers, we eat shortly, and this adds to advancing food dysfunctions. Realize that the stomach-related framework is made out of 200 million neurons in reliance on the brain and that satiety is acquired by an input circle between the mouth, the stomach, and the mind, subsequently the significance of eating gradually. I won't harp on the inquiry, you can discover more information on the weight reduction page, and it is a subject talked about during the meeting.

• **The passionate hub:** It is doubtlessly the one that will intrigue you the most and that you know the least. As said before, the stomach has a neural insight interconnected with the mind. Feelings in the body memory can influence feelings of anxiety all in all and specifically the working of the gut. A few groups will have stomachs tied by stress, uneasiness, and dread and will, in general, get in shape; others unexpectedly will take asylum in food to discover a wellspring of brief conciliation.

As a decent clinician, I likewise realize that weight gained is additional protection for some individuals whose beginning is frequently found in youth, following embarrassment, we might need to be "solid"... or then again not to kindly to keep away from all peril from sexual savagery, tribal connections and so forth. In youth, there are likewise parental orders, "finish your plate to satisfy mother," the kid who needs acknowledgment comprehends that to acquire the blessings of his mom, he should fulfill him by completing his plate without tuning in to his body.

Additionally, along these lines, if there should be an occurrence of absence of parental love, desserts frequently bring comfort. These are only a couple of the components to assist you with understanding that sincerely charged occasions influence the equilibrium of the stomach-related and intestinal frameworks, causing eating disorders.

This is the reason why my weight reduction technique depends on enthusiastic purifying work enhanced with explicit work; the message I need to pass on is that the virtual gastric band is one alternative among others which isn't really fundamental on the grounds that passionate work as of now normally improves the meal frame, conducts control and builds the inspiration. In the event that you just have 10 to 15 kg to lose, this should be possible without the break of a ring. Furthermore, on the off chance that you experience the ill effects of sugar dependence, the best is to treat it with another particular convention and not the ring, which is primarily used to lessen craving yet not dependence on an item.

Remember that weight reduction is essentially multifactorial and that hypnosis is a decent option, yet notwithstanding a solid and adjusted eating regimen and that it works without clinical issues adding to this weight gain.

Concerning the gauge management and hypnosis changes, all around, the body permits admission to the memory of the feelings of lived experiences with the help of a specialist.

Another investigation emerges in the nourishing drive; there is a void, a passionate need in the nourishing drive, there is mental torment, a pain of enthusiastic emptiness, the need to safeguard against something unbearable inside the real world, dissatisfaction involved with friends and family, absence of inner security, despondency, fear of abandonment, and so forth. Thus, physiological, mental, and enthusiastic administration by means of input and nutritherapy generally gives excellent results.

Chapter 6 - Binge Eating

Hi and welcome to your entrancing weight reduction meeting, "Binge eating," which will uphold your assurance and introduce a mental gastric band so you can easily finish and adhere to your eating routine arrangement. All meetings in this health improvement plan are entrancing in nature, and they can, without much of a stretch, put you in a condition of unwinding and ingest your conscious consideration inside. Kindly don't tune in to these meetings while driving or working any device or at whatever other time, which requires your full, stir attention.

I'm the Hypnosis Guru, and I will control you through this brilliantly loosening up experience and an astonishing excursion of finding the internal strength and assets that will assist you with stimulating your inward resolve so you can normally begin shedding pounds while appreciating the interaction of progress. You are here on the grounds that you chose to be better, in a superior shape, and feel great in your body.

In some cases, we permit ourselves to fill each opening in our tummy, and commonly we have a wide range of reasons for doing as such. From old style reasons, for example, "I will begin my eating routine tomorrow," and all the best approaches to "just one more nibble." Whatever pardon we have, it is only our own consent to feel terrible later on about our weight and the manner in which we look. The most well-known motivation behind why we think of any pardon is that we are attempting to expand our feeling of solace. What's more, that is completely fine in the event that you need to expand your feeling of solace, yet pick the procedure that won't cause you to feel awful about yourself later on.

Tuning into this guided hypnosis is a decent system to restrict your food admission with the force of your psyche, so you can stop binge eating and positively begin feeling the advantages of adhering to a better way of life.

We will start this guided entrancing meeting by turning out to be intentionally mindful that we are consistently in charge and consistently have a decision. As of now, the lone decision you need to make presently is to decide to go into a profound unwinding right now, or in a couple of moments, when you make yourself more comfortable, at ease, and when you tell yourself, "I will unwind, now, completely and easily, while my psyche mind masters all that is required to stop my binge eating..."

Begin breathing in intentionally and somewhat more profound than expected; at that point, gradually push all the air out as much as you can, and once you push all the air out, stop briefly before you begin breathing in once more.

One more time, take another full breath in, intentionally and gradually push all the air out completely, and once all the air is out, pause briefly before you begin breathing in again, that is right, just like that.

Don't be amazed on the off chance that you would already be able to see that the old impulses are simply beginning to liquefy away, very slowly, as you breathe in profoundly and permit yourself to unwind.

Proceed with breathing at a consistent pace, just like you typically do, and permit the air moving all through your lungs and stomach to extend your unwinding. Imagine that each time you inhale, a sort of relaxation energy fills your head, neck, and chest and as you breathe out, that unwinding energy spreads through the remainder of your body, just like a wave.

Fill your head, neck, and chest, and as you inhale and spreading that unwinding energy everywhere on your body as it goes down your arms and belly, all the path down your legs and feet washing away your concerns and disturbing contemplations.

Proceed with your unwinding by delivering ordinary concerns and alarming thoughts, by basically guiding your concentration to your body. Make yourself agreeable before you get totally consumed by the sound of my voice that will lead you into an ideal perspective to let go, release, and free yourself totally from binge eating, and become more resolved to restrict your food admission.

As you make those last little adjustments, I might want you to get mindful of your feet intellectually; it doesn't make any difference on the off chance that you are sitting or lying down, as long as you know about the sensation in your feet at the present time.

As of now, become mindful of the sensation in your feet and imagine how light they would feel like soon after a multi-week of halting binge eating and deliberately restricting your food consumption.

Instruct every one of the little muscles in your feet to relax and as your feet become significantly more relaxed, allow that unwinding to gradually move upwards up your calves and knees, making your muscles soft and lose completely loose.

Fill that unwinding in your thighs, making you experience that lovely substantialness of totally loosened up muscles in your legs.

Unwinding and that rousing picture of restricting your food admission are climbing your torso lower back and wrap themselves tenderly around your stomach and gradually begin contracting your stomach to a size that can with your intentional restriction deciding on food consumption at the same time you feel significantly looser.

Each time you consider food and eating, you see this picture folding over your stomach firmly, so it permits just a restricted measure of food that is enough for you to remain solid and become fit.

What's more, normally, as unwinding arrives at your chest, you feel a powerful urge to breathe in profoundly and fill your lungs with air as your chest area uniformly conveys that unwinding across your shoulders and arms right to your fingertips and that shivering impression that you feel in your fingers and palms is there just to advise you that you are going to go into a brilliantly loosened up condition of mind perfect for you to totally relinquish every one of the concerns, and stop binge eating but there is no rush yet, you will do this soon.

Before you go into a superbly loosened-up perspective, I might want you to imagine that you are remaining before a flight of stairs that is driving up. You can see ten stages before you, and as I check from one to ten, you will imagine that you are climbing those stairs, and with each and new advance, your choice to restrict your food admission becomes stronger the second you hear me say, "ten" you will normally go into a superbly loosened up perspective in your body, and track down yourself in a room with a feasting table and a seat.

Beginning to climb the stairs...one...two, feeling that natural feeling of assurance ...three...four, expanding the determination behind your expectation to restrict your food intake...five...six, feeling profoundly happy with the choice to stop binge eating...seven...eight, picking just to have 20 chomps of new and better nourishment for each meal...nine, TEN...you are presently at the highest point of the flights of stairs in a room with an eating table, feeling totally loose and with a solid assurance to restrict your food admission to 20 chomps for each dinner.

This will occur on its own you don't need to do anything, yet, your body and your psyche brain will realize how to do that for you once you are prepared to let go, release and free yourself completely so that you can set aside more room for building a more grounded expectation and finish your choice to restrict your food allow and pick food that is advantageous for your prosperity.

Deliberately imagine a major green number twenty, and see it to you. Imagine that this is the number of chomps that you are taking per every dinner that you have. These twenty nibbles of painstakingly picked better food are the ideal sum for the new size of your stomach that is enveloped with that intriguing picture and restricting your food intake and halting binge eating for great.

On every meal you are going to begin, remember that large green number twenty, and you right away realize that you have the chance to appreciate this good food feast as you make your assurance to have a better way of life considerably more grounded.

Give clear directions to your psyche brain to take cues from you and help you in creating this propensity and decisions by picturing yourself doing this. Visualize that you are finding a seat at the table covered with a wide range of food, and despite the fact that everything is accessible, you are choosing to pick just quality food that is useful for your wellbeing, and you are additionally choosing to have quite recently a restricted measure of that food.

As you set yourself up to begin eating, a major green number twenty shows up before you to remind you to totally appreciate these twenty nibbles of flavorful quality food. You take the main nibble and begin biting gradually, so you can encounter every one of the flavors and fulfill your faculties.

Nineteen, you take another chomp, and you notice the new scents of your food as you bite gradually.

Eighteen, you are turning out to be more careful when you are eating, and you can see all the delicate sounds you make as you are gradually biting your quality food.

Seventeen, you are presently mindful of the multitude of developments that your mouth, tongue, and jaw are making while you are eating.

Sixteen, your Mindfulness is following your food from the second it contacts your mouth, as it makes it route over the tongue down your throat into your stomach.

Fifteen, your psyche mind picks up all that is required that will stop your binge eating problem.

You keep on eating gradually and carefully as you appreciate each bite; you are currently at number ten, and you can see that your stomach is getting full. A couple of more delectable chomps and you are presently at the number five, nearly there, but far away from old habits, so far away from old compulsions, far away from binge eating.

Presently you have one more nibble to finish your conscious food consumption limit and when you eat this last mess with you feel that your stomach is totally full, and you feel awesome about yourself. You realize that this is the correct decision for you to achieve your eating regimen objectives.

Chapter 7 - Guided Meditation

Start by considering the following.

- Where is by far most of your pressing factor taken care of?

- Where is your torture found?

- What is some segment of your body, by and large free?

- Take a full breath in as of now, inhale out.

- Breathe in additionally, out.

- Continue breathing bit by bit, without any problem.

- Rests, preferably on a bed, and let your arms, hands, and legs become limp.

Start to breathe in regularly and sensibly significantly, by then spotlight on some point just over your customary extent of vision, by then step by step let them close. Continue with fairly steady and significant breathing, let your muscles step by step and logically begin to surrender, from your feet to your neck, and soon after, fill your brain with an image that collaborates with looseness and tranquility, simultaneously breathing little by little and allowing your muscles to relax.

Now—following 5-10 minutes—you should be significantly free and now a ton "closer" to your subconscious and all that it can achieve for you.

- As of now, consider an image of yourself as you truly should be, meager, fit, and sound, and thereafter keep up that image of yourself in your brain.

- Get ready to loosen up, sitting or lying in a pleasing where you will not be disturbed.

- Interference. You're making strides towards what you need. Besides, because you're tuning in, you're revolved around change.

- I'm here to help you with doing this.

- Later on, you'll recall this moment as an extremely important occasion in your life.

- Having a critical impact, recognizing, getting more fit is basic and fun

- Delay. Weight issues are frequently a result of using sustenance to change your feelings.

- Right, when you're depleted, upset, anxious, or stressed in an unexpected way.

- You can tune in and get clear about what you really need.

- Respect yourself—taking action towards whatever that is.

- Interference. What's more, in light of the fact that your real requirements aren't seen or circled back to.

- Likewise, sustenance is used to comfort the torture of something weak in your life. Diets will not work as time goes on.

- Deferral. Hypnotherapy changes how you see yourself as it changes the significant set up confining feelings and old models which keep the load on.

- Deferral. There are two segments to this weight decrease hypnotherapy plan.

- With the objective that you'll like getting more slender and adequately become lighter, more grounded, more euphoric, and more beneficial for you, rest, you don't have to advance any endeavor at all to review what I'm expressing.

- As you significantly loosen up, your subconscious character will take in what's ideal for you—and disregard the rest—You'll take what you decisively need from this session—to feel a more blissful, lighter, and more beneficial person.

- Interference. You can loosen up significantly now—essentially taking in and out, closing your eyes softly now, and feeling the movement of your breath in your nose. Make a longer pause.

- Feel the breath spilling into your chest. Chest rising and falling

- Make a longer pause. Feeling the breath spilling into your stomach. Stomach raising and falling.

- Make a longer pause. Experience the sound of breath as you take in and out. Significantly, slowly. Listening successfully, your breath like sensitive ocean waves and continuing ahead, the tide of progress.

- Make a longer pause. Enjoy the traces of progress as you check out the voice bantering with your internal voice and feeling fairly more loose progressively pleasant as you feel your body shedding weight as it loosens up, your whole face loosening up, all of the muscles around your eyes, jaw, temple, tuning into those muscles and feeling a smooth, warm delicacy inside them.

- Rest. Look closely at your neck and how it feels. Your neck, loosening now, yielding the pressure you didn't understand you were holding there. Notice the differentiation, the softness, the softness, the warmth, the smallness inside as it loosens.

- Break. Send your thought to your shoulders and upper back. Empower yourself to surrender. The soft, warm feeling of ownership now spreads throughout your shoulders.

- Deferral. From the most noteworthy mark of your back to the foundation of your spine. Relaxing up warmth as the muscles let go, feeling lighter.

- Progressively more relaxed each time you breathe in and out, delay pleasant assumptions spreading all through your body as it changes progressively pleasant, lighter, and lighter.

- Interference. Chest and stomach are rising and falling with your fragile breath. Warm and light as they loosen up. Breathe, getting further, feeling quiet.

- Interference. Notice warmth and non-abrasiveness spilling down the two arms. Into two hands, maybe you notice some essentialness there, shuddering.

- Make a longer pause. Warmth and non-abrasiveness are gushing down the two legs. Into the two feet, as all of the muscles loosen up on the way.

- Interference. There is politeness in every cell of your body floating through this experience, beginning with one state then onto the following, viably.

- Arrange for your flight of stairs of progress—a flight of stairs with 10 phases.

- Rest. You're doing this as you would prefer. Likewise, these methods are yours. Imagine them at present before you—a great deal of 10 steps driving down to a spot you need to go to—into the comfort of your inner world.

- To acquire capability with all of the things that will uphold you.

- How do the steps look? Would they say they are stone, wooden, or created utilizing another material?

- Deferral. How does the top propel feel under your revealed feet?

- Interference. This is your flight of stairs of progress.

- Old instances of eating may have helped you previously. You can change the guides to more worthwhile ones to get what you need. What may you need to experience now?

- Interference. You have a full situation to abandon any other person's adventure.

As you go down the steps, little by little, we can count them together, loosening up creating with every movement.

1.   Ensured and maintained

2.   Logically free

3.   Viably walking around

4.   Down, further, and more significant

5.   Breathing easily

6.   Each cell loosening up

7.   Skimming down the last advances

8.   Lighter and lighter

9.   Logically weightless

10.   Feel the opportunity that goes with loosening up as you coast towards a section at the base or the steps. To elsewhere—an unfading spot.

Continue with the following.

•   A long sandy coastline relaxes up in the two headings, evaporating into faint horizons east and west. There's no past here to consider. No future to consider; you're essentially here as of now, breathing and being.

•   Deferral. The whole environment is peaceful, calm.

•   The ocean before you is turquoise.

- Hear the minimal clear waves lapping onto the shore.

- Relax your mind into complete perfection.

- Interference. Basically, it is here and now where your mind and body can become friends and group up as you lay on the sand. In the shade of impacting palms. The fragile, warm sand—cushioning your body.

- Reprieve. The temperature incredible, warm on your skin.

- Dissolving all perpetual focuses in your mind.

- Dissolving troubles interminably in your body.

- Feel this event, so free and pleasant in this charming place, retouching your body and brain.

- Respite. Take in all the space around you into each cell of your body, feeling lighter and logically cheerful with each breath.

- Respite. Skim closer to your inward world.

- All in all, it is essentially a chance to explore your own ability and what feels right to you.

- Rest. Taking in now and seeing a splendid sparkle creating inside you.

- Finish your whole body off with light and warmth.

- The light retouches you as it fills your body. Guide it to the bits of you that need extra thought, the segments of your body that are tense, in torture, or scarred.

- Make a longer pause. Imagine the cells in these parts retaining the splendid light, see them patching, getting more grounded, and more worthwhile.

- Make a longer pause. The splendid light handles you with love, supporting you, enduring all parts of you, supporting you in fellowship.

- Make a longer pause. Notice how you feel right now, any sparkle and satisfaction you're experiencing in this quiet space.

- You feel a critical serenity as you tune into your actual self, tenderly holding you, checking out your body's necessities, pleasant sensations spreading through your body.

- Make a longer pause feeling this. You can go to this spot whenever you choose to successfully roll out certain improvements for the duration of your life.

- Interference. Bring up your sanctuary.

- Picture an image here. Imagine yourself at your ideal body weight decisively as you need to look genuinely, noticing the image clearly in your mind's eye. There's no flood.

- Make a longer pause. Add to the image similarly as you're painting a picture—layer by layer each time you check out this hypnotherapy session, you'll have the alternative to include more nuances.

- Interruption. Where are you staying, towards the left, the advantage or in the middle?

- Deferral. Is the image concealing or showing high differentiation?

- Postponement. Pick your articles of clothing, the concealing, and the surface.

- Make a longer pause. Make the image life-size now, not just a picture in your mind.

- Relief. Additionally, all in all, wander into this image of yourself. Imagine yourself inside your ideal body. Look out of your own eyes inside your lighter, more profitable body.

- Respite. Inside the lighter version of you, you're looking at your lean, strong, healthy body. As of now, your ideal weight smiles to yourself.

Chapter 8 - Hypnotherapy Techniques

Hypnotherapy is the utilization of hypnosis in patients who have distress or challenges inside their minds. Those using hypnotherapy guarantee patients encountering a trance are significantly more liable to tune in to the counsel given to them. A few problems hypnotherapy treats include torment, stress, weight, weakness, and amnesia. While a significant number of these issues are mental-related, certain actual sicknesses may likewise be overseen. Hypnotherapy is a strategy the Ancient Egyptians and Indians used to do. The action in these societies would likewise have a strict vibe, and the movement included both music and dance.

In some cases, the patient-advisor relationship can trigger issues. The patient might need to satisfy the advisor, or they may figure they don't care for them. Large numbers of these contentions, be that as it may, are opposing since hypnotherapy ordinarily occurs in a clinical office. A few rising techniques are utilized in this system. Age relapse is a key strategy. The subliminal specialist will endeavor to reestablish the patient to a past state inwardly, and this is constantly done to assist the patient with recuperating what they've lost.

The subsequent strategy used in hypnotherapy is called revivification. In this methodology, the trance specialist can help patients review their past encounters.

For instance, the subliminal specialist will inquire as to whether they've at any point been fishing, and in the event that they've been, they'll begin remembering the time they've been fishing, and the hypnotherapist will not have to assemble another state. Another basic hypnotherapy approach is called coordinated symbolism. This methodology can lead the patient through a wonderful encounter. The trance specialist additionally rehashes such thoughts or standards to get the patient to accept them, and this is called reiteration.

Generally speaking, individuals are more agreeable in a fantasy state. The research has shown that when an individual can imagine what they need, they're undeniably bound to get it. For this situation, the trance inducer plans to assist the patient with accomplishing the ideal target. Hypnotherapy depends on "Hypnos," and this was the Greek divine force of rest. This strategy was primarily used to help individuals mentally and was not broadly known until the nineteenth century.

Hypnotherapy for Weight Loss

The psyche mind has monstrous command over the activities of our bodies.

What's more, over our psyche mind, we have extraordinary control. Be that as it may, would we say we are certain of how to use it? Will we comprehend our psyches enough to deal with it effectively and exploit this benefit for us? We may inquire as to whether we don't.

The conscious brain can drive a thought by dull contemplations into the psyche mind. In a specific measure of time, the thought is set to such an extent that the psyche mind pushes the body to follow up on the arrangement.

This is the essential idea on which this hypothesis is based. An entrancing expert will likewise help us in the event that we can't do this without anyone's help (fix a thought into the inner mind). Obviously, it's a lot simpler to say than to do.

First and foremost, since weight reduction hypnotherapy can seem like a smart thought, however, it can have an effect on progress and the inability to track down the correct advisor.

Try to get positive exhortation from your loved ones or specialists around there.

Furthermore, on the grounds that old propensities bite the dust really hard, and you might dare to dream that you are near the ideal outcomes following a little while or even a long time of serious treatment.

Thirdly, that toward the start of your new body, you will feel anxious, and you will awaken to thoughts of "plants" inside your psyche that get more ingrained and more grounded. This could set aside some effort to become acclimated to.

In the entirety of this, we can reason that in spite of the fact that weight reduction hypnotherapy can appear to be a beautiful simple cycle before you go into the hypothesis, there are a couple of interesting points. For one, I don't need anybody to stress over my psyche or mind.

Reasons Why Hypnotherapy for Weight Loss Works

For such a large number of individuals, weight reduction is a definitive (and impossible) target. Many items are accessible on the wellness market-supplements, dietary plans, exercise programs, and even "marvel" arrangements. A large portion of these products won't accomplish the ideal result since weight reduction is an intricate activity.

Hypnosis of weight reduction is another practical option. In contrast with other eating plans and medications, it gives a complete arrangement. Hypnotherapy examines the physiological reasons for overweight tirelessness and, in this way, creates positive results.

Great Encouragement

Every one of the limits is customary weight reduction. You'll realize what food sources to stay away from, what negative routines to surrender, and how to consistently keep tabs on your development.

In these cases, productive energy would be missing.

Hypnosis in weight reduction centers on the positive; it shifts basic examples of thought. Rather than imagining that burgers will make you fat, you will find that carrots will improve your wellbeing and give fundamental nutrients to your body.Positive mesmerizing guidance shows you how to cherish your body and appreciate great wellbeing. It is a lot simpler to keep up the framework on the off chance that you are glad and certain about it.

Adapting to Stress

Will you need to eat everything, or more, every time you are exhausted, anxious, helpless, or discouraged? If this is true, you are unlucky with food and are relying on some unacceptable coping system.

Hypnosis permits you to uncover the triggers for pressure, uneasiness, and surprisingly self-indulgence; these enthusiastic elements overwhelm you and structure your relationship with food.

Auto-cognizance permits you to get away from conditions that cause you to feel terrible. Moreover, you figure out how to adapt without going to food. A better adapting technique is, in every case, enough to get in shape and lead to a solid way of life.

Advantages of Hypnotherapy for Weight Loss

The food business is a multi-billion dollar industry and shows no signs of slowing down. What number of diets have you recently tried to throw into the ring?

Who doesn't understand that less and more is the key to weight reduction? Absolutely, we don't need "subtleties." So, why the fight? I will give you access to the mystery since, with regards to rolling out perpetual improvements, your conscious mind (which is your self-discipline) is tight; your oblivious psyche is here the genuine force to be reckoned with. At the point when the totality of the above aspects are gathered, and you have not changed at this point, it is implausible to transform, so it may very well be an ideal opportunity to attempt weight reduction hypnotherapy in the following situations.

- Enthusiastic eating.

- Eat when you're not ravenous.

- Habitual eating. (asking why you are doing this yet can't stop)

- The pattern of impulse blame discipline.

Your oblivious inclinations (which you don't think about yet are uncovered during hypnotherapy for weight reduction) spur your food relationship. As

293

youths, we may have been told "to complete everything on our plates," and these old messages can, in any case, be played. Or on the other hand, we possibly grew up with a mother who grieved her weight, or maybe we considered food to be "love," We support ourselves and "love" today when we felt frail, discouraged, restless, or forlorn.

It's not about counts calories; it's about emotions and how you "use" food to transform them, and this is the reason weight reduction hypnotherapy works admirably for feelings and thinking designs. For ladies, food is likewise their selection of medications.

It likely could be an ideal opportunity to jump and attempt hypnotherapy to get thinner for genuine freedom and an improved, safe connection to food and exercise forever.

Hypnotherapy Is the Answer for Weight Loss

For every one of the requests present-day lives force on people, weight reduction can be trying to accomplish. It is no big surprise that men, ladies, and even kids are benefiting from this current to an ever-increasing extent. The standard Western eating routine known as S.A.D. is high in sugar, fat and straightforward starches, and synthetic added substances.

This eating routine causes individuals to become heavy and triggers the disease of diabetes and other related diseases. Individuals move less. The normal resident is busy and exhausted, however insufficient really.

Stress is a huge factor in the helpless way of life decisions and can prompt negative routines. People who have put on weight are aware of what they are doing, yet it is hard to track down support if the weight continues to heap. We simply need another person to remain in their bodies (with a solid eating routine and exercise propensities) for a brief period to help push things the correct way.

Hypnosis will help here. The new individual who dwells inside his body might be them!

The training work is done at the level of the psyche, giving the mind clear ideas, intelligent thoughts to boost weight reduction, research at an obvious level to assemble new perspectives, standards, and the conventional idea so that buyers can settle on good options. Hypnosis helps a positive way of life change that brings about bodyweight decrease. It is very acceptable, therefore. Diets have been proven to be insufficient in the long run, while eating regimen change and maintenance of propensities causes positive results in weight reduction.

Hypnosis procedures for weight reduction normally include the support of inspiration and certainty-building phrases just as clear guidelines for a solid way of life. Entrancing activities frequently use representation techniques to help the customer "see" his objective weight and "feel" what it resembles. This makes them fruitful. In the event that an individual can figure he can get thinner, he can do it.

Unfortunately, numerous individuals have endeavored numerous weight control plans and fizzled, losing their self-assurance and want to remove their significance. Weight reduction Hypnosis spotlights how individuals feel when they get thinner, their readiness to do as such, and embracing another, better way of life.

Hypnosis arrangements with numerous people in an unexpected way, a few groups, react to ideas effectively and change them reliably for quite a while frame, bringing about quick weight reduction. In any case, some take longer and longer meetings to retrain the psyche mind and modify their insights about themselves, what they will do, and what they need to do. To change their way of life effectively, individuals need to do it.

Chapter 9 - Obesity and Weight Prevention

Schools and Obesity Prevention

Nourishment instruction is led in schools, and school food conditions permit youngsters to pick and eat good food sources. For instance, FV accessibility in the school cafeteria was a huge indicator of FV utilization following a 2-year intervention. Be that as it may, not all school food was controlled, and nibble candy machines were contrarily identified with everyday organic product utilization among center school youth.

An improvement in the use of lunch by students in the center's schools was noted after a neighborhood school zone mandated a change in cafeteria food strategy. Additionally, a statewide school nourishment strategy to improve school food arrangement brought expanded use of vegetables and also diminished the use of improved refreshments and bite chips. It decreased energy from dietary fat among center school students. Additionally, numerous schools give routinely booked PE exercises. Schools, in this way, are legitimate accomplices in changing youngster's eating regimens and active work designs.

Families give both the qualities and the quick climate for youngsters; they are accordingly a huge effect on weight and related information, perspectives, and practices in youth.

School-Based Nutrition Interventions

Despite the fact that obesity prevention contemplates having included a nourishment part, the vast majority of these tests have been executed in grade schools, so there is an absence of information for different youngsters. A new survey of school-based mediations that included body arrangement as a results measure discovered 11 tests that met the creator's specific methodological incorporation rules.

The multicomponent Planet Health intercession focused on expanding FV admission and diminishing the utilization of high-fat food varieties. Following two years, the predominance of obesity was lower among intercession students than among control school children. Moreover, dietary changes remembered a critical increment for FV utilization and an altogether more modest expansion in assessed energy admission each day among the mediation young ladies than among the control young ladies.

The absence of a change among the young men demonstrates that sexual orientation directed the impact, and elective systems may be required for young men. Two other center schools contemplated didn't quantify anthropometric results. However, one 2-year intercession focused on expanding FV, and low-fat food varieties didn't accomplish dietary change. Then again, a 2-year mediation that included family (three bulletins per year), understudy ecological culture (more products of the soil at school in addition to sustenance data), and individual (1-hour PC custom-made intercession every year) parts was fruitful.

Toward the finish of this 2-year study, young ladies in the intercession had lower expansions essentially in weight list z-scores than those in the control condition bunch, yet the eating regimen was not estimated. We discovered three secondary school sustenance intercessions. A social advertising mediation essentially affected FV consumption. A natural intercession expanded the accessibility of low, fat food sources in the cafeteria. The analysts revealed a higher level of down, cheap food deals in the mediation than control condition schools; nonetheless, singular understudy admission was not estimated.

No individual dietary information was gathered, yet no sodas were sold by Year 3, and plasma insulin esteems declined. A few school-based projects with both educational plans and cafeteria alterations focusing on dietary fat utilization effectively accomplished decreases in students absolute; the soaked fat utilization, kilocalories, and fat utilization, and all-out fat-just utilization.

Projects have additionally accomplished decreases in school dinner's fat substance. The entirety of the FV mediations accomplished little yet huge expansions in organic product or vegetable utilization.

The requirements include sustenance instruction objectives, active work, other school-based exercises, and nourishment rules for all food varieties and drinks accessible on school grounds. Ongoing information demonstrates that school food wellbeing approaches improve student utilization at lunch; notwithstanding, full assessments of these projects have not been performed. Such appraisal ought to be a need for future tests. These tests ought to include energy admission and use measures for the whole day and discrete periods (e.g., data by dinners, energy exhausted in the early evening, or school).

A particularly significant region of examination is where students eat more food sources or become stationary after updates in school food and active work conditions. While psychosocial dietary factors are likely to be greater in middle people, there is a general lack of data on this. Huge expansions of information were found in some research, extending the ability to order. The ability to order food by decision and verbal support from cafeteria workers have likewise been accounted for.

Generally, the writers propose that school-based intercessions can change youngster's eating regimens by carrying out new arrangements that cutoff high fat, high-sugar food varieties and give more FV and water choices. Information builds, asking abilities, and consolation from food laborers are likely the mediators of dietary change. Projects focusing on these ideas will probably help forestall youth obesity.

Families Diet and Obesity Prevention

Hardly any family-based youth obesity prevention intercessions have been accounted for in this book. Most have stressed both sustenance and active work however have exhibited just restricted achievement. A new meta-investigation of youth obesity prevention programs inferred that parental contribution was not related with fundamentally more noteworthy adequacy.

An audit of family contribution in weight that the executive's programs presumed is the vulnerability that exists in regards to how best to configure family-based intercessions. There gives off an impression of being a positive relationship between the quantity of conduct change procedures instructed and the consequences for parent and youngster weight. Given the lack of demonstrated fruitful intercessions, analyzing family connections of kids eating routine probably offers the best accessible bits of knowledge into possibly fundamental yet untested methods for using families to change kid's dietary conduct.

Family Correlates of Youth Dietary Intake

A new study presumes that nourishment has every indication of being affected by home nutrition source accessibility, especially FV. In spite of the fact that the extremes with respect to causality were unrealistic, a proposed system of impact was that accessibility expanded utilization through expanded openness in affected inclination. Food inclination has been associated with utilization, and parents assume a crucial part in creating food inclinations.

An audit of components affecting early food inclinations, or dread of new things, is a formatively suitable response in small kids. Rehashed openness and tastings can defeat neophobic responses. The social setting inside which food is offered was likewise answered to be significant in creating food inclinations. A negative social setting, for example, giving a prize to burning through a loathed food, has been appeared to bring about a diminished appreciation for that food.

Assisting parents with understanding the significance of making good food varieties accessible and tending to neophobic reactions in kids can upgrade inclinations and, at last, utilization. Demonstrating by others, especially moms has additionally been appeared to impact food inclinations.

Feast construction may likewise be an affecting element. Evidence proposes that adolescents who dine with their families have more excellent weight control plans and a lower risk of obesity. The utilization of controlling or prohibitive parental taking care of procedures has been related to diminished advancement of discretion eating instruments in youth, bringing about a more serious danger of obesity, especially in young ladies. Formative contrasts in parental impact over youth dietary practices should be viewed when planning family-based youth obesity intercessions. From incubation through youthfulness, parents have less control over youth dietary practices progressively. Therefore, family-based mediations ought to be custom fitted to the distinctions in parental impact during every period.

Family mediations from the get-go being developed are bound to be viable in view of more grounded family impacts. New techniques that emphasize changing nurturing style, giving quality food sources, and making family eating times fun and charming (all middle people) appear to hold the most guarantee for family-based obesity prevention endeavors.

Families Physical Activity and Obesity Prevention

In the most exhaustive survey of actual work relationships, various examples of discoveries with respect to what parents meant for actual work were found among kids (4-12 years of age) versus young people (13-18 years of age).

Among youngsters, no parent-related factors were reliably identified with actual work; among teenagers, parental help was in every case emphatically related, direct assistance was reliably pitifully coupled, and having freedoms to work out (a variable affected by parent decisions) was reliably feebly identified with active work. Likewise, clashing outcomes about parental or family impacts have as of late showed up.

Some portion of the irregularity seems to have come about because of the variety in family impacts (pretty much every test used unprecedented family impact measures) and actual work used. Nonetheless, parental arrangement of transportation was identified with absolute active work and interest in sports or action exercises among the two young men and young ladies. It very well might be a fundamental middle person to focus on in future intercessions.

Chapter 10 - Intuitive Eating for Effective Hypnotic Gastric Band

The best way to deal with get more fit and keep up your optimal weight expects is to make acclimations to your way of life.

The interaction is certifiably not a convenient solution, and various methodologies are indispensable in making it effective. Most importantly, mental viewpoints are vital in accomplishing positive aftereffects of the hypnotic gastric band. Similarly, working out the amazing confirmations and representation for weight reduction is imperative. By consolidating entrancing, reflection, and unwinding, you make certain to succeed. With the hypnotic gastric band, you ought to know about what, how, and when you eat.

In intuitive eating, you fabricate trust in your body to stay mindful of what, how much, and when you eat. I realize it sounds basic; however, it is important to know that eating routine insane culture impacts your convictions about food.

Therefore, you ought to disregard feast plans and weight reduction remedies and become the master of your own body. It isn't unexpected to discover calorie counters making transient accomplishments in weight reduction, however neglecting to keep up their optimal weight. Thus, they feel regretful and deterred from the methodology.

Intuitive eating fills this hole as it floats you away from diet culture rules and assists you with eliminating judgment from eating. It guides you to control yourself and be accountable for your eating. Prominently, intuitive eating has no standards, and the accompanying standards should direct you to weight reduction achievement and desire less food effortlessly.

Stay away from a diet mindset. Diets are misleading in promising quick and perpetual weight reduction. You are probably going to fault yourself when they fizzle. Keep away from outer control and accept that your own feeling of craving is the lone inward control.

Perceive hunger; it is your body's signal that you need to sustain it. Keeping the body took care of is vital to upgrade your relationship with food. Eat just to fulfill your yearning and get it going when you feel hungry.

Find a sense of contentment with your food, allow yourself to set no conditions to any band.

By eating any food, the body sets aside an effort to discover that specific food varieties are not, at this point, confined. Continuously, the food quits controlling you.

Challenge the limitations, avoid carrying on honestly of what you ought to or ought not to eat. It implies you don't commend yourself in the wake of keeping up your calorie-breaking point or feel remorseful subsequent to eating a biscuit. Food is your friend and not your adversary and is critical to immersion and energy.

Recognize your completion; if you can tell when you are eager, you likewise can tell when you are comfortably full. Your satiety ought not to be constrained by the measure of food left on the plate yet by your inside signals.

Find the fulfillment in food. In your undertaking to get thinner, you may disregard the fulfillment and delight found in eating. There is incredible substance and fulfillment in eating what we need in a helpful and welcoming climate. The experience causes you to understand that you need less food to choose you have had enough.

Try not to eat for comfort; avoid eating enthusiastically to soothe your misfortunes, as it will not make the problem go away. Comfort eating should not be a psychological sedative, as it can lead to genuine medical conditions. Focusing on different leisure activities, taking a walk, or ruminating is a part of the options to energize yourself and lift your spirits.

Honor your wellbeing; intuitive eating doesn't imply that you throw meals out the window. By recuperating and improving your relationship with food, you are in a superior situation to consolidate sustenance into your eating decisions. Above all, while adding the sustenance piece, you should stick it in the deferential self-care instead of diet attitude.

You have been conceived as an intuitive eater, so you ought to get back there through inner prompts. You should focus on perspectives, evolving convictions, practices, and fixing your relationship with food.

It is a pragmatic manual for entrancing for weight reduction: Hypnosis works by permitting you to change your oblivious musings and cycles to accomplish a particular objective. On the off chance that you need to get thinner through Hypnosis, you should impact different convictions in your psyche mind about your weight.

These convictions will assist you with conquering the apparent inconceivabilities in shedding pounds and trouble in choosing what, how, and when to eat.

Your psyche gets suggestible when in a tranced state, empowering you to access and impact your amazing subliminal suspicions. By following this guide, you will find that you have made some new and positive moves towards the new changes in your own life that you have effectively set for yourself.

Entrancing Session for Intuitive Eating and Weight Loss

Let yourself loosen up when meditations enter your psyche, you basically decide to recognize them at that point, return your regard to the sound of my voice, and the sound of my voice goes with you and stays the main sound you hear. You are starting to encounter a more profound degree of unwinding. I might want you to start presently to concentrate on your relaxing for a more profound degree of unwinding, and the sound of my voice goes with you and each word taking you more profound and more profound, and I truly don't know what your own inner state is precisely bringing to you now whether pictures, sensations or sounds as you tune in to every one of these words. I say to you now with quietness and harmony about what you experience now you can rehearse this experience by accepting that you will lose the measure of weight that you need to lose you will lose the right measure of weight you wish to lose, and you can do this effectively and normally through carefully eating solid and nutritious food.

You feel glad for yourself, you think about every one of the good things in your day to day existence, and you realize that you will make the most solid and good life for yourself and now see yourself more clear on the screen, stomach level, hips, and thighs thin and trim, legs thin and trim, you look extraordinary and feel so great you are loose and cheerful, comfortable in your skin and your psyche mind is aware of when you just ate to fulfill yearning and you returned now from this second on to possibly eat when you are genuinely eager.

Your psyche mind knows precisely how this feels and that this is the awesome best method of eating that you will possibly eat when you are really truly hungry. You possibly eat when you feel the real actual yearning in your body and when you feel this genuine craving, you eat solid indispensable food that you know is useful for your brain uses, for your body uses, for your spirit, and you know when you are really ravenous on the grounds that it is an appetite that goes ahead slowly.

A genuine craving is good and effortlessly cheerful with little bits of food, you embrace change and development, you keep your attention to the current second through feelings and sensations from a profound perspective of tranquility and harmony that empowers you to eat gradually while being mindful of the sum you are eating and biting. You feel accomplished from feast to feast consistently slimming down safely and securely, and normally, when you keep mindful of what, when, and how you eat, you are positive about the decisions you make about your appearance, so visualize yourself currently strolling out on a bright new day perhaps feeling proud and ready to go for the decisions you caused to eat strongly emanate essentiality and to feel fitter and slimmer.

You experience your own inclination in a quiet and sure state for your wellbeing decisions and increment your sensation of wellbeing and energy, and now it is the second to end this state in a moment. I will check back from one to five, and you will come out of the entrancing, bringing every one of the advantages, feeling yourself coming out gradually now one, two, three, four, you start to move and stretch, and five, eyes open wide away feeling better and secured in a collapsing snapshot of the present. With the assistance of incredible assertions and perception, you can accomplish your optimal load in the most normal manner. Try not to fret about what you eat or not yet with how you wish to look.

Try not to imagine disturbing eating or hating some sort of food. By saying solid and positive insistence, you make the psyche mind direct you to eat the correct amounts of food with balance. Note that nothing occurs without any forethought, and you need persistence and ordinary incredible confirmation and perception to encounter the effectiveness of a hypnotic gastric band.

The subsequent stage is to quit perusing and to get beginning doing whatever it is that you need to do to guarantee that your body and the weight, specifically, will be appropriately dealt with should the need emerge. In the event that you find that you actually need assistance understanding the maximum capacity of Hypnosis and reflection, you will probably have better outcomes by creating a timetable that you desire to follow, including severe cutoff times for different pieces of the assignments just as the general fulfillment of your arrangements. It is essential to set practices for weight reduction, and studies show that mind-boggling assignments that are separated into singular pieces, including singular cutoff times, have a lot more prominent possibility of being finished when contrasted with something that has an overall need of being finished yet no ongoing table for doing as such. Regardless of whether it appears to be senseless, feel free to set your own cutoff times for consummation, complete with pointers of progress and disappointment. After you have effectively finished the entirety of your necessary practices, you will be happy you did.

Chapter 11 - Shrink Stomach Without Surgery

Prior to finding ailing health, weight, coronary illness, and an assortment of issues that influence the human body, individuals eat what they need without speculation about the number of calories and deficient sustenance they put in their stomachs. Yet, with the evolving way of life, individuals are more worried about their wellbeing and the impacts of heftiness.

Weight reduction surgery isn't new, albeit a portion of our friends have had medical procedures just to get thinner, and it has been a pattern for some time. In any case, the majority of these medical procedures are a momentary answer for getting in shape.

One of the basic medical procedures that regularly help overweight individuals is a gastric detour. All the more explicitly, prohibitive gastric detours, bariatric gastric detours, and the laparoscopic gastric band are the most well-known. Prohibitive gastric detour includes appending a flexible gastric band to the stomach and diminishes food admission without influencing the stomach-related cycle. Then again, the bariatric gastric detour puts an empty band around the stomach and structures a little pocket and a slender entry that prompts the leftover piece of the stomach. You will consistently feel full when you have this system. The laparoscopic gastric band is less intrusive and uses a band through and around the stomach. On the off chance that you put movable ties around your midsection, you get a more modest stomach. The outcome is like a bariatric sidestep for gastroplasty that limits food admission.

Although numerous specialists support these techniques to get in shape in overweight patients, there is as yet a danger of surgery, and others are worried about pre-and postoperative confusions and troubles in adjusting to their new eating regimen.

One of these tasks can be lethal and irreversible. Before you choose, counsel your PCP, family, and examine your alternatives with them. Getting in shape can be accomplished with persistence, constancy, restraint, and difficult work. Indeed, even surgery doesn't offer a drawn-out arrangement however is just impermanent.

Getting thinner with practice and legitimate nourishment can assist you with accomplishing the body and wellbeing you generally needed. Come to me to accomplish your objective of getting thinner!

Would you be able to diminish the size of your stomach without gastric detour surgery? The appropriate response is yes. Gastric surgery changes your stomach's size through staples, tendons, or other careful changes to the stomach. The breaking point of the measure of food you can eat by limiting your stomach to a more modest compartment is in groups; your stomach develops as large as a golf ball.

You absolutely need to be more slender, and surgery seems like a moment fix, yet don't have any desire to set aside the entirety of your cash by not performing this surgery and attempting to help yourself by shrinking your stomach? All things considered, you made it as large by putting as much food in your mouth as you needed. The skin is flexible and stretches to the size it develops. Your stomach is likewise adaptable, extending to any estimate that compares to the measure of food you eat. The inverse is likewise evident; your stomach will shrink to retain the measure of food you put in it.

What is the genuine state of your stomach? It is roughly twelve inches in length and six inches wide at its most stretched-out point. It channels your food after it has been processed in the upper stomach-related lot, where it is handled into fuel for your body. On the off chance that your body has sufficient fuel to make all the difference for you, overabundance fuel is put away in your body as fat and cellulose.

How large can your stomach stretch? Take a gander at a gallon compartment of water. A gallon of water weighs, at any rate, eight pounds. One gallon is equivalent to sixteen cups. Your stomach can be extended to oblige at any rate a gallon, and with an ordinary overhead eating routine at each dinner, it tends to be extended to immense sizes.

Also, observe a one-liter compartment. There are multiple pounds in a liter of water and four cups of water. This is adequately huge to collect enough food for a typical dinner to bolster your body and still store the abundance of fat and cellulose. Two cups of food are all any person could need to cope with their problems in one feast. Try measuring the food you put on your plate. Put your ordinary measure of food on your plate and then measure everything. Write down this sum.

You will be astounded at the measure of food you eat. The explanation why you want to eat is that your body needs fuel to work, play, walk, and exercise. Is it accurate to say that you are right? Do you need to spend the well-deserved cash on surgery? There are numerous approaches to lessen the size of your stomach. Eat little, regular suppers.

Your stomach will not remain large in the event that you don't keep it full. It will gradually shrink to the size you need for the food you get. By gradually diminishing your stomach each day, you keep a sensation of totality. All things considered, the stomach has a major shouting voice and can deal with its requirements. Rather than spilling over this gallon-sized holder, you can fulfill it by essentially biting each chomp of food gradually. Did you realize that it requires twenty minutes for your stomach to make an impression on your mind that it has arrived at the full imprint?

Twenty minutes is quite a while to keep eating. You need to accelerate the news intermediary. Without uncertainty, your express sprinter conveys a great deal of fat and can barely arrive at the brain to press the quit eating button.

So now you have an issue. You don't have the foggiest idea when to quit eating, and you presumably disdain when your stomach cramps with the void. The best answer for this issue is to bite gradually. Bite each nibble. They can be eaten up as fast as you can scoop. For delicate food varieties, you ought to burn through in little nibbles.

Have a go at eating with a child spoon that moms feed their children with. Sounds clever. You are attempting to fulfill your stomach without limit, and you need to put the scoop down.

Meat and other strong food varieties ought to be gnawed in any event multiple times. You don't need to tally; simply bite until your food is practically similar to pureed potatoes. You can't suffocate that way.

Your stomach needs liquid to process food. Drink when eating is additionally an approach to feel new. Take some food, bite it quite well, and wash it down with a lot of water. Try not to stress; not all supplements will be eliminated from the food.

All nutrients and supplements are prepared in your lower stomach-related parcel.

Your health will depend on the type of food you eat. Your stomach is the size you permit. Less food implies fewer calories than you burn, and fewer calories bring about a deficiency of weight. This is definitely not a convenient solution. It required some investment to grow up, yet in the event that you bite gradually in one day and eat loads of little dinners, you will be quicker than you might suspect.

Scrummy Tummy is a protected and powerful strategy for getting thinner. There are various names and minor departures from this technique; however, they all use the force of their brains to persuade you that your stomach is more modest.

This is a mesmerizing method to shrink your gut by revisiting a virtual gastric band or entrancing band so you can receive the rewards without the agony, hazard, and stunning expense of real surgery.

Here you can find out more about your choice. Really expensive and distressing surgery?

The customized meeting package that guides you to your optimal weight and size, the virtual gastric banding surgery with abdominoplasty or entry-level gastric banding, can help you achieve your goals of looking less fat and more attractive.

Similarly, as a genuine activity isn't for everybody, here are a few different ways you can choose which one is appropriate for you. I'm a hypnotic weight reduction proficient, not a specialist, so I will focus on sharing what I know to help you settle on the correct choice for yourself.

You should be liberal and prepared to roll out these improvements for the entrancing virtual gastric band technique (either close to home guided picture meetings or the sound program bundle). Do you need the outcomes? Do you feel good with the expanded good consideration you get when you are slimmer and look more alluring or feel more appealing? In all honesty, some who are overweight have oblivious motivations to remain hefty.

In the event that you only need to shed pounds dependent on the things that others are saying or thinking, this isn't an ideal choice. The genuine changes come from the inside, and you need these benefits for you! Frequently your mental self-view changes first from within. This helps you look and feel the manner in which you need from an external perspective.

Nonetheless, in the event that you are open and need to exploit this strategy and recover control of your eating regimen and weight, you will be wonderfully astounded at how powerful this technique will be for you. It is conceivable that in a couple of months after you have arrived at your optimal size and weight and are happy with the outcomes, you can keep up and think back on this ideal normally and essentially. A choice you've made at this point!

The reduced stomach is sensitive to imagery suggestion. You can imagine the size of the littlest stomach and perceive how a more modest stomach implies you eat less.

You additionally feel full prior, and when days become many weeks become months, your weight and stature change, and you become more slender. You will see, feel and imagine yourself as a more slender individual who eats less, and subsequently, your psyche will stick to the script and help you plan your new picture.

The best part is that you can keep this new weight and size on the grounds that your mental self-view has been upgraded. Your inner mind will be furnished with the correct picture and plan of your body in the event that you feed your body with the correct sustenance.

Normally, lose weight fast and train your brain to eat less.

All individuals have another "you" in us. You simply need to look and quit saying "sorry" and start another attitude to get in shape normally, another outlook, and another viewpoint on your life. Your body intuitively conveys signals, so turn over your motor.

You have heard the old saying. "Eat like a ruler" for breakfast, "Eat like a sovereign for lunch, and" Eat like a homeless man for supper." It is extremely obvious in light of the fact that your body will make up for the lost time by consuming calories the entire day. If you are eager before early afternoon, you will most likely not have enough for breakfast, attempt to eat in any event 250 calories, and you will get thinner normally.

Chapter 12 - What Mindfulness Is

The principal importance of care in a more standard setting is an inclination of mindfulness, of simply being more mindful of the things around us; in any case, care can go past endeavoring to end up being more in accordance with the world and is by and by transforming into a standard piece of reflection. Getting mindful of your body, your resources, and your mental state through reflection is a fundamental cycle that simply requires the assurance and time just to check out what your body is expressing.

Stop, tune in, feel; it's as simple as that; aside from the push to pause and sit, check out the feelings and messages from your body and feel them. At the point when you do that, you would then have the option to begin to see the value in the various potential benefits of giving consideration admittance to your life.

To what limit can mindfulness benefit your life? There is an immense extent of mental and real benefits of practicing care, which can be astonishing given the ease of the preparation. It is definitely not hard to consider how 15 minutes of cautious reflection on your distress and mental state can enjoy any basic benefits on your success anyway the results are typically noticed.

Similar to different sorts of reflection, care can be an inconceivable instrument against pressure and anxiety. Studies have shown that not only is there an association between care and mental tests, but it can also likewise assist with despairing by influencing cortisol levels.

Also, a couple of schools have even taken up showing the preparation to help test-based anxiety and even improve abilities to center. Concerning the genuine side, alongside a possibly more clear cognizance of the pulsating difficulty in the body that may have been disregarded, there are likewise who consider proposing an association with cut-down circulatory strain and better safety.

There is even a kind of care thinning down to improve mindfulness and valuation for food that can help weight decrease.

There is something else completely to mindfulness that meets the eye. Care, that essential exhibit of two or three seconds to stop, tune in, and feel, is a basic idea that we would all have the option to join into our lives. Whether or not it is an occasion of checking out those damages as we wake or ruminating to control our disquiet for 20 minutes in the early evening, anyone can see the value in the consideration and the benefits, and it is so normal to see the physical and mental changes it can bring.

Chapter 13 - Changing Habits Through Hypnosis

Beat Sugar Addiction

Unreasonable sugar admission is a typical issue for individuals requiring help with weight reduction. By using a procedure like the Advanced Interactive Gastric Band technique, the Brain Training for Overcoming Sugar Addiction plan allows you to improve your sugar utilization practices by making minor, feasible upgrades.

Comprehend the Qualities

The Hormone Hypnosis programming assists you with making speedy, mindful, and oblivious changes. The product will assist you with perceiving the key chemicals that impact our wellbeing and figure out how they can impact fat gathering, processing, energy levels, rest, and constant infection. By means of this educational plan, you can find out about large hormonal wellbeing disruptors and turn out to be more mindful of your own body's necessities.

Take Advantage of Nutrition

Numerous individuals face vulnerability with regards to having the best nutritious worth from food. In the event that our bodies don't get what they need healthfully, we will attempt to eat more, regardless of whether we're done. In the Hypnosis Meets Diet application, you will acquire exhortation on the main aspects of diet that can help you settle on better dietary choices.

Gain Confidence in Sports

A few people think that it's hard to foster certainty and a motivating force to partake in sports. The Hypnosis Meets Sports programming will help you increment confidence about your capacity, increment inspiration, hold focus, formative wellbeing, train for testing conditions, and lift your prosperity about sport.

Deal with Your Weight

The Hypnosis Weight Management program works best in blend with the Simulated Gastric Band program however should be possible autonomously of this.

The course will assist you with exploring the ordinary battles of weight the executives and spotlights on solidifying restraint, holding certainty, and offsetting food utilization with work out. This product will likewise help you construct subliminal changes to keep you on target.

Lessen Alcohol Intake

Nine million individuals in England drink higher than the suggested day-by-day liquor limit. Unreasonable liquor admission can unfavorably influence your wellness, weight, and prosperity. The Minimize Alcohol Initiative chips away at separating the act of drinking liquor, expanding mindfulness about your passionate responses, and urging you to assume liability for diminishing liquor utilization.

Bring an End to the Smoking Habit

The Interactive Quit Smoking programming will help you shake the addictive reasoning examples and practices related to smoking and urge you to change your habits and achieve enduring change. The product uses an altered way to deal with focus on the basic reasons for smoking and to help you through the recuperation cycle in a customized way.

Disposing of Emotional Eating Through Hypnosis

Unfortunately, for some individuals, the undesirable propensity for using food to defeat negative feelings like exhaustion, misery, and dejection is really normal. Fortunately, you can eliminate mental eating in two different ways by the gadget of hypnosis.

As a matter of first importance, Jeffrey Rose, the Behavioral Hypnotist, and Nutritionist will guide you to address the underlying driver of enthusiastic eating. On the off chance that it is strain, misery, or sorrow, you will actually want to adapt explicitly to the psychological drives of indulging. Second, you will actually want to choose more sure approaches to adapt to it whenever you face another life battle, as opposed to searching for high food accommodation.

Hypnosis is the ideal method to give the subliminal every one of the resources and procedures for beginning a superior life rapidly and successfully. Your psyche will guide you to manage and beat any relational challenges you have in a more good style, not, at this point, baffled by both conscious and subliminal musings and feelings.

First off, you would presently don't look for food while feeling uneasiness yet can promptly like, among alternate ways, similarly as fruitful in diminishing and destroying your terrible encounters. Perhaps you're taking a walk, run, or exercise. You can play your main tune, watch a film, read an engaging book, or call a friend. You will turn out to be completely drenched in your profession or an individual undertaking that you have set out on.

Also, surprisingly, every one of these things would be nearly however amazing or more regrettable than the psychological eating seemed to be once.

You will wind up being pushed down an alternate street for social challenges, finding a way or valuable ways to change or fix the components in your day-to-day existence that had recently caused your terrible feelings. You will end up being a prevailing and fruitful wellspring of valuable upgrades that will take you to the existence you have consistently wanted for yourself, rather than effectively suffering awful things in your day-to-day existence.

You will have the inner mind esteems and abilities by hypnotherapy to adapt effectively to any new social issues that may happen and push you to search for food.

Food Addictions

As of late, the idea that an individual may be dependent on food has acquired developing prevalence. That comes from mind imaging and different investigations of the effect of indulging habitually on the brain's pleasure habitats.

Creature and human tests show that, for specific people, a similar brain award and delight focuses are invigorated by addictive substances; for example, cocaine and heroin are frequently activated by food, particularly exceptionally agreeable food varieties. Food varieties, especially tasteful, are food varieties wealthy in sugar, fat, and salt.

Very tasteful food sources enact feel-great brain synthetics like dopamine, similar to addictive substances. At the point when individuals experience satisfaction related to the upgraded transmission of dopamine by burning through specific food varieties through the brain's prize framework, they effectively want to eat once more.

Different indications of completion and joy might be superseded by the remuneration signs from effectively acceptable food varieties. As an outcome, despite the fact that they're not ravenous, individuals continue to take care of. Habitual indulging is a type of compulsive conduct that implies somebody may get associated with an action that initiates outrageous happiness (for example, devouring, drinking, or shopping).

Individuals with food addictions let go completely over their dietary examples and consume an excess of time on food and gorging or anticipate the psychological outcomes over habitual indulging.

A type of food opposition can likewise be set up by people who show side effects of food dependence. They eat to an ever-increasing extent, just to track down that less and less food fills them.

Researchers concur that the role of food compulsion in heftiness could be significant.

Nonetheless, people of normal weight may likewise be managing food dependence. Their bodies will be hereditarily designed in a real sense to help oblige the additional calories they take. Or then again, to make up for gorging, they could build their actual work.

Regardless of hindering impacts, for example, weight gain or bargained connections, individuals who are dependent on food will keep on burning through.

Also, as individuals who are dependent on medications or betting, despite the fact that they attempt to or have attempted a few times to chop down, individuals who are dependent on food would experience difficulty forestalling their activities.

Indications of Food Addiction

A survey was created by scientists at the Rudd Center for Food Science and Policy at Yale University to distinguish individuals with food addictions. Here is an example of inquiries that will help you choose if you are dependent on food. Are those demonstrations applicable to you? Do you:

• At the point when you begin burning through those food sources, you wind up eating more than anticipated.

• Continue to eat those food sources despite the fact that you're not eager any longer.

• Eat up to the stage where you feel tired.

- Stress over not devouring particular sorts of food sources, or stress over dispensing with such sorts of food varieties.

- Make a special effort to get them on the grounds that those food sources aren't accessible.

The survey additionally inquiries concerning the impact on your own existence of your relationship with food; in the event that these conditions allude to you ask yourself if you eat those food varieties time after time, or in such incredible amounts that rather than a living, investing energy with the family, or appreciating relaxation action, you begin devouring food.

You keep away from work or social conditions where, out of dread of gorging, such food sources are accessible.

Rather than food and dozing, you experience difficulty working productively at your work or training.

The survey questions with respect to indications of social disconnection: at the point when you cut back on specific food varieties (barring jazzed drinks), for instance, you will experience signs, for example, tension, unsettling, other actual manifestations.

The poll likewise tries to check the impact on your sensations of food decisions. Are those conditions concern you?

Issues like misery, nervousness, self-hatred, or blame are brought about by eating food.

To diminish unsavory feelings or increment fulfillment, you need to burn through an ever-increasing number of calories.

Devouring a similar measure of food would not diminish awful considerations or, as it used to, increment fulfillment.

Would hypnotherapy be able to be used for food addiction? Definitely! No doubt! As per this report, there was a bigger increment of individuals going through hypnotherapy for gorging than at any rate 70% of customers looking for non-mesmerizing consideration.

Hypnotherapy will assist you with overcoming your dependence on food. Here are a couple of ways that hypnotherapy attempts to hold us back from eating excessively.

• **Careful eating:** Food addictions lead individuals, without thought, to gorge. Until we do not provide an explanation of our activities, it turns into an allurement.

• **The brain might be molded to remain conscious through hypnosis:** At the point when you eat, you'll figure out how to know your longings, how full you generally are, and how to remain conscious. Care can make you aware of your activities, with the goal that when you feed, how frequently you devour, and the amount you feed, you will oversee them.

Chapter 14 - How to Deal With Food Addiction and Achieve

Losing weight is not easy for anyone, and it's even more difficult when you're dealing with food addiction and food controlling your life. If you're looking for a gastric band procedure to help deal with these problems, The Hypnotic Gastric Band may be the right choice for you.

Hypnotic Gastric Band surgery is a non-surgical, non-invasive procedure that helps control weight by limiting how much food can be consumed at one time. The only part of the stomach that leaves the operating room is a very small pouch above your belly button called an "A-Pouch." When this pouch fills, it signals to your brain that you're full.

Then you may ask, "What about the rest of my stomach? How does it fit into the equation?" The rest of your stomach is transformed into a new organ called the "Hypothalamic Stomach." When your Hypothalamic Stomach fills up, it signals to your brain that you're full. This means that with The Hypnotic Gastric Band, portion control is taken out of the equation.

The Hypnotic Gastric Band surgery is performed in a hospital and takes approximately 1-2 hours to complete. You will be asleep for the procedure, but during that time, Dr. Sutton will place an inflatable band around your A-Pouch and suture it into place. This band will then be connected to a port placed subcutaneously under your skin, approximately 3 inches above the incision line. After surgery, you are taken to the recovery room and monitored for one hour before being sent back to your room.

The Hypnotic Gastric Band procedure can be performed on its own or in conjunction with conventional gastric procedures such as the Roux-en-Y gastric bypass or vertical sleeve gastrectomy. Before deciding on a gastric band, it's important that you speak with Dr. Sutton about your options and decide what's best for you. He will take into account your life expectancy, level of activity, and how quickly you would like to lose weight.

The Hypnotic Gastric Band procedure is very safe, with a mortality rate of less than one death per 1,000 procedures completed. Patients have complications in less than 2 percent of cases. Within the first year after surgery, you are required to visit Dr. Sutton once a month for six months and once every three months after that. This ensures that your band is working properly and is monitored for safety purposes as well as to make sure you are continuing on your journey to weight loss success.

One of the biggest reasons why patients choose The Hypnotic Gastric Band over other types of weight-loss surgeries is that it is effective and has been proven to work. In a six-month study, patients lost an average of 49 percent of their excess weight. Overall, 83 percent of patients were able to lose at least half their excess weight in one year. Another proven benefit of The Hypnotic Gastric Band is that it's reversible, in case you decide you want to remove your band and resume eating normally.

Chapter 15 - Long Term Sustainable Weight Loss

Anybody that needs to get in shape faces most notably horrible adversaries who are cravings and hunger. This is additionally felt as food yearnings for various food types like sweet, sound, or, much more terrible, junk foods like chocolate; thus, the word "chocoholic."

Above all else, it's these food longings that make you overweight. However, the desires are additionally amplified when you start eating less, as it has been shown that when you don't take enough calories, food yearnings are increased, especially yearnings for unhealthy sweets and greasy foods.

As an outcome, when you eat, you are considerably more liable to pick something incredibly calorific, hence fixing your low-calorie system's weight-loss acquire.

It is further compounded by the way you shed pounds, your body tries to fight back (a resistance tool you created when the food turned out to be scarce) and hinders your digestion, while food cravings expand, especially cravings for foods high in carbohydrates, fats, and sugars.

Every one of these physiological factors consolidates to make it exceptionally hard for the calorie counter to settle on lower-calorie food decisions and support weight loss.

In reality, the generally heard expressions of "food yearnings" and food addiction or "chocoholic" have become states absolutely on the grounds that insight is like medication addicts. The impulse to eat, especially foods high in carbohydrates and fats, might be more ingrained than the "urges" of the heroin addict.

The appallingly low eating routine achievement rates are additional proof of the troubles of keeping away from food desires. In five years, 95% of healthy food nuts recuperate their weight and more. In a long time, by far, most of us can't battle them viably, making our weight-loss objectives appear to be unreachable.

I, for one, saw that while I realize the best foods to fill me with fewer calories and I attempted to include whatever number of these kinds of foods as would be prudent in my eating regimen, I actually experienced starch desires and sugar items that took me over my weight loss calorie cap.

I frequently found that I now and again didn't have the opportunity to plan lower-calorie options or that lower-calorie options were simply not accessible (for example like eating on the run), or that I really loved dinners that were higher in calories and didn't consider lower-calorie choices. For instance, with my eggs and sandwiches, I truly incline toward buttered toast!

Wouldn't it be such a great deal simpler on the off chance that we could take a pill that would permit us to burn through more carb foods without the eventual caloric outcomes? (For example, weight gain)

All things considered, after my broad and intensive investigation into the best weight-loss strategies and basic survey, I'm certain there is an assortment of enhancements that make the weight-loss measure simpler.

Perhaps the most energizing enhancement I tried is a medication that assists with decreasing the ingestion of dietary starches. It's all acceptable, solid, an incentive for cash, result-free, proficient for long-term use, and has amazing weight-loss-helping execution. And, most fundamentally, for the customer, logical information can be looked at to help their cases of adequacy.

Section a day and a half

Tips From Hypnosis Weight Loss Programs

One of the fundamental factors in guaranteeing you lead a glad, safe way of life is weight the board. At the point when you're an enthusiastic eater, it's harder to direct your weight. There is a wide range of healthful territories that lead to weight the board, making it simpler to stay away from passionate eating and securely get more fit.

• The primary thing to remember is the addictive impact that food has on you. You may experience desires that regularly feel wild, and you can desire to get food addiction, very much like a smoker is dependent on smoking.

• Try to control your feelings and emotions appropriately and train your mind not to react to unsavory or awkward feelings by basically burning through food (your choice brain drug) to quiet down.

• Eating fewer carbs kills your digestion and may possibly make you gain weight. Actually, consuming fewer calories only works in the present moment and brings down your delicate confidence.

• Change the manner in which you think ladies seem to think uniquely in contrast to overweight or corpulent men. They don't add feeling to food and don't use food to self-sedate and feel much improved.

• Learn elective methods for de-pushing and quieting instead of eating. Recognize your eating triggers.

• Avoid or stay away from the food you know makes you gauge, fulfill your longings, and promote enthusiastic eating or commonly snack foods, cakes, treats, and so on. I likewise test for food hypersensitivity or food affectability. Indeed, even quality foods can prompt your food addiction and weight gain.

• The most straightforward approach to shed pounds will see you eliminating something extremely normal from your eating routine and delivering long periods of pointless fat exercise at the rec center. Recall brain and body activities like yoga, pilates, or in any event, strolling in a pleasant park will ponder for your care, confidence, and body. Relax more.

• Set aside some effort to reconnect with yourself. The vast majority don't have the foggiest idea how to unwind appropriately and believe it's enough sitting before the screen—it's most certainly not. Study some fundamental reflection methods to totally unwind.

• Try not to compare yourself with others. At the point when you're getting in shape, it's significant not to contrast your weight with people around you. In case you're discontent with your weight, contrasting yourself with the thin young ladies you find in magazines or on TV that prolong your recuperation interaction by changing your way of life propensities with eating, exercise, and brain control, you'll see it a lot simpler to stop passionate eating and lose the weight you need a lot quicker and longer-term.

• At the point when you've learned methods to manage eating causes and yearnings, passionate eating will end.

• In an individual who controls their feelings and has more good methods of adapting to negative feelings, passionate eating can't flourish, or it is improbable. Before you know it, you'll be eating instinctively and freeing yourself from emotional eating and an abundance of muscle to fat in a great way.

Is it accurate to say that you are tired of getting the normal, worn-out weight loss guidance? Searching for some quick tips to help enable yourself to stop an occasional weight gain? Why not follow to find out about some quick, safe weight loss tips?

1. Eliminate Five Pounds Before a Significant Case

In case you're typically healthy, yet need a couple of pounds off to put your best self forward before a significant occasion like New Year's Eve or a class get-together, probably the ideal approach to do it is to clean your body.

Avoid bread and pasta the prior week, eat a lot of crude vegetables and servings of mixed greens, keep lean protein in the blend, and drink at any rate eight ounces of water a day. You will not just end up slimmer; you'll feel 100% more sure and more secure.

As a matter of fact, your weight changes during the day, so your smartest option is never on the scale, just when restoratively fitting. Shedding five pounds quickly will cause you to feel fabulous, yet you can likewise begin eating fewer carbs. In the event that you've at any point gone on the outing, will you not at any point get off the eating regimen for a thrill ride?

2. Weight Without Diet

It's more than you thought. Eating less junk food makes you prone to problems. Skip the diets and count. Expect to eat ordinary, tight portions three times a day, 4 hours apart.

3. Know the Exercise

An energetic one-mile walk, 30 minutes of moving, or pursuing the children around in a label game; try to save it from the outset for 20 to 30 minutes and then add the following seven days consistently.

4. Right-Start Your Day

Cutting calories during getaways also means skipping dinners. Regrettably, this makes it difficult for digestion to speed up. Try not to miss breakfast while you are trying to shed pounds, and don't choose "sustenance bar" consolation.

All things being equal, give your body a raw dose of protein from fresh, natural products and a whole grain base. A part of the most loved morning meals is a boiled egg or microwave fried egg, a bowl of whole-grain oatmeal with fresh organic products, cantaloupe, or peaches.

You get the fit protein that allows you to remain alert, assembling the muscle that consumes the fat, the sugar that your mind desires, the starches it needs to deal with, and adding cancer prevention agent nutrients to help it keep focused and healthy.

5. Take Top Notch Dietary Enhancements Everyday

There's no option for eating a decent blend, everything being equal, yet holding back on the rudiments is very simple when endeavoring to get more fit. Make sure the body doesn't come up short on the supplements it needs since you cut calories. A sound dietary enhancement contains nutrients and cancer prevention agents to improve the structure of your cells.

An expansive multivitamin would give the least suggested day-by-day measures of nutrients A, B6, B12, C, E, and K. While at it, get out in the sun, at any rate for ten minutes every day is enough to help the body produce the vitamin D it needs. Then again, a ton of work has shown that a great number of people have a low vitamin D deficit, and they can likewise take nutrient D enhancements.

6. Eat Vegetables

Especially lettuce. However, don't depend on ice sheet lettuce or plates of mixed greens. Look for braised, steamed, or flame-broiled for something other than what's expected from the ordinary plate of mixed greens.

6. Set a Hopeful Solid Objective

Instead of reasoning or discussing how to "shed 5 pounds," plan to gauge your weight; for instance, take your present weight, deduct 5, and trust you as of now, measure that sum.

On the off chance that you experience issues accepting this, figuring out how to utilize Hypnosis will assist you with developing yourself securely and serenely. A prepared hypnotherapist utilizing an approved Hypnosis preparing method with genuine customer results will show you how in a far-reaching weight loss program.

7. Eliminate Disappointment Propensities

Weight loss disappointment because of past disappointments. It actuates an example of frustration or "dissatisfaction assumption" for new practices.

One of my #1 statements from Dr. Ste Stephen Covey is, "You can't consider the circumstance you've acted in!" Just making a move on these tips can make critical upgrades in mentality, weight, and shape. What do you do on the off chance that you make the above moves, yet you don't?

Chapter 16 - Gastric Band Hypnosis Script

You take in, and out, and in, and out. As you do, you wind up loosening up to an ever-increasing extent. Close your eyes and take a full breath. As you take a full breath through your nose, you understand that you can smell the aroma of sterile alcohol surrounding you. It smells like somebody has splashed the entire room in scouring liquor to clean it, and you can smell the sharp fragrance of hardened steel surrounding you. You take in, and you smell gloves on somebody's hand.

You can see an exceptionally brilliant light right above you. It is practically unthinkable for you to see past the splendor above you, regardless of whether you need to. The remainder of the room past the light is dull. You can hear voices discussing groundwork for a medical procedure. You feel a hand contact yours, and when you turn, you see an individual in greenish-blue scours, with a face cover and a bandana over their hair to keep it set up.

"We will start the system. Is it true that you are prepared?"

You gesture your head to the individual.

"You will feel a little squeeze as we embed the IV, OK?" The individual close to you say. "And afterward, you will check to ten and nod off."

You gesture your head once more. You feel consummately calm where you are. You are not stressed at all as you are there. You realize that you are in extraordinary hands and that they will deal with you exactly how you need to. You realize that they will assist you with being put on a way toward a better life, and you are prepared to accept it.

You feel the squeeze in your arm, trailed by cool fluid moving through your vein directly in the space that it was set. You feel tension on your arm where they tape the IV into place so you can't thump it off. You begin to feel somewhat hefty and floaty as whatever is in the IV streams into your body.

At that point, they put a veil over your mouth and nose. It is large and cool, and it presses into the skin around your face. It is pushed somewhat harder than you expected to make a tight seal, and afterward, you hear them teach you to check-in reverse from ten to quiet yourself down.

"Ten…" you start, feeling somewhat dazed. You are loose.

"Nine…" You are feeling heavier now than you did before like you are sinking onto the surgical table.

"Eight…" You are getting much more drained than you were previously, and your eyelids are getting weighty. You can't keep them open anymore.

"Seven…" The entire body feels hefty and like it can't move.

"Six…" You can scarcely say a word by then.

"Five…" And the entire world disappears. You can't move any longer. You are stuck where you are, and you feel calm.

You are finished and utter unwinding right now. You are not apprehensive or stressed. You are not in torment or awkward. Your eyes are shut. However, you know that individuals around you are talking.

"We should make the entry point," you hear one of them say, and unexpectedly, you feel tension on your stomach. You feel simply pressure—no agony. You can feel it in a few better places on your body. You grope it close to your stomach, at that point, a couple of more places too. "We are placing in four entry points so we can get the band in," the specialist states. "We will actually want to do as such with this laparoscopic camera."

You feel the pulling and pressing factor again as they place their camera where it should be. "Since it is there, we can perceive what we are doing. Do you see the stomach there?"

You can hear the group express their agreement and affirmation.

"Great. We will put a band around this part here," he expressed. "We will isolate that upper piece of the stomach from the lower part so the patient can't eat as much food anytime. We are making the stomach's volume more modest, so the patient should eat less and, consequently, will shed pounds. Any inquiries?"

Another person begins to talk. "Will it hurt?"

"It very well may be awkward for a couple of days after the technique, yet they ought to be completely agreeable. We do this laparoscopically, so there is less disturbance during recovery. It ought to be a straightforward methodology. Additional inquiries?"

There is quietness, so the specialist returns to work. You can feel pressure in your middle. It isn't awkward—simply unfamiliar. The specialist works with little instruments that permit them to get to your stomach without opening you up so much, and that permits them to treat you simpler.

"We have the band arranged now," the specialist says, following a couple of moments. They didn't take long to track down the correct spot by any stretch of the imagination. Also, as they do as such, they secure the band around your stomach. You feel pressure around your stomach as its ability for food has been drastically diminished.

"What's more, it's finished." The specialist pulls back, and you feel an odd pulling in your stomach in four spots and afterward settling. The little devices have been taken out from inside you. You can dubiously smell the aroma of blood among the tempered steel and sterile alcohol, and you feel tension on top of every one of the four cut destinations. You can feel that they are doing this to get the draining dealt with.

You are entirely loose, and however you can feel pressure, you are not in torment. You know about the way that you can feel the peculiar tension on your stomach that has cut the measure of room that you can fill down the middle. You can feel that you can presently don't eat such a lot, and you perceive that this is an immediate consequence of the band being put there for you. You are straightforwardly mindful of the certainty that you have gotten that band arranged and that your stomach's volume is presently drastically diminished, and that you won't eat such a lot.

"The patient might have the option to burn-through around 1 cup of food now. An ordinary stomach holds up to 4. However, it would appear that we are finished. The time has come to take the patient to recovery."

And afterward, you are uninformed of whatever else.

You awaken gradually, feeling tired and moderate. You feel hefty, yet you are as yet in no agony. You are agreeable and all set forward. You are all set.

"Try not to move such a lot," somebody says close to you, and you see an attendant there, dealing with you and attempting to get you familiar. "Is it safe to say that you are in torment?"

You shake your head no. You are very agreeable; however, your stomach feels a lot more modest.

"Great. We need to get you to eat to guarantee that the medical procedure has worked. Is it accurate to say that you are prepared?"

You gesture your head, and they give you a little cup. "It's brimming with stock," they advise you, and you make a gesture once more. You take a taste. Your stomach feels awkwardly full as of now. You understand that you can't devour close to however much you could previously. It is bizarre; however, you see that eventually, you must choose between limited options. You need to eat less so you can get more fit.

Over the course of the following not many weeks, you can just burn through a modest quantity of food anytime. You ought to be exceptionally cautious with the amount you eat, and in the event that you indulge, you will get yourself regurgitating. You will wind up attempting to get past the food. You will wind up not being able to keep as much in your stomach. From the start, it is suggested that you just eat fluid food sources so you can acclimate to your stomach being this new size. It isn't excruciating— simply unique.

You won't feel torment—simply extraordinary. You will feel a pressing factor, and you will feel that your stomach is not, at this point, the size that it used to be. You will feel that you are done going to be as eager. You can't be ravenous when there isn't as much room in your stomach any longer. From this point forward, parcel control is everything. Bit control

343

will keep you sound, and it will keep you ready to eat however much you ought to be. It will control your eating routine and ensure that you will just eat similarly however much you required.

You take in and out; your stomach feels tighter. It feels more modest. You take in and out; you understand that you just drank half of your stock before you were full and, at this point, ready to have no more any longer.

You take in and out, and you understand that you are en route to assuming back responsibility for your own weight and life unequivocally. You take in and out, and you are feeling looser.

You are informed that you are permitted to return home yet to resist the urge to stress about the nourishment for the following, not many days. You are released quickly without any entanglements, and you are allowed to return home.

At the point when you return home, you are in no agony. You never feel any agony. Simply pressure. You never feel yourself getting injured. You simply feel that you are fuller more quickly. Without fail, after only a couple of nibbles, you will begin to get full. Each time you drink, you just have a couple of sips too.

You feel incredible. You feel quiet. You feel better in your own body as you understand that you are on target to being solid. You take in. You inhale out. What's more, you feel good.

The time has come to fire awakening now. You take in, and out, and in, and out. And you understand that you are on target to the existence that you need.

Take in and out. Take deep in. Take deep, out. Rehash to yourself:

- I'm equipped for eating less.

- I will eat less.

- I won't eat close to however much I did previously.

- I will get more fit.

- I have a gastric band on my stomach.

- I may have the option to eat a limited quantity of food at some random time, and I will eat it gradually and cautiously.

- I might have the option to eat a tad at a time, and that's alright.

- I will be the individual that I need to be.

Chapter 17 - Hypnosis for Fighting Cravings Script

Welcome to this hypnosis script for fighting off your cravings. This hypnosis script is planned to be used at home and not while driving or doing whatever else that may require your entire consideration. As you tune in to this script, you will be tenderly hushed into a condition of unwinding and have your brain delicately moved toward the objectives that will assist you with bettering yourself. Recall that this script will possibly work if your psyche is open and on the off chance that you are willing and open to the messages that are being given to you. Achievement in the present circumstance is altogether reliant upon you and what you are doing. However, the achievement is conceivable as long as you are willing. To start, you should ensure that you are in the correct attitude, the correct area, and you are prepared to tune in. Assuming you are prepared now, if it's not too much trouble, continue!

Start by getting yourself comfortable any place you mean to tune in to this script. Ensure that you needn't bother with anything and that you are someplace that hushes up advertisement faintly lit, so you are not intruded. If it's not too much trouble, turn your telephone off or quiet the ringer and ensure that you have no interruptions around you. At the point when you are comfortable and loose, and you're prepared to begin, take a full breath, and we should start!

Take a major, full breath. Feel the air make a trip through your nose to your lungs and let the oxygen travel through your body. Each breath that you take will go all through your entire body. Relax. You feel it going into your arms. It goes through your corridors right down to your fingertips.

Relax. Feel it go through your neck, your middle, and your midsection.

Relax. Feel it work its way down your legs and right to your feet.

Feel it in your toes. Each breath conveys with its unwinding. It conveys with it the sensation of satisfaction and unwinding.

Take a full breath in. You feel much more loosened up at this point. Your body is quiet. Inhale out.

Also, take in. Feel yourself relinquishing any of your concerns that are disturbing you. Give your pressures and stresses access to your body, float back to your lungs, and breathe out them away. With each breath out, you inhale out that strain, and with each breath in, you take in unwinding.

Stay there and relax. In and out, and in, and out. You are comfortable. You are loose.

Check out yourself. You are in an incredibly huge field that is encircled by tall grass. There are blossoms to a great extent in your field. You can see that there are butterflies and honey bees flying about to a great extent, languidly floating from one plant to another. The air is fresh and clean. It is quiet there around there. It is comfortable, calm, and is ideal for unwinding. You realize that you can be entirely content there. You feel comfortable.

The sky above you is a perfect, clear blue. The sun isn't excessively sweltering or excessively cold—it is perfect. You feel impeccably calm there. You need to remain there forever. Harmony is overpowering. You feel as though you would be glad never to move again. You are content there.

As you unwind, you hear a few birds singing close to you. They are tweeting their tune noticeable all around. It is wonderful and fresh. You can hear the grass stirring around as the ideal percussion to it. You can hear your breath traveling every which way, murmuring past your lips.

You feel something. Profound inside you, you feel something that needs to drag you away from that happiness. You feel something that is attempting to drive you away, to remove you from the spot that you are. It needs to make a huge difference. You can feel it somewhere down in your mind. It is in your mouth, a sensation of strain. It is an inclination of yearning. It is an inclination of urgency. You feel the requirement for your number one food overpowering you. You want to get that food, whatever it is. You feel your mouth is watering. You need it.

You feel the hankering. It gets more grounded and more grounded, and as the hankering comes, you see the sky obfuscating up above you. The mists come in, and with each whirlwind, another influx of wanting falls over you. The hankering feels like it could take you over. You would prefer not to surrender to it, yet you feel like it is excessively difficult to. The hankering is the dim mists over your head. It is covering out the light. It compromises a tempest above you.

You take a full breath. You can feel the hankering in your whole body. It has covered you, head to toe. What's more, as you inhale, you can handle it. You take a full breath and push it down. Your breath drives the hankering away from your toes. You take in and out. You push the hankering out of your lower legs and out of your legs. You take in and out. What's more, you push it out of your pelvis and your stomach.

You inhale and feel your head begin to clear. You push it out of your mouth, pushing the hankering down. You smother it. The hankering is gathering inside you, profound inside your chest as you relax. You gather it until it seems like it is a lot to hold anymore, and you pull it away. You consolidate it down into your hands.

You imagine yourself grasping your hankering. You can see it in that general area before you. It is dim and dull, very much like the mists above you.

The hankering is substantial. It burdens you. It pulls you down further and more profound, and you feel like it is difficult to receive in return. You feel your feet sinking into the dirt under the heaviness of the hankering; however, notwithstanding trying, you can't release it. It adheres to your hand, similar to half-dried paste, and regardless of how you attempt to push it off, it simply sticks to an ever-increasing extent. It stalls out that you feel it pushing back, scaling your wrists. In the event that you're not cautious, you understand that it may assume control over your entire body once more.

You take in and out. You take a gander at the ball in your grasp. You watch and see it whirling around in your grasp. Similarly, as you are prepared to surrender, you take a full breath. As you take that full breath, you understand something: Your breath is pushing it off of you. Your full breath begins to disengage it from you.

Your full breath permits you to escape from it. With each full breath, you can feel yourself acquiring more and more authority over the thing you are doing.

You can push the sensations of discomfort, and you can assume responsibility for yourself. You take in, and out, and in, and out. And as you do as such, you gain the power to toss the entire ball; you should do it.

The ball isolates from your hands. It feels soft to the touch, and as it could suck you directly back up in the event that you're not cautious. However, you pull it away from plain view. You pull the ball in and hold it tight, developing the force in your grasp. You breathe hard and deep. At that moment, gathering all the might you can muster in your arms, you inhale once more, what is more, one more time.

You develop the purpose, and with each breath, you feel more confident.

You don't need to allow this load to hold you down. You don't need to allow yourself to sink. You have the solidarity to retaliate. You have the solidarity to stand up and be the individual that you need to be. You have the solidarity to pound that hankering in the event that you need to.

Inside your hands, you push ready of wanting. It begins to disintegrate inside your hands. You push more diligently, and it begins to contract. With each full breath you take, you can feel yourself conquering the hankering. You feel the hankering contracting more and more moderately. You feel the hankering getting simpler to oversee.

It isn't as substantial. It doesn't feel as tacky. It feels somewhat simpler to oversee, yet it's actually an ideal opportunity to toss it. You realize that you can make it go further a lot away from you.

Thus, you pull your arms back. You inhale deeply. At that moment, with all the strength you can muster, you throw the bundle of desire as far as you can. You push it away as far as you can. As it flies out of your hand, it zooms through the air. You watch as the bundle of desire flies away, getting more far and farther. As you get more separation from the hankering increasingly, you feel much improved. You feel more in charge as it goes further away.

As the packet of desire flies further away from you, you feel more secure. You feel more like you are controlling yourself as opposed to allowing your hankering to control you.

The ball continues to zoom through the sky as though it's not limited by gravity by any means.

It flies increasingly elevated, getting more modest and more modest. Also, soon, you can see where it flew through the cover of mists above you. You can see the beams of daylight get through the sky in the opening where the mists were penetrated, and as the daylight channels down through the sky, you feel harmony. You feel more grounded. You feel like it is simpler for you to adapt.

You take a full breath, and you watch the opening get greater and greater in the sky. Each breath assists you with getting out of the sky further constantly. Every breath assists with making the mists vanish. Furthermore, before you know it, the mists have gone. The sky above you is clear and blue once more, and you feel quiet. You crushed the hankering and moved beyond it.

In the sky above you, you can see a rainbow spreading across the sky. You can feel it giving you expectation and fulfillment; it is endorsing the way that you figured out how to overcome the hankering. It is showing you that you had the strength.

You slowly inhale in and loll in the light above you. You appreciate the glow of the daylight, remunerating you. It leaves you feeling more certain and more joyful in your place. With a grin to yourself, you compliment yourself for crushing the hankering, and you invite the glow and bliss inside you. You invite the smoothness. You feel loose as you lounge in the sun, and you gradually begin to get back to that quiet and calm condition of happiness in your field. The brightness and quieting air got back with the absence of mists, and you are prepared to make the most of your time there.

Chapter 18 - Craving Food and Emotional Eating Psychology

The idea of food cravings is one critical factor that can influence hunger. For overweight weight watchers, this exceptional inclination to eat a specific food shows up powerful, and a few theories have introduced why this is so. Physiological theories portray the nourishing and homeostatic part of food cravings and clarify why cravings might be more present in individuals denied of food.

A few food's psychoactive abilities to cause cravings are identified with an example of self-prescription and thought to mitigate a focal serotonin lack.

Mental theories stress the part of negative feelings (e.g., outrage) as foundations for cravings, and theories of learning declare that cravings are a useful, learned response to signals (tactile, situational) and a pleasurable result for cravings. What is clear here is that food cravings are a multi-dimensional and dynamic wonder, one that may include components of the relative multitude of hypotheses recommended.

Whatever the reason, it is recommended that food cravings are oftentimes associated with food use and inclination for high-fat foods and raised Body Mass Index (BMI). Food craving has been discovered to be related to body weight, even in non-clinical tests, showing the significant job of craving in food admission.

For future anticipation of heftiness, early recognition of raised weight lists (BMIs), clinical dangers, and undesirable eating and active work examples might be fundamental. A central point of contention is a job that food cravings can play in supporting undesirable eating propensities found in other eating conduct issues; glut taking care of, bulimia, and stoutness.

Food cravings, weight gain, and lost connection, if this isn't examined, there is far-reaching and amazing information about the ascent in overall heftiness levels and the normal results. Youngsters are particularly noted as profoundly in danger for potential long-haul medical problems.

While dietary limitation, more smart dieting propensities, and active work have consistently been thought to be the answer for the heftiness scourge in grown-ups, young people, and youngsters, long haul meta-investigation and follow-up research show that weight loss isn't supported (and in reality, the additional time that passes between the finish of an eating routine and follow-up, the more weight is recovered, Mann et al., 2007. Unfortunately, some other tests show that diet is as yet a solid pointer to potential weight gain.

An examination led as of late by Patricia Goodspeed Grant (2008) managed the mental, social, and social commitments to over-utilization in stout individuals. She discovered eating for comfort to the very big-boned is established in the use of food to oversee emotional torment encounters and troublesome family and social connections. Her members showed that the "freedom to focus on close to home issues simultaneously as weight loss" was missing from all recuperation administrations they had attempted.

It appears to be that this thought and the issue of tending to the mental causes or emotional components that reason individuals to indulge is a missing connection in the treatment of overweight and heftiness. It is just insufficient to depend on willpower and schooling.

356

Inspiration Problems

People are guided exclusively by feelings (i.e., sensations). There are basically three sorts of feelings; great, antagonistic, and unpalatable. The support we get from the negative inclination is to push towards a tendency that we don't have however that we do like. We switch on from the unpalatable preference by supplanting it with another great (or impartial) feeling.

Yearning is an uncomfortable sensation (for the vast majority) and is adjusted by the great impression of taking care of and the flavor of food (for the vast majority). This, among other fundamental jobs, is so we can live separately, just as collectively. The majority of us incline toward lovely feelings over disagreeable feelings. Be that as it may, fun upgrades aren't constantly connected to the outcome they were intended to accomplish.

Numerous individuals feed, not on the grounds that they need nourishment, but since they feel an uncomfortable feeling like dismissal, seclusion, pity, sadness, dread, disillusionment, uselessness, misfortune, vulnerability, or misery. The over-utilization of emotional food additionally adds to fat-acquire and other medical problems. This could then make an endless loop of more emotional eating to deal with the emotional impacts of getting overweight and feel unfortunate.

Overabundance eating and gorging are additionally an aftereffect of dissatisfaction and dull propensities for adolescents. Food or refreshments are utilized to decrease dullness. They could likewise be utilized as a way of dealing with stress to adapt to uneasiness, sadness, stress, and struggle-related issues. While they may feel comforted in the wake of eating an amount of food, the individual has not tended to the fundamental reason for those issues. This gives a circle of remuneration to using food to improve feelings. There is no clarification, therefore, why they will not reoccur later on. This can transform the issue into a horrendous circle.

At the point when a parent manages their own emotional issues by drinking and/or overeating, all things considered, the youngster will do so too. This methodology is being demonstrated for adapting. Parents likewise think that it's difficult to bear the disappointment or to endure of their newborn child and are headed to remove this. For instance, if food is regularly used as a method of doing this, "It doesn't matter that we welcome a chocolate dessert," a parent may set interaction of quieting uncomfortable feelings with the delight of eating. This can set up an eating example to control the feelings once more. This is fundamentally an issue when there's no genuine conversation about the dissatisfaction or torment of the kid, and all things considered, food is simply being offered.

Have an idea at this moment. Why do you need to quit eating emotionally? You may adapt quickly, or you may have to think for some time. Finish for all to hear this sentence:

Because of my feelings, when I quit eating, I will.

Your reaction/s will give you some knowledge into how roused you are.

In case you're motivated to charming results, you may have made statements like:

• I'll have the option to purchase clothes as-is in shops when I quit eating in the light of my feelings

• I'll be fulfilled in the event that I quit eating because of my feelings.

If you are inspired away from the adverse outcomes, your reactions may reflect:

- If I quit eating in response to my feelings, I'm done going to feel uncomfortable in my clothes

- I will discard my "fat" clothes when I quit eating because of my feelings

You most likely have seen the themes here. Moving towards pleasurable outcomes or away from an adverse result influences how we think, feel, and act.

You can discover you have a blend of going to specific results and away from others. That is ok as well. Regularly than not, we are moved one way, essentially subliminally.

In people, by and large, inspiration was likewise shown to exist either as an inner trademark or as an outer factor. Inner inspiration is the left prefrontal flap that is identified with neural hardware; sensations of accomplishment, energy for work, euphoria in our day are completely associated with the left prefrontal cortex. It is that mind region that administers rousing conduct. It debilitates sensations of cynicism and advances activity. Actually, certain individuals characteristically have a serious level of this internal inspiration; the individuals who focus on the inward sensations of bliss will achieve them in spite of any challenges they may experience en route. Others, however, require more than this.

Outside impetus to create great activity is an outer force or incitement.

These can include financial advantages, for example, rewards, substantial or significant acknowledgment, grants, or other motivators. The truth of the matter is, with these transient impetuses empowering conduct, it has been shown that no measure of remuneration or recognition can inspire individuals to use their full capacity to keep running after their objectives (Goleman et al., 2002). What does it cost, then?

With work out, you may have seen that regardless of what number of fitness coaches you employ, what number of inspirational exercise tapes you purchase, or classes you join in, you, at last, lose interest and return to your old conduct.

That is on the grounds that every one of these issues is outside inspiration types. There's nothing amiss with them; a few groups are blossoming with outer inspiration and doing it well indeed. However, often, when you try not to get the drive from an outside source, your direct drops off.

In the event that you had a fitness coach at the door consistently for the remainder of your life and a culinary specialist in the kitchen preparing solid adjusted meals forever, then sure, you'd be enlivened to get thinner and get fitter. For the vast majority of us, such full-time help isn't a reality.

Often individuals find the inward motivation that they need to get in shape from an outside source, and that can assist them with the beginning. Here's the story about Mercedes.

For years Mercedes had attempted to shed pounds. She was a neighborhood library agent and making the most of her work and food without limit. Throughout the long term, she discovered a generally inactive way of life, with no activity and a great deal of perusing in her leisure time that the pounds had dropped on. She was a cultivated cook and was satisfied to plan meals for herself from the library's connoisseur magazines.

She wasn't too worried about her weight, yet she would, in any case, do something about it toward the rear of her brain. It wasn't until she recalled that every evening she focused on a successive guest to the library.

Jon has selected bookkeeping for his last tests of the year, and as he actually lived with his rambunctious, more youthful brothers and sisters at home, he began to take harmony and calm to the library each evening. He saw that Mercedes was truly proficient and accommodating in tracking down the suitable examination programs for him, and they fostered a decent relationship.

Chapter 19 - Mindfulness Exercises to Improve Your Emotional Well-Being

In this bustling world, where we are continually presented with new innovations, the psyche habitually moves from one side to another, dispersing our contemplations and feelings, which can cause us to feel overpowered, apprehensive, and surprisingly restless.

Western social order's lifestyle puts us on autopilot, guaranteeing that days pass by without understanding what's going on inside or around us. We drag, stroll through life ceaselessly briefly to inspect ourselves inside, ceaselessly considering our requirements. As yet ruminating, sticking to dreams, not reality.

Live on Autopilot Is an Awful Choice

Living on autopilot, living by latency, and going a little crazy by routine can be entirely agreeable for the time being. It is simpler for the days to pass, and don't confront the dread of talking with your partner about what you feel. Or then again, it is less convoluted to go overboard by every day than to perceive that you are pitiful, correct? The planets will be adjusted to tackle your issues.

In any case, living a long way from the present, that is, with the breastplate on and without feeling anything, can be negative over the long haul, since when something occurs that shakes us (for instance, we get fired from work or our partner leaves us). At that point, the time has come to step on with feet on the ground. Furthermore, living in assumptions can make us enormously miserable.

Mindfulness, more than methods, is a way of thinking about life. Mindfulness practice is a way of thinking of life, a mentality that should be received to reconnect with oneself, in excess of a bunch of strategies to be right now. It is an adapting style that drives individual qualities, which serves to self-manage conduct and become more acquainted with one another better, as well as establishing a climate helpful for well-being.

As such, Full Attention is a conscious and deliberate approach to tune into what is happening inside us and around us and permits us to expose automatisms and advance the basic turn of events. A couple of moments daily isn't such a lot.

For certain individuals who live endlessly pushed, discovering 5 minutes per day to associate with oneself can be confounded. Be that as it may, contributing 10, 15, or 20 minutes every day for your own well-being isn't to such an extent. As of now referenced, the significant thing in the act of this control, paying little heed to the procedures used, is to embrace the Mindfulness disposition, which moves consideration right now, without judging, and with sympathy towards oneself and towards others.

Five Mindfulness Exercises for More Prominent Well-Being

1. Mindfulness in a Solitary Moment

This activity is ideal in the event that you are starting in Mindfulness practice; for what it's worth as you progress in learning mindfulness, it is ideal for expanding the training time until you reach around 15 or 20 minutes per day. What's more, since it is just a single moment, you can rehearse this activity anyplace and whenever of the day-by-day life.

2. Landing Breath at This Very Moment

This activity is ideal for killing the autopilot. In rehearsing it, the attention is on the current second and stops the steady progression of musings, memories, pictures, or thoughts. It is ideal for releasing the gathered voltage in an extremely straightforward manner.

It is important to focus into consideration on relaxing to complete this technique. A delicate, profound, and consistent motivation should be made through the nose. When loading up with air, promptly discharge the air through the mouth with power, however, without driving the throat. At the point when we notice an interruption (which is typical), we see what it is that grabbed our eye, and we got back to the breath once more.

3. Mindfulness Breakfast

It is normal to get up toward the beginning of the day with autopilot. You get up, scrub down, get dressed, eat, clean your teeth, and one more day at work. Indeed, one more day! You can end this negative propensity by performing Mindfulness in the first part of the day.

Subsequently, you will confront the day in an unexpected way. For this, it is fundamental that you sit in a peaceful spot and turn off the TV so you are quiet. You should likewise have the laptop away. It's about not having interruptions. At the point when you prepare for breakfast, attempt to concentrate on the flavors, the scents, the touch of food, or drink, feel them! Thusly, you will be with consideration right now, and you will see the distinction.

4. Thoughtfulness Regarding the Hints Existing Apart from Everything Else

This activity comprises of intentionally noticing the sounds that happen in our current circumstances. Along these lines, it is tied in with tuning in, hearing them as they sound without attempting to recognize them, passing judgment on them as charming or horrendous, or contemplating them. With no exertion, the sounds are noticed, and other outer insights are left to the side. While seeing an interruption, we see what's going on with everything that grabbed our eye, and we return again to tune in to the sounds, depending only on the breath of that second

Clearly, when tuning in to sounds that enter our ears, musings and feelings emerge identified with what we are hearing, so this activity attempts to know the quietness and the sound in a non-reasonable (without speculation) yet the experiential way (feeling them).

5. Body scanner

With this activity, we attempt to connect with the experience of our body, all things considered, without deciding, without dismissing horrendous sensations or adhering to charming ones. This activity is likewise called a body output or body check.

It is important to sit in an agreeable stance to do this, with your back straight, despite the fact that it is likewise conceivable to embrace the lying stance. At that point, close your eyes, focus on the breath, and make the excursion through the body. This sort of contemplation is prudent to be guided.

How Could Contemplation Help Us in Regular Daily Existence

Reflection is at its pinnacle, and many have started to appreciate all that contemplation can give consistently. Numerous investigations show its advantages for diminishing pressure, improving rest rhythms, decreasing cortisol levels, improving picking up, reinforcing memory, and, also, making life fuller and more conscious.

An illustration of this is an investigation led at the University of California Santa Barbara, which showed that with only a couple of a long time of contemplation, participant's consideration and memory improved during the thinking meeting in which a benchmark was applied around here.

Notwithstanding every one of the logical advances and studies committed to this space, there are still individuals who question or appear to be hesitant to begin this action. A portion of the fantasies encompassing these strategies is simply wide thoughts, however not certain. Then, we will perceive how reflection can help us in our day-by-day lives.

Advantages and Guidelines of Daily Meditation

Reflecting

It is simple. It could be somewhat more convoluted from the outset, so it will be simpler on the off chance that we let ourselves be guided and attempted to comprehend it as a fixation on the breath or quietly rehash a mantra to make the errand simpler.

The objective isn't to quiet the psyche. The objective is to discover quiet inside the contemplations. Change the focal point of consideration when different contemplations come. As you recognize less with your contemplations and stories, you feel more harmony and get open to additional opportunities, giving you more elbow room to make the most of your environmental factors each day.

In only a couple of training moments, you can get numerous advantages.

Logical tests show that with only two months, there are less nervousness, more settled, and spaces of the brain identified with memory, compassion, mindfulness, and stress guideline. Professionals additionally improve rest, fixation, lower circulatory strain, stress, and uneasiness, and improve invulnerable capacity. In 2011, Sara Lazar's examination group at Harvard University showed that mindfulness practice could change brain structure. Following the 8-week Mindfulness-Based Stress Decrease (MBSR) course, hippocampal thickening (a design that assumes a critical part in learning and memory), and different spaces of significance for guideline and Emotional preparing.

Contemplation assists us with being and staying. Pondering is reconnecting with your actual self, something contrary to getting away from the occasion. You need to give one minute of your time. Reflecting is a chance to stop, and with only a couple of minutes, you sort out and quiet your brain prior to making a move.

Wide Assortment of Ways

Meditation can be drilled diversely and in various positions. Standing, strolling, doing yoga, mindfulness, and so on, it is simply important to track down the best practice that suits everyone.

368

What occurs on the off chance that we feel that the psyche doesn't stop thinking? In a short time, we can arrive at 300 musings, a sum that immerses anybody's brain. Then again, used to working at max throttle, diminishing it takes practice and tolerance. Note the advantage. You need to depend on the interaction since it requires some investment. Appreciate the little advances and joys that reflection offers.

Discover the model that works for everyone. It's smarter to spend only 10 minutes than to last 30 since somebody said this is the correct one.

Reflection Is a Procedure for Everybody

A portion of the genuine advantages that reflection can fix in our day by day lives can be appreciated by following a couple of basic advances:

•   Try not to be challenging for yourself.

•   Have no assumptions; simply watch the occasion.

•   Try not to demand on the off chance that you don't arrive at internal quiet.

•   Stay alone, if conceivable, in a calm spot.

•   Step by step instructions to transform contemplation into your everyday schedule

Transforming reflection into your day-by-day schedule can be a convoluted test on the grounds that the essential time isn't generally accessible; however, whenever it is accomplished, the physical and psychological well-being benefits are quick.

The beneficial outcomes of contemplation go past the abstract and emotional. Logical tests have demonstrated its convenience to diminish the pressure and hurtful symptoms it causes in our bodies.

Stress makes the body produce significant degrees of cortisol, a chemical that unreasonably makes inflammatory cycles that cause muscle, migraine, chest torment, and stomach upset. Also, cortisol causes sleep deprivation, uneasiness, touchiness and diminishes sexual craving.

Chapter 20 - How Your Healthy Self Can Recover and Heal Your Eating Disorders

Treatment for voraciously consuming food needs proficient help and/or to put forth a concentrated effort help strategy. Experts who can help are a therapist, nutritionist, advisor, doctor, and trained professional. A therapist would help in diagnosing any basic mental issue that might be causing the issue or one that has been created because of the gorging issue. A nutritionist is expected to address any dietary inadequacies or uneven characters that came about because of the gorges.

In general, many people gorge on unhealthy foods, such as those high in sodium and sugar. The assistance of a nutritionist is enrolled to make the important dietary changes. An advisor would help sort through the feelings that reason the issue and manage the impacts on psychological wellness. A doctor is required to surrender an overall check and see any actual health issues that might be available because of gorging. This includes pulse checking, heftiness-related issues, organ damage, and so on. An expert on eating disorders and overeating is urgent in aiding an individual to roll out manageable improvements in life to keep the issue from repeating. Additionally, some portion of the cycle is in managing weight issues. There might be a need to lose a portion of the weight. This ought to be securely and under the careful checking of an expert.

The entirety of the experts referenced above is required for the effective treatment of voraciously consuming food. This is on the grounds that the issue not just influences one part of an individual's life and health. Working with every one of these experts tends to the entirety of the variables that add to the issue. That includes managing passionate triggers. Treatment likewise includes learning new and more compelling approaches to adapt.

Systems for Self-Help and Support

Despite what treatment is used to treat the issue, self-help assumes a vital part. An individual is possibly viably treated if there is a dynamic investment. The will, responsibility, and exertion to be freed of the overeating desires should come from the person. Really at that time will medicine and treatment approaches become compelling.

An individual ought to foster approaches to assist the self with controlling the gorges.

This problem is, in reality, totally different from different kinds of disorders or addictions. One cannot avoid food. One will consistently be enticed to return to overeating. Food is vital for living, and one cannot or should avoid it. Altogether, for effective treatment, one ought to foster better ways of dealing with stress and more inspirational perspectives towards food and practices around food. The key is to figure out how to meet nourishing necessities when eating and not tied in with addressing feelings or managing passionate contentions.

Self-Image

The initial step is to foster a positive self-picture. I love the body for what it is. Try not to get excessively influenced by cultural pressing factors and standards for size 0 dresses and stick-meager bodies. Each individual is extraordinary, and body shape, size, and weight all contrast. Acknowledge what one has and keep it healthy, as opposed to pursuing down some unthinkable standard for magnificence.

Here are a couple of tips to begin on cherishing the self, acknowledgment, and developing a self-picture:

Wear casual garments. The dressing should be a method for communicating one's thoughts and not a mission to adjust to cultural pressing factors and assumptions. Indeed, a ton of enthusiastic misery and stuff can be taken out once this idea is embraced. Have a positive outlook on the garments you wear. It ought to reflect how you feel and what your character is.

Quit getting on the scale. Avoid it. In the event that on weight observing, leave the weight checks to the experts. Try not to continue to step on that scale a few times a day. This will possibly purpose pain and disappointment when assumptions are not met. The attention ought to be on getting a healthier body, not on how much weight is lost.

Quit taking a gander at design magazines, TV, or motion pictures. These are infamous for propagating a culture fixated on thin bodies. Media sets a ridiculous standard of what magnificence ought to resemble and what body is awesome.

These are all dreams that nobody great, particularly one who battles with self-regard, self-perception, and eating disorders.

Cherish and spoil the body; what a better approach to show love and acknowledgment of one's body than to give it the best consideration and spoiling. Get another fragrance, go to a spa for a body rub, a facial, nail treatment/pedicure, or a straightforward hairstyle. This will help rethink the self. It is one acceptable approach to take a gander at the self from a viewpoint.

Be dynamic. Take part in exercise or interests that keep both the brain and the body dynamic. It very well may be selecting yoga classes, mastering another art or expertise, checking another book, going out with family or friends, go to the seashore, go trekking or climbing, and so forth. This assists an individual with finding abilities and capacities that can help support self-regard.

Offering Help to Others

Recovered food eaters or loved ones of a food eater can help by lending their assistance. They are usually the ones who notice the warning signs that their loved one is having an eating problem, such as the ones below:

•   Keep secret supplies of food in the most unreliable spots, particularly unhealthy shoddy food.

•   Discovering void food coverings and bundles yet not really seeing their cherished eat.

•   Cabinets and fridges routinely cleared out Grocery things or higher than expected bills.

Regularly, it is hard to tell when to step in and where to begin interceding. Here are a few hints on how to help somebody who has a gorging issue:

Empower talk

Expect the first run through defying an individual associated with a gorging issue to oppose, deny or make light of the issue. Try the following time again.

Discover freedoms to show that the practices are seen, and that one will listen carefully.

Urge to Look for Help

Remaining excessively well before seeing assistance can spoil more. Other illnesses are likely to be created because of gorging designs, such as heart problems and obesity. Urge your loved one to seek the help of a professional. Better yet, offer to go with them to the health specialist.

Stay Away from Guilt Outings Talks and Abuses

The individual with the eating issue is, as of now, experiencing blame, disgrace, and low self-regard. Try not to add to these negativities with all the negative talk, offending about the behavior, scrutinizing body weight or shape, and giving mean remarks about the eating propensities. These will not help by any means.

Set a Genuine Model

Get the individual with the eating problem to be healthier by going along with them in their excursion. Improve by eating better, as well.

The support is vital towards the way to recovery. Individuals in the victim's life can help in this objective or compound the issue. With the correct information, understanding, and resources, the problem can be successfully addressed.

All in all, what else does hypnotic gastric banding consider? On the off chance that you need to make your body a fat-consuming device, refined sugar should have stayed away from forestalling carbs like bread, sorts of pasta, and cake. Starch turns quickly into sugar. The body can store fat just if there is insulin and sugar in the body, just on the off chance that you have consumed carbs. The best method to make a slimmer body is, along these lines, to eat the food that nature has given to you; fit protein meat, fish, poultry, eggs, organic product, vegetables, and so forth. You don't have to restrict the sum in light of the fact that your body can not store fat except if there are carbs. A gastric band, accordingly, deters you from eating food varieties that consume fat and urges you to eat the same food sources that make your muscle to fat ratio. However, weight reduction quite often levels with a highly debilitating gastric band—Vanessa Feltz's gastric banding as of late detailed this issue.

Here's the affirmed answer. The hypnotic gastric band framework changes the size of your stomach yet additionally assists you with getting familiar with and appreciate healthier food. Hypnotic gastric banding is a healthier, long-haul, non-shifty decision. Changing your body genuinely cannot give you long-haul results, yet you can appreciate healthier choices by attending to the fundamental issue that caused overeating.

Chapter 21 - Meditation and Hypnosis

"Meditation is only hypnosis without an idea." Most trance specialists will disclose to you that.

And albeit this might be valid in a few (not very many) cases, tragically, this assessment is communicated on the grounds that it portrays just an exceptionally restricted part of meditation and doesn't consider the incredible number of types of meditation that exist. It additionally doesn't consider the real essence of most types of meditation.

To delineate this, I would propose that you consider the inconceivable number of guided meditations offered, sold, and advanced by different benefit and philanthropic associations. Obviously, to completely understand the ramifications, one needs to consider the creation of the greater part of these guided meditations, which contain some key components:

• For the most part, it intended to make an elective condition of cognizance.

• For the most part, they are planned with a particular life/meditation objective as a primary concern.

• These objectives are now and again even sought after as a representation if imagined.

• It tends to be overseen without help from anyone else or by another person or in a gathering setting with incredible achievement.

At the point when you check this plainly, there is quite often an objective to be sought after in guided meditations. It should likewise be perceived that objectives can't be accomplished without a proposition to push the expert the correct way. Obviously, there are different types of meditation in which the idea fundamentally assumes a subordinate part. Notwithstanding, it ought to be noticed that meditation without an objective is largely insignificant, and consequently, most types of meditation are rehearsed with a particular objective. And it isn't astonishing that there must likewise be a proposition in these.

Another illustration of this would be a straightforward meditation application for unwinding. (a genuinely normal practice). For this situation, and objective remaining parts.

"Unwinding." And albeit the idea is, for the most part, not passed on during the meditation, it is by and large pre-meditation ideas that are then executed during meditation and by and large with the ideal outcomes.

So it would not be exactly reasonable to diminish meditation to a pointless exercise in the definition. Obviously, this helps me to remember another perspective. Is there a contrast between Hypnosis and meditation? All things considered, they appear to have comparable essential properties. And assuming this is the case, what's the distinction if there, right?

Albeit the responses to these inquiries are fairly more perplexing, it ought to be noticed that while meditation may not be perceived now, meditation is a less formalized type of Hypnosis and is viewed as Hypnosis in many analogies, particularly when you take a gander at the qualities of normal meditation.

In the event that you take a gander at this similarity, you should realize that meditation ought to do exactly the same thing as Hypnosis. It likewise centers on making mental states where the psyche can be controlled to accomplish the objectives set. One thing to remember, in any case, is that this is by and large rehearsed in a significantly less proper setting and considerably more in an individual circumstance that is basically like self-hypnosis. Obviously, there are social scenes in which meditation is rehearsed, by and large, in a guided way. In any case, they actually hold comparative properties and, accordingly, can be just about as compelling as most types of Hypnosis rehearsed.

In light of this, it appears to be that there is essentially no qualification to be made in the definition aside from their use for health purposes.

1.   Hypnosis can be used remedially to control and control the patient's responses. This empowers immediate and quick versatile mental treatment in a controlled climate. This additionally offers specialists the chance to treat more extreme psychological sicknesses that meditation would not be reasonable for. This is accomplished through the making of outer control through Hypnosis that advances the safe mental mending of patients with real and genuine ailments. This additionally offers a genuinely straightforward option in contrast to meditation for the individuals who don't have the internal capacity and solidarity to the entrance/ruminate over themselves.

2.   Meditation can likewise be used as a restorative option; however, it requires more expert inward abilities.

Given the idea of meditation and the huge similitudes between meditation and Hypnosis, meditation can be used as effectively as most self-hypnosis methods and even some restorative uses like relapse and different structures. Progressed meditators are accessible from related hypnotherapy. An expert can accomplish results like that of hypnotherapy with meditation, for instance, when he says: "Help you quit smoking." However, with regards to more genuine dysfunctional behaviors, hypnotherapy is without a doubt more qualified to treating issues that may emerge, as the specialist is capable from an external perspective to control and ad-lib a meeting on a case-by-case basis.

In the event that I acknowledge this, I would propose that meditators are not reluctant to investigate their brains and capacities using meditation as a stage and to expand them to what exactly is generally viewed as self-hypnosis procedures. In the event that you do this cautiously, you can accomplish substantially more of your meditation in a lot more limited time. Particularly when procedures of the two sexual orientations are joined, when the emphasis is on inward limit instead of the customary hypnosis necessity for outer control. Applying this likewise offers you a novel chance to set your own hypnosis/meditation objectives, which is normally impractical with subliminal specialists as they, for the most part, need to choose what is best for you.

Obviously, there will consistently be space for outer hypnosis/meditation. In the event that the specialist can be trusted, it can likewise bring astounding advantages and may result fairly quicker than anticipated from endeavors to do it without anyone else's help.

Figuring out how to get thinner forever isn't, in every case, simple. Long after you arrive at your weight objective, you either need to keep up or hazard landing right where it began. There is something that numerous individuals disregard the worth of their possibilities. Your disposition and outlook can make a critical commitment to inspiration and achievement in the event that you need to realize how to get more fit forever, the first figure out how to appropriately handle the errand, and be intellectually ready for any deterrent that comes to your direction.

Consider your objectives and abilities. No, you will not sound insane when you talk with yourself. Here and there, it is useful to rehash what you need to do. On the off chance that you need to realize how to get thinner for all time, start with this straightforward procedure. Make a short expression that you can advise yourself. This ought to be done toward the beginning of the day or before bed (or perhaps both).

While attempting this procedure, remember that the words you say have an effect. Stay away from words like "I feel" or "I think" and stick to good and firm words like "I can" and "I will." You need to make a 100% good and certain message that you will impart to yourself. On the off chance that you figure out how to get more fit forever, you can say something like, "I will get in shape this week" or "I can arrive at my optimal weight."

Whenever you've tracked down a short, simple to-recall state that is totally sure, it's an ideal opportunity to try it. Rehash the request multiple times on set occasions (either before bed or when you awaken). Fourteen functions admirably on the grounds that there are enough reiterations to keep the idea in your mind, however insufficient to sound dull. The key is to say each word and not be kidding!

You don't need to glance in the mirror or anything; say the sentence orally so you can hear and say it simultaneously.

By figuring out how to get thinner forever, you are continually assisting with carrying out a scope of inspirational resources to guarantee a positive outcome. In the event that your psyche is in the perfect spot, your body will follow you. Attempt to consider something individual and substantial to help you to remember your objectives and endeavors. For instance, while you're busy working, you can purchase a tag. The intelligent sort of being used in houses functions admirably in light of the fact that they are bigger and more particular.

Pick the number that relates to the number of pounds you need to lose in seven days. It isn't prescribed to use stickers that demonstrate your objective load in the event that another person sees them. Spot the sticker where you can, without much of a stretch, discover it. These persuasive tips can assist you with getting in shape forever in the event that you experience the ill effects of Hypnosis or hypnotherapy so you can carry on with a better life!

In the event that you experience the ill effects of Hypnosis or hypnotherapy, you have most likely seen a new consideration that gastric band hypnosis methods have gotten.

The vast majority of you know about the gastric band, a medical procedure. Here, an inflatable silicone gadget is put around the highest point of the stomach to assist you with getting more fit. At the point when you place the band, a little pocket is made on the stomach.

This pack contains around a large portion of a cup of food. (The normal stomach contains around 6 cups of food). The sack rapidly loads up with food, and the belt eases back the section of food from the pack to the lower stomach. At the point when the upper piece of the stomach registers as full, it makes an impression on the mind that the whole stomach is full. This assists the individual with going hungry less regularly, feel full quicker and for a more extended period, eat more modest segments, and thus get more fit after some time.

Albeit this activity is more secure and less obtrusive than other comparable tasks, like stomach cramps, it is as yet not without chances. Likewise, the significantly related expenses are an expected obstruction for some individuals.

By offering another option, hypnotherapy can eliminate these hindrances. Rather than going through this activity, a clinical trance specialist can persuade his patient subliminal that he has gone through this system. They can lead you into a trance and guide you through the strategy as though it had occurred. On a conscious level, you will find that you have gotten hypnotherapy, however on an oblivious level, you will accept that you have had a medical procedure.

Chapter 22 - How to Stop Emotional Eating

People eat for various reasons. For you to stop emotional eating, you need to comprehend what triggers it. Comprehend what conditions, feelings, or spots trigger the enthusiastic hunger.

Energetic eating is by and large set off by adverse conclusions and, once in a while, by sure feelings, for example, repaying yourself for achievement.

Explanations Behind Enthusiastic Eating

• Stress, by far most, will overall eat when centered, and there is a substantial defense for it. Right when stress is progressing, critical degrees of cortisol, a pressing factor chemical, are conveyed. The cortisol gives you wants for sharp, sweet, and oily sustenances that will raise your energy and delight levels.

• **Boredom:** This happens when you are dormant and don't haveanything to do. You may eat to overcome the exhaustion. You feel empty and unfulfilled, so you eat to kill the exhaustion and get that vibe of fulfillment.

• **Childhood penchants:** You may review esteemed memories about food. A couple of parents use goodies to compensate kids for doing useful things; possibly your people remunerated you with a chocolate each time you got good grades. You may get the affinity from youth.

• **Social effects:** Eating with allies is a phenomenal technique to blend and have some happy occasions, yet it can incite overeating once in a while. It will be straightforward for you to glut when your colleagues enjoy also, or you will enjoy calming your nerves. In case family members or buddies ask you to humor, it's definitely not hard to do it.

• **Stuffing feelings:** Eating can be a technique for calming negative feelings you may have, as a shock, shame, sadness, harshness, and so forth. By focusing in on eating, you get to neglect to recall those feelings momentarily.

The Best Strategy to Control Enthusiastic Eating

One basic technique for doing this is by keeping an eating diary and an aura diary. Each time you comprehend you have eaten awful meals, record it. Later remember what feelings made you eat. As time passes by, you will have the alternative to perceive inclinations or, then again, feelings that made you enjoy food. At the point when you comprehend what triggers your enthusiastic eating, you can start going after how to stop it and discover more beneficial eating ways.

1. Discover Substitute Ways to Deal With Your Feelings

If you can't find another strategy for dealing with your feelings without including food, by then, it will be practically hard to stop this penchant. One explanation burns-through fewer calories crash and burn is because they offer wise food counsel tolerating that the primary concern protecting you from eating right is the shortfall of data. This simply kind of direction works if you can handle your dietary examples. Recognizing your triggers and understanding your cycle isn't adequate to control enthusiastic eating.

You need to find alternative strategies for dealing with your feelings. Right when engaged or forlorn, you can call or join with a partner that makes you feel much better, visit places you like, check an interesting book, watch a spoof show, or play with your pet.

2. Defer When Longings Come

This may not be just about as basic as it sounds since when the tendency for the food hits, it is all you may consider. You need to eat in that broad region and a short time later. Require at any rate 5 minutes before you give up to the craving; this offers you a chance to consider the vulnerable decision you will make. Inside that period, you can modify your viewpoint and make an unrivaled choice. On the off chance that 5 minutes is an incredible arrangement for you, start with 2 minutes and increase the time as you improve with it.

3. Sort Out Some Way to Recognize Extraordinary and Horrendous Feelings

Enthusiastic eating comes from not having the alternative to deal with your feelings on the head. Find a partner or a specialist with who you can check issues that you have. Having the choice to recognize dreadful and decent slants without including food will help you with making strides.

4. Take an Interest in Strong Lifestyle Tendencies

Exercise, rest, and enough sleep will simplify it for you to deal with any issue that you may encounter, whether enthusiastic or physical. Set aside a few minutes for a 30 minutes practice on any occasion five days of the week, loosen up, and get rest of 7 to 8 hours reliably. It is moreover basic to circle yourself with positive people who will motivate you and help you with dealing with your issues.

Simple and Rapid Weight Loss Ideas

Need some clear and quick weight decrease considerations that you can use to change your body completely? Getting fit as a fiddle speedy is an authoritative goal of practically every single person who is centered on eating less shoddy nourishment.

What you look like impacts your certainty and how others see you; having excess weight can cause distress and prosperity risks, so it is fundamental to get alive and well, as of now. At whatever point you have experienced weight decrease, you will see a giant number of positive changes in your everyday presence; you'll have more sureness and have the alternative to continue with life to its fullest.

Independientemente de las ideas de disminución de peso rápido que utilice, comprenda que el movimiento y la rutina de alimentación modificada son las dos claves más grandes para la reducción de la grasa y el peso. La mayoría de nosotros entendemos que si comemos un número más notable de calorías de las que debemos, vamos a aumentar la grasa. Hay innumerables artículos por ahí que están preparados para hacer la diferencia y lograr más esbeltez, sin embargo, muchos están confundidos, y las consideraciones ofrecidas son difíciles de ejecutar. El objetivo de este texto es darle algunas consideraciones claras de disminución de peso rápido que puede entrelazar en su estilo de vida ordinario con eficacia, ayudándole a ser más delgado sin el trastorno.

These six fundamental and quick weight loss thoughts will have you losing more pounds faster than you ever suspected possible; all it takes is a little work! So how about we get started?.

1. Go Food Shopping After You Have Eaten

Exactly when you visit the market on an empty stomach, you will be tempted to buy an over-the-top measure of food; a considerable amount of this will be trash-type food which fixes our hunger however offer close to zero dietary advantages.

2. Don't Wander Out From Home Hungry

Exactly when you leave your home "hungry," you are increasing the load; we recently referred to in the first of our quick weight decrease musings that yearning can coordinate your food choices. Have a light snack, for example, a touch of a natural item or some cut fruits or veggies before eating out at the bistro; you'll not be as inclined to be tempted by the most stuffing banquet, and chances are you'll evade the treat menu.

3. When Eating Out Stay Away From the Dressings and Sauces

Maybe have them as an idea in retrospect. Dressings and sauces stacked over servings of blended greens or vegetables can cause a strong dinner to be changed into a disturbing one. A huge part of these sauces and dressings contain a great proportion of calories hampering your weight decrease tries. If you ought to have a dressing with your plate of blended greens, demand a low-fat one or far superior requesting your sauces and low-calorie dressings as an untimely idea.

4. Drink Six to Eight Glasses of Water a Day

Water is so basically critical for weight decrease. I am extremely astounded that most calorie counters disregard drinking enough, dismissing the forward of our fat weight decrease contemplations. Water makes you digest food and flushes out harms. When you drink more, you will truly diminish fluid upkeep, preventing that puffed-out, broadened look.

5. You Don't Have to Finish Everything on Your Plate

Despite what your mother may have told you, you don't help the desperate masses by finishing everything on your plate at eating times. This kind of mindset is enormously negative to weight decrease. Eat until you are full and subsequently stop.

6. Take Your Involvement in Your Food

Do whatever it takes not to hustle through your dinners; your brain needs an ideal chance to select that your body is full. This can require as long as 20 minutes to loosen up, take as much time as it is required, and capitalize on your food.

Well, the writing is on the wall; 6 essential and speedy weight decrease considerations to help you with changing your shape. If you are captivating in getting more from your weight decrease plans, I propose you visit Extreme Weight Loss which includes a whole host of speedy weight decrease considerations, exercise routines, and food counsel, all totally free! Change your affinities and change your body. Good luck.

How to shed pounds safely with self-hypnosis? So would you say you are unglued to lose excess weight? Fortunately, there is a way for you to fall into shape without encountering the difficulty and troubles it may cause through oneself hypnotizing weight decrease methodology. Selfentrancing weight decrease is the ideal reaction for any individual who needs to shed those two or three pounds quickly and with no issue.

You, as of now, have a bit of the quick weight decrease considerations to help you with changing your body, yet stop there's extra! Track down the hid fat adversity advantaged bits of knowledge that the top health specialists need to put something aside for themselves by visiting Fat Burning Tips.

Chapter 23 - Hypnosis and the Power of the Mind

Hypnosis is an absolutely regular expression that empowers direct admittance to the psyche mind, where our example-making frameworks of learned conduct dwell. With hypnosis, then, in our completely conscious state, we can sidestep what a delayed or roaming re-learning project would require.

There is no actual interruption; it is essentially a difference in mental mindfulness that is self-considered. Hypnosis is, in this way, a falsely improved condition of suggestibility that looks like rest. It's not resting, nonetheless.

While there is no unmistakable "awareness" definition, one idea is that the ordinary condition of cognizance of an individual is the one wherein the person burns through the greater part of their waking hours. An adjusted condition of mindfulness is one in which the individual plainly feels a subjective change in their psychological working example.

With three special cases, the condition of hypnosis is indistinguishable from the condition of full awareness:

• The fixation will be completely engaged (without the typical thinking interruptions, waking conscious mode)

• They will loosen up each muscle

• The keenness of the faculties, hearing, contact, and smell is improved.

As hypnosis is an absolutely characteristic expression, the subject won't be abandoned to a ceaseless trance by an abrupt withdrawal of the trance specialist. All things being equal, the mindful subject will be either so shocked by the subliminal specialist's vanishing as to be enticed to open their eyes and convert to ordinary cognizance, or, alternately, to appreciate a quiet rest from which they will normally stir.

Significantly, the customer is in charge, and the trance inducer can't think or do anything against the desire of the subject.

Using Hypnosis to Transform Your Mind

Master keys are intended to open various locks; they are an all-inclusive instrument here and there, on the off chance that just there was a gadget like that to help us open our minds; it is called hypnosis. Luckily, there is one! A typical condition of insight that is protected, effortless, and powerfully adaptable in therapeutic systems (hypnotherapy) in actuating mental, passionate, and even actual improvement, for example, an expert key for the mind.

Here's the reason you should attempt hypnosis today. The recorded use of hypnosis as a tool for change and healing dates back more than 7000 years.

Hypnotherapy has since ebbed and streamed in prevalence, here and there thriving, nearly vanishing now and again, however continually getting by across societies, geologies, innovations, and time itself, and for an extremely basic explanation; it works!

Today, hypnotherapy is resurgent again. The logical premise through which the brain creates and profits by mesmerizing trance is uncovered by specialists and experts around the world, subsequently removing hypnosis and hypnotherapy from the elusive and otherworldly domain and into the standard of current medical care and health.

Breaking the Myths

Hypnosis "consistently brings out dreams of consuming eyes, swinging watches, goofy stage-show tricks, helpless plot-lines in terrible movies, the apparition of blacking out and being constrained to act without wanting to, being caught in a zombie-like netherworld, or in any event, getting moved by Satan himself, in spite of the advanced science, however, for some."

Luckily, all the old and total babble of these ideas is quickly surrendering to current science's chilly, hard rationale. The facts confirm that without wanting to, nobody can enter hypnosis, and they can't lose their mind's control or stall out or be moved by.

The entire reason for hypnotherapy, unexpectedly, is to help customer's increment power over both their mind and body and along these lines their lives likewise.

We Are All Hypnotized Every Day

A few groups are stunned to find that the entire life, essentially, we all go through hypnosis without anyone else. At whatever point you get into a pleasant novel, "daydream" or dream, find yourself crashing into your carport, then don't remember arriving, or seeing a film or TV show that makes you giggle or sob, you're most likely in hypnosis!

There is by all accounts a significant qualification, obviously, between daydreaming on the thruway and rising above a daily existence restricting emergency. However, it's simply a nebulous vision.

Since hypnosis is basically a perspective that may emerge by a guide (the trance specialist) or through one's own (self-hypnosis) unexpectedly or set off through reason, similar to an expert key, the impact is more about the lock it is used on.

Attempt a Little Self Hypnosis Right Now

Need to check hypnosis out? In the security of your own home, here's the way to spellbind yourself.

1.   Seat unobtrusively in a situation without unsettling influences or commotion, inside or outside.

2.   Close and totally loosen up the eyes; cause the covers to feel so weighty that they won't open.

3.   Presently, with your jaw, do likewise. As though the bones and muscles are gelatin, let it fall.

4.   Loosen up the neck and shoulders, then arms and hands, middle, butt, upper and lower legs, and feet gradually, delicately, and consistently by first straining and then completely loosening up the pressure in the muscles of each field.

5.   To begin with, focus your mind on your eyes once more. Gaze softly upward to within your eyebrow and breathe in; when you discharge your breath, say basically, "Absolutely quiet, profound rest." You're in gentle hypnosis. That's it.

6.   Count1, 2, 3, 4, 5 open arms, wide alert to come out

You're here. Congrats, you've recently been mesmerized.

Profound Sleep and How It Works

Entering hypnosis implies participating in and fostering a neural "sidestep" to homeostasis, our inherent and often persistent abhorrence for change and the obscure, both the conscious psychological and subliminally programmed segments of the mind.

However long they are as per our desires, we arrive at a condition of changed yet insightful cognizance almost like reflection, strongly focused, available, and flawlessly touchy to new discernments, ideas, activities, and feelings, both mental and physical.

The conscious and subliminal minds play out a sort of neuronal gathering meeting with homeostasis essentially "killed," another "strategy" is formed, talked about, and approved, and then, with adequate consolation, normally an assortment of meetings combined with straightforward, ordinary exercises, the brain viably reinvents itself.

Thus, both synaptic pliancy the limit of our brain to rework itself-and the strength and energy of the mind/body dynamic are purposely mishandled and controlled.

The Most Effective Method to Use Hypnosis in Your Life

However, why put effort into hypnosis? The future applications of therapeutic hypnosis are most varied. An incomplete summary includes:

• Undesirable/unfortunate propensities are settled (e.g., smoking, nail-gnawing).

• Change propensities for activities and feelings.

• Overcome fears and doubts.

• Developing trust in yourself and confidence.

• Improve consideration, accentuation, and profitability in games, instruction, or at work.

• For clinical/dental problems and persistent agony, absence of pain, and anesthesia.

• Limit harm to organs, absence of blood, and improving recuperation from dental and surgeries.

• Facilitate the symptoms of radiation therapy and chemotherapy.

• Oversee (here and there disposing of) various conditions like headache, IBS, unsettling resistant influences, asthma, sensitivity, sexual brokenness, and a lot more that are ordinarily hard to treat.

The Takeaway

There are, obviously, restrictions to the viability of hypnotherapy, like any instrument or system, anyway adaptable. A few people and circumstances don't react, and it is certainly not wizardry, but instead, it might act so effectively that it can sound that way. Genuine desire, the capacity to go through initiated hypnosis, trust in a useful result, and devotion to the therapy cycle are fundamental for progress.

Obviously, these conditions seem, by all accounts, to be a little cost to pay for the large numbers that profit from a theoretically extraordinary result, feeling aroused and carrying on with life the manner in which they need as opposed to feeling caught and powerless about their issues. It's an awesome method to feel, and it's something that we as a whole have the right to do. Today, try hypnosis and transform yourself.

Reinventing Your Mind Through Hypnosis

Figure out how by taking advantage of profound cognizance and getting to the covered up, 95 percent of your mind, to change your life. Find out about reasonable and motivating strategies for genuine change and enduring impacts to reinvent your mind.

By tuning into your psyche mind, follow this free and clever workshop to figure out how to change yourself.

For concrete, long haul results, set up sped up change and accomplish more prominent satisfaction. Hypnotherapy empowers you to develop an existence of fortitude and self-realization, from arriving at individual objectives and settling self-harm to mental assistance and recuperating from injuries.

Enter the leading group of authorized clinical hypnotherapist Shivam Ray and gain proficiency with the psyche mind's secrets. Find how our day-by-day encounters and the "scripts" for our lives are made by the "programming" of the psyche mind and how to change this programming to change you completely. Find the psyche mind's mysterious power, which is multiple times more powerful than the conscious mind. From past lives and in utero encounters, the psyche mind holds every one of the mysteries for a total change to achieve valid and enduring results.

- The lingo of the psyche mind, how your inner mind thinking can be found and re-composed

- How the psyche mind directs our considerations, ideas, and activities

- Self-harm, compulsory mind versus conscious mind

- Rehashing life propensities are framed by past injuries and natural feelings

- Synthetic Evidence. Regeneration by the Mind the body

- How covered-up musings (ailments and infections) are sent in the body

- Past and future between daily routine experiences; how the current life is affected

- How your excursion produces life in utero encounters and memories

Chapter 24 - Keep as Fit as You Think You Are for Weight Loss

For a great number of people, nonetheless, this is the place where we measure. It is additionally regularly the last where weight is taken out, also, despite the fact that perhaps nature implied that we were in any event to some degree pear-formed.

You would need to take a gander at a reach that had a sizable amount of hips and thighs for each model; the look that most ladies need today is exquisite bends, restricted base, and level stomach. Not many of us love the idea despite the fact that it ought to be female. However, in case you're swelling and overweight where you'd prefer to be level, don't be miserable. Coming up next are tips for raising your weight loss fat and thinning your thighs.

•   Ensure your eating routine is low in fat. In the wake of warnings to burn less fat in the course of recent years, a large portion of us actually overeats, basically on the basis that it is a high-calorie food and pleasure.

•   As grown-ups, just about 20% of our food consumption needs to come from fat, so abundances are as yet kept beneath the midsection for ladies in any event. This is on the grounds that the female estrogen chemical exchanges the chemical, while fat has all the earmarks of being put away in the center of the body.

•   Scale back espresso and tea. Caffeine, a profoundly addictive drug, puts additional weight on the kidneys, and they can't purify the body appropriately. The outcome is that waste containing water, otherwise called cellulite, stays in fat cells.

• Also, fat cells in hips and thighs are twice as extensive as those somewhere else; they swell up for additional. Look for two cups of tea or some espresso daily; drink morning ideally. Others attempt natural teas. Liquor, for the most part, adds calories and brings fat.

• Drink a lot of water to flush out toxins. Numerous individuals consider plain water so unpleasant to drink that they prefer to forget it; however, in the event that you add it into your ordinary everyday practice, it turns into a propensity. Get six to eight glasses of water to drink regularly. Frequently take a glass of water before sleep time.

• Stop the dairy items you can. You needn't bother with them as they're tacky, thick, bodily fluid forming, hindering your framework. Just babies need milk. Additionally, a ton of current dairy and poultry created is loaded down with antimicrobials and chemicals to forestall diseases. What's useful for creatures can't be useful for people, so it's difficult for our bodies to dispose of trash.

• Cut weight loss on sugar as much as possible. Some sugar is without a supplement. For pleasantness, use brown sugar or natural nectar. Eliminate chocolate and afterward take more organic products.

• Eat high-fiber food sources. The most recent test has shown that one weight-loss approach is to amplify fiber consumption. The impact is around 150 additional calories daily lost from increased stool size.

• It is likewise seen more weight loss when high fiber food contains peas, entire bread, brown rice, entire potatoes, green vegetables, and organic products. On the off chance that you can deal with it, seven days in length high-crude eating regimen of new products of the soil vegetables can drive your lymphatic frameworks quickly.

• Keep up with the times. Office staffs are more at risk than at any time in recent history, as working word processors consume far less power than old-school typewriters. Start moving past the workplace like clockwork. Start balancing your knees with your elbows. On the off chance it is possible, put some telephone guides under your feet and practice deep breathing, and it makes a difference. This will help keep the body new and safe, too.

• Fitness strolling, which seems to supplant running, will manage knees, particularly in the event that you can do it quickly enough. You need to walk 4 to 5 miles an hour to consume off any considerable fat. Yet, 15 to 30 minutes daily would likewise yield positive outcomes.

• Numerous exercise centers have hip-conditioners. Machines where you place a weight inside your leg, at that point give moving it a shot. You'll take note of the distinction in the event that you keep up the effort. From the start, it's a persistent effort, yet gradually, when you use the instrument, you'll feel muscles unwinding.

Solid Habits for Fast Weight Loss in a Matter of Days

On the off chance that you need to shed pounds fast, you will try not to look for codes, wizardry deceives, or wonderful pills. Any fitness or diet master will reveal to you that you need great weight loss propensities.

In the event that you need to shed 10 pounds or 50, it's tied in with being lean, however keeping the additional weight off for great. Furthermore, this can possibly happen when you're prepared to live securely. Here are six stages to better your wellbeing and get in good shape.

- To get lean, you need to get typical, which means adding more leafy foods to your eating routine. New vegetables and natural products are plentiful in complex sugars and micronutrients, including nutrients and minerals.

- Most prominently, they are low-calorie and fiber-rich. For all the sustenance in a total serving of organic products or vegetables, you'll stay full more and be more averse to over-eat. The outcome: your calorie admission will decrease, and you're progressing nicely for weight loss.

- Consider adding additional natural products or vegetables to your #1 dinners like grain breakfast, pasta, or prepares. You may likewise have some steamed vegetables with dinner or pastry new organic product salad.

- Begin going literally. That is the thing that you need to never really get thinner. Regardless of whether you're going cycling with friends, using your bicycle to travel regularly, or adding an energetic stroll into your everyday practice, some form of cardiovascular exercise is vital to getting thin.

- For a sound eating regimen, you'll have the option to diminish calories and increase your digestion a couple of focuses, however for fast weight loss, you need a drastic lift in the calories you consume each day, which can just come through a high-impact workout.

- For nothing else, it includes greater development in your regular day-to-day existence, like using the stairwell, leaving your vehicle farther away from your objective, and hanging tight for orders.

Get Rid of Sugar

Eliminate prepared food sources you may have dependent on is easier said than done, yet it's an indispensable advance in case you're not kidding about getting great weight loss propensities.

Try not to surrender your number one treats altogether. These switches are ordinarily not durable. All things being equal, think about decreasing bits of handled food sources in every dinner and supplant them with a more adjusted food choice; on the off chance that lunch tomorrow is a burger dinner, substitute soft drink with a decent homemade banana smoothie.

Get Stronger

It is perceived muscles consume a larger number of calories than fat. In this way, the more slender muscle you acquire, the higher your digestion will be, and with a better capacity to burn calories, you will improve.

Take a stab at incorporating two 15-30-minute strength instructional meetings into your week-by-week plan. Your body shape will likewise change once your muscles are conditioned, and you'll feel better, more remarkable, and hotter.

You don't actually have to perspire in an exercise center, however. There are some strength practices you can perform in your own front room, use your own body weight (squats, leg raises, pushups, seat plunges, and so forth). With these four safe weight loss rehearses, you can get thinner easily and hold it off for great.

Fruitful Weight Loss With Hypnosis

Hypnosis can be a compelling weight-loss gadget, especially when joined with a good dieting plan and exercise. A great many people have worries about using hypnosis in light of various legends in papers, motion pictures, and Stage Hypnosis.

While investigating specific benefits and uses of hypnosis for weight loss, how about we address basic hypnosis issues that the normal individual has.

Hypnosis is a sound, tried strategy used for centuries. It's a tranced state or adjusted condition of awareness, similar to some other trance state you experience regularly. Indeed, regular, we are holding nothing back and out of trance states. Staring off into space's a light trance. A more profound trance state happens just before rest when one's exceptionally loose.

Hypnotic specialists make a tranced state by aiding the customer to quiet the body and conscious brain and direct concentration toward the psyche mind. It assists us with going to the base of issues and make upgrades further. Others feel hefty in the body during Hypnosis; others report feeling lighter.

What's most ordinary is feeling exceptionally quiet, cheerful, and relaxed. In the event that an individual isn't oblivious in a Hypnosis state, they can open their eyes whenever.

While with a more profound trance, sounds are more inaccessible, an individual might be aware of commotions outside and inside the room.

One of the points of entrancing is to bypass the conscious psyche while cooperating with the more profound piece of the brain, the psyche mind. At the point when the body is comfortable, the psyche mind turns out to be more open to ideas.

For what reason is the psyche mind not the same as the conscious brain? The conscious psyche works while we're alert and aware of our environmental factors. It's likewise our savvy person, chatting part. The psyche mind contains nothing of our current cognizance. This may include early ideologies, memories, and abilities that are not needed in conscious awareness. It's the place where our dreams come from.

The entire lives, we are holding nothing back and out of trance states, so it's characteristic and typical for us. Frequently a man doesn't enter an entrancing state in light of the fact that there is inadequate certainty and connection between the customer and trance specialist.

A beneficial contention is that a man isn't "spellbound." The client chooses to acknowledge or deny the hypnotherapist's recommendation, remaining totally in control. While an individual is more open to ideas in an entrancing state, they can't be constrained to do whatever is in opposition to their good or moral code. Stage hypnotic specialists have done a lot to advance a customer's appearance of force.

The people who participate are purposely chosen by the hypnotherapist as consistent, agreeable, or extroverted. Subjects understand that they are in front of an audience for amusement and are probably not going to "ruin the arrangement." Although stage trance specialists use entrancing strategies, and numerous members are in trance express, the control factor is a deception.

The primary concern is that when you're in a condition of Hypnosis, it's not possible for anyone to cause you to do anything incorrectly for you. Please acknowledge or deny any ideas.

Chapter 25 - Losing Weight With Hypnotic Gastric Band

Presently, the entirety of this may sound extraordinarily convincing. In any case, it is simply going to occur in the event that you really work to lose the weight, and you really need to. It appears to be an awesome choice for the vast majority, yet actually, you need to comprehend that it will, in any case, require work and upkeep. In the event that you decide to use gastric band hypnosis, you are focusing on guaranteeing that your brain and body are better only because of the way that you will be changing your attitude and the relationship with the food that you burn through. Will it work for you?

The appropriate response is a resonating possibly—yet in the event that you are submitted, it will.

Within this part, we will take a gander at whatever it will take for you to sort out some way to get thinner with gastric band hypnosis. It is something that you should do cautiously and purposely, and you should set aside the effort to really attempt to make it work for you. Yet, in the event that you understand what you are doing, you can guarantee that, at last, you can and will get to that mark of progress.

We will initially go over what you can expect with the experience that you will have. This will help you realize what will occur throughout this book and how you can get past everything. At that point, we will go over the adequacy of gastric band hypnosis and why and how it can get those impacts that you need. At last, we will investigate a portion of the manners

409

in which you can anticipate that gastric band hypnosis should prompt weight loss.

What's in Store With Gastric Band Hypnosis

In the event that you are seeing a subliminal specialist, you can anticipate that your process should go pretty correspondingly. You will have a few meetings with a hypnotist who will help direct you on your excursion and to assist you with getting whatever it is that you desire to accomplish. You will find that your advisor is there to help you. The person in question will help by becoming acquainted with your past endeavors to get thinner.

Try not to feel excessively alarmed or awkward in the event that you are posed a few inquiries that you would consider to be intrusive or meddling—your advisor needs to ensure that they are on the correct page to guarantee that you are really getting the treatment that you need. They need to think about your past disappointments, so they can ensure that you succeed this time around.

Your specialist will assist you with sorting out how best to treat your weight gain with the goal that you can begin losing weight. The actual strategy is intended to cause you to feel like you really got the treatment. On the off chance that you go to a hypnotic specialist, they may go over all that occurs in an ordinary medical procedure. They may request that you go to a genuine working room, getting ready as you typically would. You will go through everything, bit by bit, and the specialist will gradually spellbind you. You will be talked into that condition of unwinding, and once there, the advisor will depict the cycle of the whole activity, bit by bit, from being put under to making cuts, fitting the band, and fixing the injury. You will be portrayed while being presented to the ordinary sounds and fragrances of the working room, assisting with promoting convince your subliminal that you are there, and it is going on.

Simultaneously, the specialist is probably going to examine self-assurance boosting minutes too and will work with you to find yourself mixed up with that condition of unwinding. Once there, you will actually want to quiet down and unwind. They may likewise show you some self-hypnosis methods that you can use at home too to guarantee that you can stay aware of your weight loss.

After the treatment, you should feel quiet. You ought not to feel any torment or distress—simply that condition of unwinding that you were in during the hypnosis.

The expectation is that through this interaction, you will begin to feel fuller sooner when you are eating, permitting the treatment to work for you. For the individuals who indulge, it very well may be hard to perceive when you are genuinely full, or on the off chance that you are a solace eater or a fatigue eater, you might be eating, paying little mind to the actual craving level. Notwithstanding, in any case, figuring out how to perceive the impressions of craving and completion should occur, and that is something that requires some serious energy. You will be urged to eat carefully and purposely as you do—this is to ideally make that feeling of realizing how your body reacts to the food that you eat and when your body is in reality full.

Know if It Will Work

Obviously, this carries us to the following question—is gastric band hypnosis appropriate for you? Numerous individuals trust that this will be the sorcery arrangement that they can use that will assist them with flourishing—they trust that they will actually want to appreciate this treatment and mysteriously be fit for losing their weight, yet the appropriate response is, it is dependent upon you. While hypnotherapy can help a ton of issues, it possibly works on the off chance that you effectively need to change your propensities. It is incredible for fixing issues identified with gorging, for example, feeling like it is decent enthusiastic support that you can use when you are pushed, blameworthy, or in any case, feeling adverse.

In any case, over the long run, you can work with how you deal with yourself, and you will actually want to take that responsibility that you required.

Remember that gastric band hypnosis is a promise to losing weight. Very much like some other responsibility, it will require significant investment and exertion. It will be troublesome on occasions, and that is OK. At last, it will be your level of responsibility that will guarantee that you are in good shape and prepared to make things work for you effectively. You will simply be prepared to submit however much you can. What would you be able to advise yourself to assist you with feeling like you can do this? At last, it will require a level of self-assurance.

This will possibly work for you on the off chance that you are willing and capable. In the event that you put stock in the treatment interaction and you trust in the hypnosis that you get, you will be bound to effectively get past your treatment and see those outcomes that you are searching for. You should approach with a receptive outlook to get that additional impact that you are searching for. At the point when you do this, you are bound to roll out those improvements that you need. You will be bound to genuinely assimilate whatever your subliminal specialist has said to you in the event that you put stock in them and the interaction. This is the reason it is a smart thought to explore the advisors around there in the event that you go down the conventional way; you will need to ensure that you can produce that affinity that you need with them, and that implies having the option to feel greater with individuals that you are near.

Eventually, in the event that you are somebody who is committed and able to keep a receptive outlook, this type of hypnosis is amazingly incredible and can truly assist with rolling out those improvements that you need or need to see. On the off chance that you have confidence all the while and you have that level of trust with your advisor, you are substantially more prone to retain the messages that you need and start the positive changes to your way of life that hypnosis will empower. It is just when you begin to receive those responses to what exactly will be reasonable that you begin to perceive what the correct answer is. Keep in mind, regardless of whether this isn't the choice for you; there is a decent possibility that there is an alternative out there for you.

How Gastric Band Hypnosis Leads to Weight Loss

Gastric band hypnosis works since it is a way that you will actually want to make that weight loss that you need. As we've set up, you need to have the correct outlook to get the correct outcomes. For what reason may you inquire? Straightforward, our outlook is everything. The considerations that we have affected our activities, and thus, even the most oblivious musings become a portion of our most exceedingly awful adversaries some of the time. Perhaps you have an idea that you are not sufficient, for instance—that sort of thought would straightforwardly and effectively damage all that you are attempting to work for.

At the point when you think contrarily, you feel terrible. At the point when you feel awful, you may fall into propensities for awful eating that could be immensely tricky for you. We as a whole have ways that we handle pressure and antagonism, regardless of whether it is through indulging, messing around, dawdling, smoking, drinking, or whatever else. A few groups foster better strategies for dealing with their pressure, like working out.

What is your way of dealing with stress when things get unpleasant? After a battle with your accomplice, do you rush to the refrigerator for the container of frozen yogurt and a jug of wine? Provided that this is true, you may end up battling with your weight in a little while. These are detrimental routines that are normally imbued in your psyche and may have even come from how you were brought up as a kid. What's the significance here for you? It implies that you should track down another approach to abrogate those negative routines to fix the issue.

On the off chance that you are a pressure eater, next to no will help you keep the weight off in the event that you are continually going after the frozen yogurt and treats following a monotonous day.

There is an excellent possibility that someplace within you, you have that propensity included in your oblivious brain, implying that the solitary way that you can fix the issue for yourself is to beat those detrimental routines. This is the means by which hypnosis will assist you with losing weight—it will work with you to guarantee that as you go, you will actually want to sort out how it is that you can deal with fix those detrimental routines.

Hypnotherapy works by revamping those propensities that you need to make choices. Rather than going after the frozen yogurt when you are pushed, for instance, you could decide to go exercise, all things considered. Through all-around made hypnotherapy, you could essentially urge yourself to sort out how you can deal with improving the circumstance. You could decide to purposefully pick better food varieties to eat rather than the bad ones. Or then again, you could decide to eat with some restraint as opposed to whatever else. There are so numerous ways that you can work with yourself to up your feelings and responses.

Chapter 26 - Hypnosis for Healthier Mindset Script

Welcome to this hypnosis script for the improvement of a healthier psyche.

This hypnosis script is proposed to be used at home and not while driving or doing whatever else that may require your entire consideration. As you tune in to this script, you will be tenderly hushed into a condition of unwinding and have your psyche delicately moved toward the objectives that will assist you with bettering yourself.

Recall that this script will possibly work if your psyche is open and on the off chance that you are willing and open to the messages that are being given to you. Accomplishment in the present circumstance is completely reliant upon you and what you are doing. Yet, the achievement is conceivable as long as you are willing. To start, you should ensure that you are in the correct mindset, the correct area, and you are prepared to tune in. On the off chance that you are prepared now, if it's not too much trouble, continue!

Start by getting yourself comfortable any place you plan to tune in to this script. Ensure that you needn't bother with anything and that you are someplace that is quiet and faintly lit, so you are not intruded. If it's not too much trouble, turn your telephone off or silence the ringer and ensure that you have no interruptions around you. At the point when you are comfortable and loose, and you're prepared to begin, take a full breath, and how about we start!

Take in a decent, full breath. Feel it enter through your nose and let it escape through your lips. As you inhale, you feel calm. You feel focused and quiet. You felt empowered and prepared to get past your day. You take in and out once more. You take in and out. As you do this, you feel yourself settling down. You feel yourself feeling quieter. You feel yourself settling down in your spot.

Take in and feel the entirety of your pressure moving through your body. As you breathe in, imagine that you are holding the entirety of the strain in your lungs. At that point, inhale out. Breathe out and feel the pressure begin to scatter around you. Release everything. Rehash this and once more. With each full breath that you take, you feel like your strain is scattering away from you. You feel significantly more substance in yourself.

Take in and inhale out once more. Furthermore, once more. You feel totally loose. You have never felt this loose. You close your eyes. Furthermore, when you open them once more, you are someplace new.

You are standing outside of a house. The house appears as though it would be more pleasant on the off chance that it was dealt with. The old, white paint is stripping off of it, and it would appear that it's unquestionably seen some more promising times. As you approach the house, you notice that the weeds haven't been pulled, and the grass has been permitted to grow interminably.

There are cobwebs and leaves all over the place. You're almost certain nobody at any point deals with the house.

Yet, you feel strangely attracted to it. You need to realize what is inside. You gradually open up the entryway, looking inside. Nobody is there.

There is nobody around anyplace, and you are almost certain that the house is vacant beside you. The house is empty. It is a major room with nothing in it, and the isolated spot to go is down a flight of stairs. You take a gander at the flight of stairs and feel like you need to go down. Something inside yourself is pushing you to stroll down the steps, and you begin going. You make one stride, at that point one more and again. You continue driving yourself to stroll down the steps.

You venture out. You feel your apprehension and dread dissolving away from you. You leave it there. You require the subsequent advance. You feel smoothness surrounding you. As you walk, you feel like you are comfortable where you are.

You make the third stride. You feel looser. You are at home where you are. Something about the space you are in feels recognizable.

You make the fourth stride. It's hazier; however, that is ok.

You make the fifth stride. Somewhere far off, you can see that there is a weak blue gleam toward the finish of the steps.

You make the 6th stride. You can hear the buzzing of PCs surrounding you.

You make the seventh stride. You are exceptionally loose. You feel great where you are.

You make the eighth stride. You feel prepared to perceive what is ground floor.

As you venture into the room, you see that there is a book there. The book is on a platform, and there are screens on the dividers. The screens show a wide range of various numbers, and they show you a lot of information. They likewise show you the perspective on the room around you. You can see that the data is recorded with information, for example, "Calories," and has an advancement bar on it.

There are progress bars for a wide range of various wholesome realities. There is one for fat and one for sugar, and one for pretty much everything identified with the food that you burn through. It is there to help you track the amount you eat.

You can see that the calories bar is full. It is blazing red and showing a number and message: "143% everyday suggestion burned-through." As you take a gander at the words across the screen, you understand what you are taking a gander at. You are taking a gander at something that is showing the food that you have burned through. It is showing you how much or how little of each piece of your day-by-day admission you've consumed. You can see that you have effectively eaten more than you ought to have. On the screens, you can check that there are issues with the food sources that you have eaten. Nothing seems, by all accounts, to be aligned, and you can see that the yearning measure on your screen additionally shows outrageous craving. They aren't exactly arranged, and the craving for food is by all accounts higher than what is required.

You peer down, and you see that the book is a guidance manual. It is a manual for guaranteeing that you are eating the perfect measure of food to keep yourself healthier. The guide will disclose to you how you can begin programming your body to eat the perfect measure of food. It is a manual for figuring out how to control your body and ensuring that your body will work the correct way.

You get the book and open it up. Within it, you see a wide range of directions. There are codes that must be composed. There is a major console before the greatest screen, and you see it there before you. You simply need to type in the correct messages to guarantee that your body and brain will be adjusted.

The main code you type in is "Adjust stomach volume to hunger level," and as you do, the craving disperses. You feel yourself evolving, as well. You feel yourself getting less eager, and as you get less ravenous, you feel more in charge of yourself.

The following code you type in is "Decrease huger level to calorie level." As you type this in, you see that the appetite is currently connected to the calories and that you won't feel hungry when your body needn't bother with more calories.

The third code is "Square longings and adjusts need for good food varieties." As you type this in, you feel any desires that you have disappeared. You needn't bother with any low-quality nourishment any longer. You don't have to have desserts and greasy food varieties.

You will desire healthier food sources. You will feel the requirement for great products of the soil that will assist you with remaining sound. You will have the self-discipline to choose the healthier food varieties regardless of whether you have the decision for low-quality nourishment as well.

At the point when you do this, you see that the entirety of the alerts on the screen begin to disseminate away. You see that the screens begin to try and out. Rather than red alerts everywhere, you see heaps of green across the diagrams. They are showing that you have recalibrated your body and that your body will be prepared to deal with you. Your body will help you as long as you hear yourself out during it.

You take a gander at your outlines and grin. You are now feeling more confident.

You can see that you are willing and ready to be the individual that you need to be and that you can get more fit on the off chance that you tune in to your body. You can see that your body has a truly dependable way that it can direct your craving. You simply need to ensure that you are focusing on your prompts. Any time that you begin questioning your capacity to see how much food you need to eat, you can get back to this room. You are as far as you could tell, and that PC screen that you are taking a gander at is your body. It shows you that you don't need to be so questionable about your necessities. You can get back to that screen and take a gander at it for yourself, so you can find what you truly need. You can see that you don't have to eat, and that implies that you can fight the temptation. You can advise yourself that the food that you eat is to keep your body energized and running appropriately. You can ensure that you're eating regimen is healthier, and that implies that you'll be sound.

With your body adjusted and your brain feeling quiet, you can fire awakening. You can believe that your body will mention to you what you need and the number of food sources that you should eat. You can guarantee that you are burning through exactly what you need. You can see that you can restrict yourself just by figuring out how to tune in to your body.

You take a full breath. You feel somewhat more settled as you do as such. You feel focused. You feel confident that you can keep yourself sound.

You feel sure that you can permit yourself to get thinner. You feel satisfied that you can be fruitful in restricting your eating routine. You think your mindset is evolving.

You feel yourself confiding in yourself increasingly more with what you are eating. You feel yourself resting easy thinking about your body.

You take in and out, and you reveal to yourself that you can deal with yourself. You take in and out, and you feel significantly more settled with where you are.

You take a full breath once more. At that point, you feel like you're prepared to confront your day. You take in and out. You disclose to yourself that you can be more grounded for yourself. You take in and out, and you advise yourself that you have the psychological fortitude to keep yourself healthier.

Chapter 27 - I Can Be Hypnotized to Lose Weight

Weight-loss hypnosis can help you shed an additional couple of pounds when it is essential for a weight-loss plan, which consists of diet, exercise, and counseling. However, definitely, it's difficult to say because there's insufficient solid scientific evidence about weight-loss hypnosis alone.

Hypnosis is like being in a trance, a condition of profound relaxation and concentration. Hypnosis is normally done using verbal repetition and mental images with the assistance of a hypnotherapist.

Your attention is highly focused when you're under hypnosis, so you're more open to suggestions like lifestyle changes that may assist you with losing weight.

A couple of studies tried the use of hypnosis for weight loss. Numerous reports showed just humble weight loss of more than a year and a half, with a normal loss of around 6 pounds (2.7 kilograms). However, the validity of a portion of these trials was tested, making it impossible to survey the real effectiveness of weight-loss hypnosis.

In any case, a new exploration, which showed just moderate weight loss results, discovered that patients undergoing hypnosis had lower inflammation levels, higher satiety, and better quality of life. Those might be mechanisms by which weight might be influenced by hypnosis. In request to better comprehend the potential part of hypnosis in weight the executives, further studies are required.

As a rule, weight loss is best achieved through diet and exercise. At the point when you have tried diet and exercise, however, are still struggling to arrive at your objective of weight loss, address your medical care professional about different choices or improvements in lifestyle that you might make.

Relying on hypnosis for weight loss alone is unlikely to result in appreciable weight loss; however, using it as an adjunct to an overall lifestyle approach may be worth exploring by some.

Hypnotic Trance

Hypnotic trance is, basically, to some degree close to fantasizing. Looking out the window and not actually centered, maybe thinking about a holiday you're planning or imagining to take care of a difficult yourself. At the point when you're lost in a book or movie, you're up to speed in what you see. However, you don't have the foggiest idea about the slip by of time. Drive familiar streets, however, not knowing the last couple of miles of driving until you arrive at the destination. Painting, gardening, cooking, biking, gymnastics, the list might be unending.

Which goes on in our brains when it occurs? We're loose and ok with what we're doing, and without being mindful. We're concentrating on a point, utilizing our great creative mind also, concocting the right game plans and considerations for us.

The conscious piece of our mind is free, and the sub-conscious part is increasingly open and touchy to our opinion. Rest inducing contemplation can be helpful here.

First, I can't put somebody in a trance who would not like to unwind, some fantasy busting. The demonstrations of stage hypnosis look sophisticated and try to demonstrate that the hypnotist in front of an audience has mind command over the subject. Until execution, these demonstrations do a ton of study and questioning. They need attractive individuals and are more excited to go in front of an audience; these individuals have effectively convinced themselves that this will work, and they need the experience.

If you would prefer not to unwind, somebody will not assume control over your brain by showing you a pocket watch and clicking their fingers; coincidentally, I don't have a pocket watch, and I don't state 3 2 1, and you're back in the room!

I can send them a calming compact disc to listen to at home whenever I've visited a customer.

It assists their brain with listening to my voice while feeling good drifting off to rest at night. In a hypnotherapy session in my treatment room, I don't focus on their current issue by probing, getting an understanding of their aspirations or best wishes. At that point, I ask how different their lives will be if this issue is diminished or even gone.

This inquiry gets the client to use their optimistic brain segment and creativity to explain what's going to be different. I can't give advice or suggestions, and I will not give them; this is their life that is altogether different from mine. For them, my ideas will not work, and vice versa.

At the point when I've been given information about the thing they're going to do another way, they bounce onto my love seat, and I'm talking to them. This is additionally another issue for individuals, regardless of whether they're going to say something they don't need or are embarrassed about. You don't talk the trance, simply listen and unwind.

I'll talk about the different pieces of your body during the trance, asking you to quiet them in turn. At that point, I request that you stroll down a couple of steps into more profound relaxation and then go on an excursion, maybe a beach, a mountain, a sailing boat, that is to allow your brain to use its imagination. I don't mention "the issue," if you don't stress over the issue, you're going to concoct different solutions because that is the thing that our optimistic brain segment is built to do. It is something they would continue to do while in a trance, yet on a much more profound degree, because the client was dreaming about their options prior to trance.

Negative thinking interferes with adjusted brain activity as we talk about our issues. We get terrified; our pulse gets higher, we inhale rapidly and shallowly, and we get hot and attacked. At the point when we have brain haze, we can't focus, and we can't quiet down.

At the point when we unwind, the pulse eases back, our breathing is without rushing, we feel great and mollified, and afterward, our brain has the opportunity to figure out our best options and course in a logical manner that is right for us. We presently feel like we have a guide, a way that is right for us, and we are currently inspired.

If I left the room during trance and didn't return, the customer wouldn't remain in a trance and not "awaken." Their subconscious will relatively quickly note or modify the silence and make that individual mindful. It's similar when we're sleeping deeply, yet an abrupt change will quickly animate us. Again that is the subconscious that makes us conscious that something is off-base; it's still searching.

I can interact with the vast majority, and a great many people can get a trance degree. If you have a physical symptom, like incessant migraines, windedness, or worries about your stomach, I will consistently inquire as to whether you have seen a doctor preclude medical issues. I cannot work with clients who are, as of now, experiencing psychotic episodes, and if you have schizophrenia, I would likewise have to communicate with your specialist.

How Hypnosis Feels Like and Its Safety

Like different conditions of consciousness, common waking mindfulness, rest, dreaming, and addiction from various substances, the hypnosis experience is unique to the individual undergoing it. And keeping in mind that there are characteristics of the hypnotic express that are regular among hypnotized people, it is never precisely the equivalent from one individual to another, nor is it equivalent each time a similar individual is hypnotized.

Like any remaining nations, the setting and environment are highly influenced and are entirely unpredictable. Nonetheless, numerous individuals are put off attempting hypnotherapy because they have seen stage hypnotism or anything like it on television and stress that they may lose control if they are hypnotized, do anything humiliating or find the experience awkward. The opposite is valid a significant part of the time. Hypnotherapeutic hypnosis varies from stage hypnosis, which is induced for an audience's entertainment.

This article discusses a few specific emotions and thought designs that individuals seem to experience while undergoing therapeutic hypnosis. Since individuals experience hypnosis differently each time they are hypnotized, the explanation is not going to be a definite match constantly for each hypnotic topic. If you recommend Hypnotherapy, however, it will give you an idea of what's in store.

Relaxation

This is a vital part of hypnosis and requires stimulation of the mind and the body. Hypnosis doesn't necessarily induce relaxation essentially. Maybe, the hypnotic induction measure involves you following instructions from the hypnotherapist to quiet your mind and body. The hypnotherapist, for instance, may indicate a sensation of heaviness in at least one space of your body. Since hypnosis is a collaborative cycle between the hypnotherapist and the client, you may feel likely to experience a sensation of heaviness indicated in the body part(s), yet in reality, it is you, not the therapist, that induces the relaxation.

Unlike the way in which hypnosis is as often as possible depicted, where a hypnotic subject carries out a hypnotist's instructions, the hypnotherapist's suggestions are generally passed on as an invitation, not an order. At the point when you think of the hypnotherapist's advice, you might find yourself thinking something like, "It would generally be excellent to loosen up right currently," at that point, find it simple to relinquish anxiety and unwind. There is no "must-have" in it.

Sharp Emphasis

Another component of hypnosis is a different kind of focused concentration on the mind. Similarly, as with relaxation, this is totally affected by the hypnotized individual, not the therapist. Since Hypnotherapy ordinarily occurs in a quiet private room, the emphasis on the therapist's words is, for the most part, exceptionally typical and straightforward. Numerous individuals find it simple to relinquish distractions and focus their attention on the topic about which the hypnotherapist is speaking.

The therapist is qualified to direct the perspectives in a particular manner and is demonstrated to be useful in overcoming addictive addiction, managing pain, or dealing with a variety of other mental, emotional, and behavioral issues. Individuals under hypnosis will continue by and a large focus on what the therapist recommends.

Chapter 28 - Yoga or Meditation

We are frequently focused on our regular daily existence, work, and family obligations. We have chosen to turn our lives around by doing an additional movement that permits us to track down the much-wanted sensation of unwinding. In this, we are confronted with a genuinely basic difficulty, yoga or meditation.

Unquestionably, this choice isn't basic, and it turns out to be substantially more perplexing when we don't have the correct information.

The media and mainstream society, all in all, place the two orders as the cream and cream of the counter-pressure battle. Be that as it may, both have their disparities and are expected for very surprising crowds. What is the action that creates more genuine feelings of serenity? How about we see.

Meditation

It implies unwinding and profound development. Meditation includes a genuinely huge set of practices focused on the individual, mental, and otherworldly development of individuals.

Specialists from various societies comprehend it as a self-preparing to arrive at high conditions of comprehension and behavior. Reflection, thoughtful reasoning, and authority of feelings are its fundamental targets in practically all societies. For this, there are numerous schools, controls, and methods.

From this point of view, we should comprehend it as order inside the reflective inclinations of Hinduism. We discuss a solitary method of discovering fulfillment, true serenity, and, all things considered, the unwinding of the specialist.

Yoga

Unwind through the dominance of the body and stances. Yoga is a Hindu control or school where meditation and obviously the sensation of unwinding are particular. This millenary practice has its origin in India and includes the control of the psyche through the space of the body.

Therefore, its experts resort to stances, figures, and force levels that increment with learning. The thought is to rule the development and have all-out body control while intelligent and quiet states are reached.

Maybe one of its benefits over customary meditation methods is that it works straightforwardly with the body. This reality can ensure a little exercise and include more of your practices.

Yoga or meditation? Every individual is essentially unique. Choosing between yoga and meditation doesn't just have to do with knowing the qualities of each control. Maybe, the important thing is to confirm the psychological and substantial aptitudes, just as the conditions of every person.

Somewhat more retired individuals, like older people, will have an ideal opportunity to rehearse the stances and conquer them. Possibly, the same is true for wellness enthusiasts and other comparable profiles. In addition, our own preferences and inspirations will characterize our decision.

What persuasive effect does it have on lowering pulse and stress? Pulse and stress states can be controlled when we experience vibes that summon harmony, quietness, and joy. According to this, both yoga and other meditation activities can accomplish this sort of beneficial outcome on the body.

Logical exploration proposes that the two exercises can calm people down. Furthermore, that can be found in certain indicators that are used to gauge our condition of wellbeing.

Also, on a mental level, yoga or meditation? According to a mental point of view, this can likewise be a very familiar element. Truth be told, all that will rely upon the sort of tolerance and the disorder that you need to work. For instance, an individual who is hyperactive will discover in each practice an alternate incitement.

In any case, in the event that it is a question of working on the mentality and temperament of a sick person or patient of some kind of disability, it is clear that yoga will not be a more satisfactory option. The reality of not having the option to finish the stances can act adversely on the confidence of the specialist. The music treatment or breathing may work.

In this sense, the main standard is undoubtedly the personal and not the contrasts between each. Both work with breathing, reflection, muscular tension, and, most importantly, are essential for meditation from a broad perspective. All will depend on the difficulty we need to handle, the way we work it, and, obviously, our individual existence and inclinations.

Reasons Why Yoga Is Ideal for Overweight People

1. Improves Relaxing

Yoga practice will permit you to loosen up more and simpler. This makes it simpler to lose fat by running and adding a solid eating regimen.

Being more mindful of your breathing and healthy living additionally helps supplements to enter the entire body more effectively. This works more viably and keeps away the rise of supplement insufficiency diseases.

2. Improve Your Security and Confidence

Yoga is an ideal method to make your life sounder. It is additionally useful for overweight individuals as it can likewise assist you with boosting confidence and wellbeing. The advancement you make truly and profoundly in the act of yoga is important to restore your mindfulness and your lifestyle. You will monitor your body and lift your personal satisfaction through actual work.

3. Battle Melancholy

People who are overweight may have poor confidence, which raises the probability of despondency. It is on the grounds that they feel terrible about their bodies or their actual appearance. Yoga is useful in light of the fact that it assists with treating gentle sorrow. It is likewise an approach to unwind, contemplate, construct certainty, and keep a functioning life.

4. Diminish Pressure

The customary breathing and meditation workout, which are important in your stances and in your yoga classes, assist you with reducing pressure and unwind. You should focus more on working genuinely and sincerely for your prosperity and have a solid objective.

The time spent in meditation and profound breathing decreases cortisol (the pressure hormone) significantly. Carrying natural air to your lungs consistently permits you to settle on choices and face day by day difficulties.

5. Decreases Actual Discomfort

Constant yoga can lessen cerebral troubles, circulatory tension and help battle fatigue and sleep disorder. This is a direct result of the expansion of oxygenation of the mind and the arrival of toxins made by profound and delicate relaxation.

Therefore, as you advance in your yoga exercises, you will have more certainty to do different things that assist you with getting more fit. You will be loaded with excitement and motivation for smart dieting and great living propensities.

6. You Will See Reformist Changes

It makes no difference in the weight or size of your butt, as there is no hindrance to accomplishing the task. Don't expect anything more from your body in your yoga classes than it can deliver. Likewise, you can achieve more testing postures by gaining versatility and safety.

Yoga is ideal for overweight people as it works to improve strength, adaptability, and balance. You will see progressions little by little, and it's great as you get acclimated to them and don't get disappointed.

7. It Is a Low Affect Action

Yoga is an incredible enhancement to solid ways of living, but extreme changes in lifestyle are not required. As the training progresses, the positions get more complicated.

Although there are amateur postures, instructors make changes according to the actual capabilities of their students. It helps you to continue your training at an ideal point, and you are not baffled by the ordeal of having those postures. You should bring the measure of time in this errand.

8. Has Consequences for the Endocrine Framework

Each yoga act influences one piece of the body at the degrees of muscles, nerves, and hormones. Large numbers of them are recommended, for instance, in the event that you have thyroid disorders.

So if hormonal issues are one of the reasons for your overweight, you ought to think about yoga as a solid exercise for battling it. In the present circumstance, we propose that you assess which positions will help manage your condition before you start the training. You ought to likewise address your professor about the abovementioned.

9. Battle Uneasiness

We have actually recorded the extraordinary and calming advantages of yoga, which is the reason it is viewed as a workout that can lessen an individual's nervousness. It is all thanks to the meditation and profound breathing that gives the discipline.

The effect of yoga on the sensory system will help you focus on expanding your active work and inclination to eat relentlessly, more formally known as gluttony.

10. Assists You With Meeting Your Objectives

In the event that you need to do active work while being healthy or in the event that you need to get more fit, yoga is ideal for that purpose. Aside from being a soft activity, it is likewise a profound upgrade, with the goal that your discipline will expand.

Doing yoga will give you snapshots of relaxation and reflection that will propel you forward. It will likewise enable you to calmly await the consequences of your work.

What stances would you be able to get more fit with? Rehearsing yoga can assist you with reinforcing your muscles, improve your adaptability, inhale appropriately, and by and large feel good. Yoga for overweight individuals is valuable since acceptable outcomes can be accomplished without extraordinary actual effort or solid impacts.

Figures to Lose a Couple of Pounds by Rehearsing the Accompanying Postures

- **The corpse unwinding stance (Savasana):** It is ideal for an unwinding, quiet body and brain.

- **Candle (Sarvangasana):** Regulates digestion and invigorates the thyroid. Reinforces and fortifies the back and leg muscles. It improves blood circulation, cleanses the blood, and decreases obstructions.

- **Transformed pelvis (Viparita Karani Mudra):** It effectively affects thyroid capacity and improves circulatory issues. It likewise offers security and passionate discretion.

- **The Fish (Matsyasana):** Helps direct thyroid capacity. It likewise influences the pituitary, adrenal, and pineal organs.

- **The furrow (halasana):** It straightforwardly influences the fat in the midsection and assists with lessening it. It additionally controls the capacity of the thyroid, liver, and spleen.

- **The Cobra (Bhujanghasana):** Regulates the adrenal organs and the thyroid. It fixes and invigorates the abs. Strengthens the spine and fixes the tailbone.

Conclusion

Hypnotic gastric banding is a quick in and out of your hospital stay procedure that can lead to dramatic weight loss. The amount of weight you lose would be comparable to 1 or 2 years of diet and exercise. This procedure drastically changes how the body reacts to food intake by teaching the body it's not getting any more food until fat stores are exhausted.

The process involves placing a large silicone band around your stomach, creating an empty space inside your stomach for food to enter two times per week. Once a week, you will fill the band with liquids and then use your finger to pull out the silicone band, and voila, no more food for an hour. After that 1 hour period, food is reintroduced to the stomach via your finger.

The band is initially placed in a hospital setting by a nurse or doctor. You may be required to stay overnight. In most cases, it takes about four weeks of attending two times per week for hypnosis before you can safely leave for home use. A three or four month's course of hypnosis is required to ensure safety and regain the weight you have lost. By the end of your sessions, you will be able to fill and deflate your band several times a day with a simple clicker that looks like a TV remote control.

Hypnotic Gastric Banding surgery has many benefits. When compared to gastric bypass, which is another weight loss surgery, hypnotic gastric banding has very few complications, such as nausea and vomiting, abdominal swelling, and leakage of saline (which is what fills up your empty stomach space). It can be done in one hour without any cutting or staples. The procedure leaves no physical scars on the body. Hypnotic Gastric

Banding is reversible. That means you can have the band removed if necessary.

One of the risks, as with any surgical procedure, is bleeding, which is a rare complication. Infection is always a risk after surgery, and there is a chance for rejection or breakage of the silicone band. There can also be some leakage of saline from time to time that will require additional visits to your doctor and slight adjustments to your weekly diet. You should not drive yourself following your surgery until you know how long it takes for you to return home safely from our office, which is only minutes away from the hospital. A positive attitude is a key to success in this procedure.

Hypnotic Gastric Banding has been used for over 20 years. It is a safe procedure but is not appropriate for everyone. You should only have this surgery if you are motivated enough to do two times per week of hypnosis following your surgery. If you are the type of person that can't even motivate yourself to buy a diet book and hasn't lost the weight on your own, then this is not for you.

If most of your weight is in your gut and not in other places, then the stomach band will not work well for you due to the fact that it works by restricting how much food enters the gut. In that case, hypnosis can be used to train the body to wait until your full stomach before allowing more food.

The total amount of pounds lost depends on how long you are using your hypnotic gastric band system. The longer you use it, the greater amount of weight will be lost. For a person who is obese and has a normal-sized stomach size, reducing those extra pounds in 1 year of use of the hypnotic gastric band system would equate to losing about 10% of their body weight per year if that person were on a regular diet and exercise plan.

If your weight is localized in your gut, you would most likely lose more than that amount. Once the weight is off, you will not regain it unless you fall into a period of depression and/or stop using your system. The hypnotic gastric band system works by re-programming the body into believing it is not getting enough food to maintain the current weight.

In time, the brain will reduce appetite and slow the metabolism down to a level that matches what food you are allowed to eat per hour via your band system. You will become much less hungry overnight and experience a newfound energy level that was not possible previously when you had extra pounds.

The hypnotic gastric band system is a great tool that can help you lose weight long term. If your motivation levels are high enough to allow the hypnosis sessions and use of the band, you will find success with this procedure.

It is the end. Thank you for enduring to the furthest limit of Hypnotic Gastric Band. Experience The Secrets to Rapid Weight Loss and Crave Healthy Food with Hypnosis and Meditation; how about we trust it was informative and ready to furnish you with the entirety of the instruments you need to accomplish your objectives, whatever it is that they might be. Since you've completed, this book doesn't mean there isn't anything left to learn on the subject; growing your viewpoints is the best way to discover the authority you look for.

Made in United States
Orlando, FL
19 March 2023

31201070R00243